F·R·I·E·N·D·S

...'til the end

The One With All Ten Years

By David Wild

long list of names below. That only seems right since making *Friends* itself is a form of collaboration, a team contact sport in which, I hope, everybody wins.

First and foremost, this book would be unimaginable without the participation of the *Friends* cast—Jennifer Aniston, Courteney Cox, Lisa Kudrow, Matt LeBlanc, Matthew Perry, and David Schwimmer—as well as their already busy representatives and assistants who put up with a flurry of *Columbo*-like requests: Marc Gurvitz, Doug Chapin, Joe Libonati, Scott Howard, Marika Cahn, Carolyn McGuinness, Ina Treciokas, Cynthia Pett-Dante, and Alletta Kriak. I promise to stop calling now—at least until the next book, sometime later this century.

Kevin Bright, Marta Kauffman, and David Crane made their first mistake when they asked me to do a *Friends* book ten years ago. I thank them for allowing me to now be a recurring if annoying character in their lives. Among the many people at Bright Kauffman Crane who were invaluable in getting this book done and done right are my longtime friend Todd Stevens, Colleen Mahan, Andy Johnson, Eric Goldberg, Missy Krehbiel, and Wendy Knoller.

And of course, like the show itself, the book wouldn't exist without all the great writer/producers including Shana Goldberg-Meehan, Scott Silveri, Andrew Reich, and Ted Cohen. And let's hear it for Jamie O'Connor who came back to BKC in order to get this book going.

How many people does it take to make a *Friends* book? Well, it may be my name on the cover—I'm humble, but my fine agent Sarah Lazin insisted—yet in truth the person who had the vision and dedication to actually pull this off was not me but Skye Van Raalte-Herzog at Warner Bros. Worldwide Publishing. Skye is the best friend, editor, and Panamanian warlord that a book could have. Indeed, everyone at WB Publishing pulled together to free up Skye's time so she could make this happen—Paula Allen, Melanie O'Brien, Kevin Bricklin, Victoria Selover, Connie Baldwin, Denny Singleton, Martha Carreon, Lila Takayanagi, and Brittany Barr who saved the day when she came in late in the game to help us win. We couldn't have done it without her.

At Warner Bros. Television, there are many to thank, including Bruce Rosenblum, Peter Roth, newlywed Phil Gonzales, Sharan Magnuson, Brett Shuemaker, Melissa Bella, Nia Figueroa, Steve Sonn, Alex Newman, and *Friends* longtime chief photographer Danny Feld whose photos are all over this book. He also took a picture of me on the Central Perk set—minutes later the set was taken down. Coincidence? I think not.

Many people had to step up to the plate to make this book happen, especially at Warner Bros. Consumer Products: President Dan Romanelli, Executive Vice President Mark Matheny, Steve Fogelson, and our best advocate Michelle Sucillon.

And let's not forget the folks who are actually publishing this book, Time Inc. Home Entertainment: Rob Gursha, Richard Fraiman, Tom Mifsud, and Victoria Alfonso who gave the book a great, loving home.

The book looks good thanks to a few designers: James Gilbert, a visionary, and Martine Trélaün, a savior. A big *grazie* to Massimiliano Masa who added an Italian flair to a few spreads. This is a colorful book but it wouldn't look nearly as good without Greg Moore, Jim Morrow, and their team at Final Film, for their painstaking work on every single photo.

Thanks to some other fine folks who had my back: Lauren Johnson, a true *Friends* authority, copyeditor Susan Jonaitis, transcriber Dale Hoffer, proofreader Janelle Herrick, and Phil McKenna of Warner Home Video who generously offered up his photo stash at the last minute.

Finally, I'd like to thank my wife Fran for being the ultimate Friend and turning me onto the show in the first place. Without her friendship—and frankly a little more—we wouldn't have our beloved sons Alec and Andrew—who like the song says, are always there for me.

—David Wild, 2004

ACKNOWLEDGMENTS

TABLE OF CONTENTS

Think where man's glory most begins and ends,
And say my glory was I had such friends.
—William Butler Yeats,
"The Municipal Gallery Re-visited"

An Introduction Between FRIENDS

I'll be there for you
When the rain starts to pour
I'll be there for you
Like I've been there before
—The theme to Friends

What is it we're looking for when we turn on the TV?

To be turned on ourselves? To decompress? To be endlessly entertained? All of the above?

Arguably what's really driving us to push all those buttons is the very human yearning for some curious sense of companionship. Sure, the friendship that TV provides is by its very nature artificial, but who among us can deny that it can be strangely comforting all the same?

For ten years now, *Friends* has offered millions of us countless laughs, a few tears, and above all else, that unusual yet powerful sense of community. Those of us who have followed the lives and mating habits of Ross, Rachel, Chandler, Monica, Joey, and Phoebe have connected *Friends* with an enduring power that has reaffirmed TV's unique ability to bring us together out of thin air. Thanks to some wonderful writing, vivid acting, and creative production, the story of these six lovely—albeit fictional—individuals has somehow become our own story.

Sure, *Friends* has become a pop culture phenomenon and a cottage industry—a large and rather well-appointed cottage at that. But in the end, this phenomenon is not about being the last great American export. The connection we feel with the show is the most heartening success story here. And that is what will keep *Friends* alive in our hearts—and in eternal syndication—forever. Finally, the curiously intimate connection between *Friends* and its viewers is the show's greatest legacy, its central perk, if you will—more so than all the fashionable haircuts, the fetching magazine covers, the high-profile contract negotiations, and the celebrity gossip that have been popular distractions along the way.

The community this show brought together has become genuinely global as the circle of *Friends* continues to grow—very fitting for a wildly appealing sitcom that has tapped into some desires best described as universal. In November 2003—just as the countdown to the *Friends* finale was beginning in earnest—China Central Television announced it would finally begin broadcasting *Friends* to the world's biggest potential audience this year. In China, it was reported, the show would be called *Laoyougi*, which translates as *Old Friends' Story*. At press time, it was unclear how the Chinese State broadcaster will translate "going commando"—as Joey refers to the American constitutional right not to wear underwear. So to any new Chinese *Friends* fans reading this book, I hereby reach out with the ultimate words of friendship—"How *you* doin'?"

In our age marked by television that appeals to some of our lower and least appealing instincts, reality really *does* bite sometimes. *Friends* is a show that has brought new excitement and energy to some TV traditions that should be Must See: good acting, good writing, good producing, good humor, good intentions. This was a show about people—less about action than interaction. Through its highs and lows—through fame and fortune—this show with the friendly name kept the faith with its audience. It made us smile. It made us laugh at ourselves. It made us care about some other people, even if they only existed in our hearts and minds. And if we occasionally got frustrated with them—hey, I believe that happens with real friends too. Through it all, they were, true to their words, there for us.

Friends has explored, with great wit and style, the ways in which friendship becomes, in essence, another sort of family. Talk to the people who took part in the group activity of making *Friends*—as I've done over the years and here once again—and you'll find some appropriately friendly folks who realize they have been part of something not just massively successful, but also something special. *Friends* has been, for many of these men and women, the ride of a lifetime. From the very beginning, 'til the journey's end, they brought us all along for that ride. Somehow they used their talents to reach through the screen and touch many of our lives for the better. And finally, that's what friends—real and imagined—are for.

—David Wild

Los Angeles, 2004

In the Beginning: Having fled her impending nuptials, Rachel explains in "The Pilot" how she realized her fiancé Barry looked like Mr. Potato Head.

SEASON ONE

IN THE BEGINNING,

there was a runaway bride. By the end of the first season, *Friends* was a runaway smash.

In between, the show enjoyed what can only be described as a dream season, both on-screen and off. While bringing to life some of the most classic *Friends* episodes ever—"The One With the Butt," "The One With the Blackout," "The One With All the Poker," "The One With the Ick Factor," "The One With the Birth," and "The One Where Rachel Finds Out" among them—the cast and creators successfully managed to avoid making "The One That Sucked." As we laughed at these and other early *Friendly* situations, millions of us took Ross and Monica Geller, Rachel Green, Chandler Bing, Phoebe Buffay, and Joey Tribbiani to heart.

"I'm really proud of the fact that we hit the ground running," says *Friends* Executive Producer and Co-Creator David Crane of the show's wildly impressive debut season. "There are many episodes that first season that I absolutely adore to this day. I see them in reruns and I just go *goddamn*, that sure worked."

Things were working so well for *Friends* during Season One that Jennifer Aniston recalls, "We didn't really know how well it was going until reruns ran in the summertime. We just knew that this was a great show. We knew *we* loved it. We were *so* into each other and doing the work that we were sort of side-swiped when the show exploded. We were not paying attention to out *there*. We were just focused on in *here*. We were thinking, 'If *we're* having this much fun, hopefully it's translating.' "

"Obviously I'm always going to remember the first season most fondly of all because it was the beginning of it all," says Matthew Perry. "Clearly it was one hell of a nice introduction."

Bound together by fate and/or the *Friends'* casting process, the show's six stars actually started becoming fast friends as the season progressed. The story that initially helped propel the *Friends* juggernaut was the relationship between Ross and Rachel. Theirs was a one-way love affair for almost the whole season, with Rachel curiously unaware of Ross's deep and growing feelings for her. In actuality, Rachel wasn't exactly the only one who didn't see the relationship coming. It turns out that the show's writers didn't quite see it either.

"*We* didn't realize Ross and Rachel would happen in the beginning," recalls Executive Producer and Co-Creator Marta Kauffman. "When we first wrote the pilot, it was supposed to be Monica and Joey.

But chemistry gives you certain ideas and a TV show does gradually take on a life of its own. It's an interesting process. The characters begin to tell *you* where they're going to go. That's how Ross and Rachel became our central romantic figures. And that love story did help get the show really going. We followed what we saw happening."

"*Everybody* was interested in Ross and Rachel," recalls Courteney Cox. "*We* were all interested in their relationship."

There was much to love about Season One—fine writing, great cast chemistry, strong direction, wonderful performances, and, lest we forget, a monkey named Marcel. On top of all that, Lisa Kudrow notes, the Ross-Rachel story line "just gave people something to invest in while they were watching *Friends* and having fun. They ended up getting involved with that couple as if they were people they knew."

Why did we love Ross and Rachel?

"We really liked each other, David and I," offers Aniston. "We both were so excited. Maybe it's unrequited love that touches people? Rooting for two people that you *know* should be together. And Marta and David were smart enough to keep them apart as long as they could. Everybody was finally like, 'Just *do* it already.' It was good manipulation on the writers' part to keep them apart as long as possible."

For all these reasons and more—including a rather cozy slot on NBC's powerhouse Thursday night schedule—the show built from a promising start to become a major hit. Along the way, the media soon jumped on the bandwagon. Gradually, a sort of *Friends*mania began to build.

"For me personally, the moment of realization was the first time I was driving in my car and I heard our theme song playing on the radio," remembers *Friends* Executive Producer Kevin Bright. "Obviously we had gotten a lot of press up until that point, but for me, *that* was when I realized we were going beyond just being a television show. I remember sitting in my car thinking, '*Wow*, we're a hit song on the radio too.' "

Still, it wasn't terribly hard to stay humble, especially thanks to the conditions inside the show's original soundstage on the Warner Bros. lot. "I remember the first season getting ready for the show shaving," says Matt LeBlanc. "There's one men's room and one women's room for everyone in the building—the crew, grips, set dressing, wardrobe, lighting, producers, writers, actors. One men's room. One toilet. Back then there was literally no room for star trips."

Things were happening for the show, and they were happening fast. In May, the cast graced the cover of *Rolling Stone*—an early indicator that they were becoming something more like rock stars than sitcom stars.

In the final episode of Season One, "The One Where Rachel Finds Out," Phoebe finds out how much money Joey will be paid for some sperm donations, and she tells him, "Wow, you're going to be making money hand over fist."

Soon, Joey wouldn't be the only one.

season

A Very Big Splash: The Gang of Six shakes things up on a cold and windy night during the filming of their first fountain frolic for the show's opening credits. Of that first frolic, Matthew Perry says, "You've got six people in a fountain at 4:00 in the morning, who are about to embark on a journey and they just have no idea what's in store for them."

Game Face: Ross is about to take a rough hit at the Rangers game Joey and Chandler have taken him to in "The One With George Stephanopoulos." Ross is hurt but happier after an obnoxious ER nurse shares his pain.

Light Her Fire: In "The One With the Blackout," Phoebe doesn't curse the darkness. Instead she sings one of her greatest hits ever. "New York City has no power and the milk is getting sour… but to me, it's not scary 'cause I stay away from dairy."

The Ride Ain't Free: Joey asks, "Hey Mon, wanna take a ride in my car?" in "The One With the Blackout," which David Schwimmer reports is one of his favorite episodes.

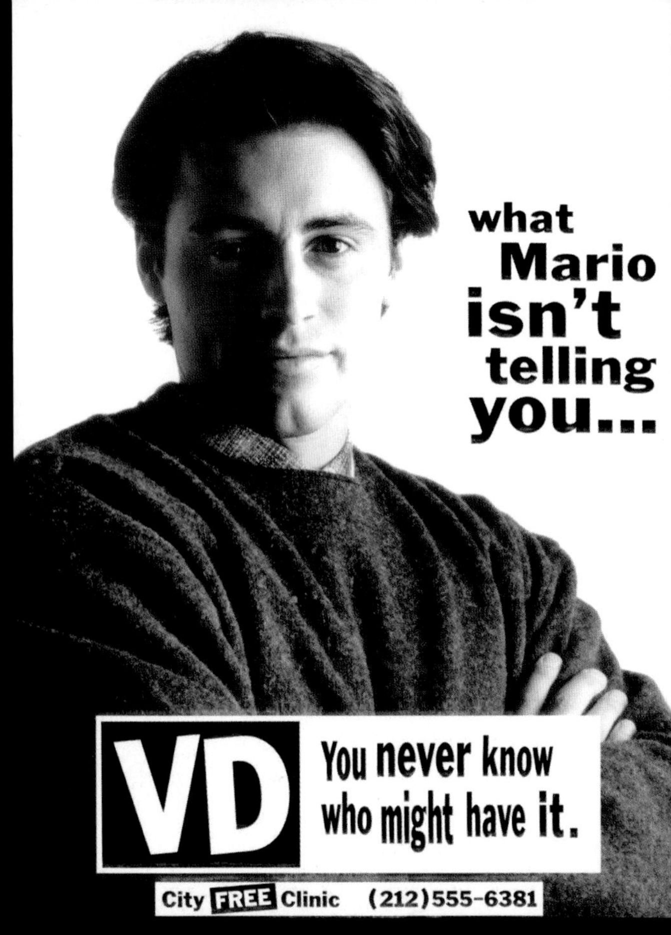

Poster Boy: Joey ends up with the venereal role of a lifetime in "The One Where Underdog Gets Away."

Too Much Information: In "The One With Mrs. Bing," the gang—and Paolo—hears that Chandler's mother enjoys Kung Pao Chicken after sex during her revealing appearance on *The Tonight Show* with Jay Leno. Cosimo Fusco, who played Paolo, reveals that "People tried to kiss me just because I'd touched Rachel—men and women. There's a lot of envy out there."

Of Bonds and Bets: Famed TV director and producer James Burrows with Courteney Cox on the *Friends* set when it all began. Burrows—who directed the *Friends* pilot and ten other episodes during the show's first season, as well as appearing uncredited as Joey's director in "The One With the Butt"—took the cast to Vegas before fame hit. "If you see any of my shows, it's really important to me that the cast bond," he explains. "It makes my life easier. And if they enjoy one another off stage, you're going to see that on stage. We took a trip to Vegas. I remember I said, 'We're going to have dinner in Vegas,' and they all wanted that. So I asked Les Moonves who was running the studio then, 'Can we get the Warner Bros. plane?' And Les was gracious enough to do that, knowing that little perks along the way always help. With *Friends*, you knew from the instant we shot the pilot how electrifying the six of them were together. So we got on the plane and we had dinner at Wolfgang Puck's restaurant there. And I remember telling the cast, 'This is your last shot at anonymity.' And it was true. I also remember they all needed money to gamble. So a couple of them wrote me checks, because I had some cash. The biggest check I got was for $200. So times have changed."

A Real Mother: Always a paragon of decorum, Nora Tyler Bing greets an arriving Ross with a sensitive "I heard about your divorce…Lesbian, huh?" in "The One With Mrs. Bing." Morgan Fairchild—who played Chandler's sexy mom Nora Bing—reveals, "When they first called I thought, 'Oh my God, I'm too young to play this guy's mother.' But I had seen the show and it's such a good show, so I thought it would be fun to do. Then I got on the set and Matthew said, 'You don't remember me but my father is John Bennett Perry and I used to visit you on the set of *Flamingo Road*.' His dad played the sheriff on *Flamingo Road* and also was on *Falcon Crest*. So then I started thinking, maybe I *am* old enough to play his mother."

He's a Believer: Ross sings the Monkees theme song to his son-to-be in "The One Where Underdog Gets Away." "People stop me all the time," says Jessica Hecht, who played Susan. "It is really extraordinary how many people watch the show. And of all the TV I've done, it's the most genuinely positive experience I've had on a sitcom set because it feels great to be recognized for something you can feel so good about. I feel so honored to be a part of *Friends*." Jane Sibbett, who played Carol, recalls, "During my first or second episode, it was raining hard—big puddles all over the Warner Bros. lot and the girls—Courteney, Jen, and Lisa had to go and play in the puddles. It was so great seeing them come back sopping wet from their heads to their toes, sides aching with that delirious laughter, having to hold each other up it was so funny, that I suddenly had this clear picture, that with that kind of giddy fun, if they could hold onto that, if they could bottle that joy, they could do anything in this world. And they did, didn't they? Every week."

Monkeying Around: Ross rushes Marcel to the hospital after swallowing some Scrabble letters and is finally convinced that he might make a good dad after all in "The One With Two Parts—Part 2."

A Prescription for Happiness: Always a big fan of the medical profession, Rachel asks, "Aren't you a little too cute to be a doctor?" in "The One With Two Parts—Part 2." George Clooney and Noah Wyle guested as the cute doctors.

SIX of ONE

WRITTEN BY

MARTA KAUFFMAN
&
DAVID CRANE

Bright Kauffman Crane productions

SIX OF ONE

The producers have asked that you take a minute to answer following questions.

Are you... (Circle ONE only)
Male 1
Female 2

What is your age? (Circle ONE only)
18-34 1
35-49 2
50+ 3

1. Please circle the number next to any word below which describes your opinions about the **Monica** story, in which she has sex with a guy on the first date. (Circle as many as apply)

Realistic .... 1 Enjoyable 6
Relatable .... 2 Predictable 7
Original .... 3 Confusing 8
Offensive .... 4 Boring 9
Adult .... 5 Believable 10

2. In this episode of SIX OF ONE, Monica had sex with Paul on their first date. In thinking about this story, would you... (Circle ONE only)

keep the story the way it is 1

prefer it if Monica and Paul did not sleep together, but made plans to spend the weekend together at the mountains instead 2

prefer that Monica and Paul not sleep together 3

Thank You

Opening Night: The original program for *Friends*, which was at that point called, *Six of One*, and a questionnaire regarding Monica's contested virtue, were given to focus groups brought in to evaluate the pilot before it aired on NBC.

"I Will Always Have Gum": Monica greets her new nephew Ben in "The One With the Birth."

a dream season

The Clothes Make the Friend: These are the original sketches of the cast by costume designer Debra McGuire.

The Secret of *Friends'* Success: According to James Burrows, "It's the same as I attribute the success of *Taxi* or *Cheers* or *Frasier* or *Will & Grace*. You have an ensemble that's seamless. There's no person you can't go to with a joke, and each one of them has a distinct character, and they play off each other, their rhythms fall into one another. That's just like lightning in a bottle. At those first rehearsals they looked like they'd been together for 20 years."

EPISODE GUIDE

Episode 1: **"The Pilot"**
Written by Marta Kauffman & David Crane
Directed by James Burrows
Original Airdate: September 22, 1994

Episode 2: **"The One With the Sonogram at the End"**
Written by Marta Kauffman & David Crane
Directed by James Burrows
Original Airdate: September 29, 1994

Episode 3: **"The One With the Thumb"**
Written by Jeffrey Astrof & Mike Sikowitz
Directed by James Burrows
Original Airdate: October 6, 1994

Episode 4: **"The One With George Stephanopoulos"**
Written by Alexa Junge
Directed by James Burrows
Original Airdate: October 13, 1994

Episode 5: **"The One With the East German Laundry Detergent"**
Written by Jeff Greenstein & Jeff Strauss
Directed by Pamela Fryman
Original Airdate: October 20, 1994

Episode 6: **"The One With the Butt"**
Written by Adam Chase & Ira Ungerleider
Directed by Arlene Sanford
Original Airdate: October 27, 1994

Episode 7: **"The One With the Blackout"**
Written by Jeffrey Astrof & Mike Sikowitz
Directed by James Burrows
Original Airdate: November 3, 1994

Episode 8: **"The One Where Nana Dies Twice"**
Written by Marta Kauffman & David Crane
Directed by James Burrows
Original Airdate: November 10, 1994

Episode 9: **"The One Where Underdog Gets Away"**
Written by Jeff Greenstein & Jeff Strauss
Directed by James Burrows
Original Airdate: November 17, 1994

Episode 10: **"The One With the Monkey"**
Written by Adam Chase & Ira Ungerleider
Directed by Peter Bonerz
Original Airdate: December 15, 1994

Episode 11: **"The One With Mrs. Bing"**
Written by Alexa Junge
Directed by James Burrows
Original Airdate: January 5, 1995

Episode 12: **"The One With the Dozen Lasagnas"**
Written by Jeffrey Astrof & Mike Sikowitz and Adam Chase & Ira Ungerleider
Directed by Paul Lazarus
Original Airdate: January 12, 1995

Episode 13: **"The One With the Boobies"**
Written by Alexa Junge
Directed by Alan Myerson
Original Airdate: January 19, 1995

Episode 14: **"The One With the Candy Hearts"**
Written by Bill Lawrence
Directed by James Burrows
Original Airdate: February 9, 1995

Episode 15: **"The One With the Stoned Guy"**
Written by Jeff Greenstein & Jeff Strauss
Directed by Alan Myerson
Original Airdate: February 16, 1995

Episode 16: **"The One With Two Parts–Part 1"**
Written by Marta Kauffman & David Crane
Directed by Michael Lembeck
Original Airdate: February 23, 1995

Episode 17: **"The One With Two Parts–Part 2"**
Written by Marta Kauffman & David Crane
Directed by Michael Lembeck
Original Airdate: February 23, 1995

Episode 18: **"The One With All the Poker"**
Written by Jeffrey Astrof & Mike Sikowitz
Directed by James Burrows
Original Airdate: March 2, 1995

Episode 19: **"The One Where the Monkey Gets Away"**
Written by Jeffrey Astrof & Mike Sikowitz
Directed by Peter Bonerz
Original Airdate: March 9, 1995

Episode 20: **"The One With the Evil Orthodontist"**
Written by Doty Abrams
Directed by Peter Bonerz
Original Airdate: April 6, 1995

Episode 21: **"The One With Fake Monica"**
Written by Adam Chase & Ira Ungerleider
Directed by Gail Mancuso
Original Airdate: April 27, 1995

Episode 22: **"The One With the Ick Factor"**
Written by Alexa Junge
Directed by Robby Benson
Original Airdate: May 4, 1995

Episode 23: **"The One With the Birth"**
Teleplay by Jeff Greenstein & Jeff Strauss
Story by Marta Kauffman & David Crane
Directed by James Burrows
Original Airdate: May 11, 1995

Episode 24: **"The One Where Rachel Finds Out"**
Written by Chris Brown
Directed by Kevin S. Bright
Original Airdate: May 18, 1995

jennifer

ANISTON

The F·R·I·E·N·D·S Exit Interview

"I believe Jen to be one of the finest comediennes ever," says David Schwimmer, after a decade of playing Ross to her Rachel. "Her timing, her instincts are so, *so* good, and so on the money. She has this rare combination: not many girls that attractive are that funny and have that much heart. She's got the emotional life underneath it to match the funny. And she's adorable. It's a triple threat."

How did it feel to start your last season of *Friends*?

Like going back to school, day one, senior year. It felt like that, it really did. Like oh my gosh, we're graduating. There's been something really beautiful about this final year. It feels very good, but strange. Believe me, this is the longest I've ever been in high school.

In television, it's pretty unusual to do anything for ten years.

I know. **How about it's unusual in life to do anything for ten years.**

True enough. Can you describe what it has been like for you and Rachel to grow up in public together?

It's something that you realize in hindsight. It's like a gift that you can't even imagine. You're right, though, it *is* growing up in public with people, because I was 23 years old when I started. Now here we are in our 30s and some of us have been married, and some babies have been born, and our lives are sort of hanging out there in public.

What, Jennifer, you're telling me you married?

Yes, I *did*, I got married.

Congratulations. Well, you've certainly managed to keep that news low-key.

Yeah, I tried to keep it *really* secret. I'm glad it worked. But yes, it's surreal—it *really* is. And I think having been on

oh my gosh, we're graduating

this show, gosh, you are very vulnerable. You're out there. But you're also blessed. The experience is so *many* things, and oddly enough, **what's so weird about this show is that so much of our lives get in there.** I don't know how the writers do this. They're either psychic or they have bugs in all of our homes.

Or possibly both.

But somehow—our writers know us so well—our personal lives sort of end up on air.

There is that weird mind meld that happens on certain shows.

Definitely. You know the whole thing about art imitating life and life imitating art is just so true. It is surreal how many things have happened that way around here. We won't go into details, but whether it was a relationship thing, or a parental thing, a situation in our lives is somehow always being played out on the show. And it all happened without us talking about it. It's weird. So the short answer is, **it did really truly feel like I was growing up in front of everybody.** There have been some bumps through the years—some major heartaches, and life lessons—yet thankfully we're all still alive and still here.

Kiss and Tell: Rachel describes every step of her amazing first kiss with Ross in "The One With the List." She tells the girls, "First, they [Ross's hands] started on my waist and then they slid up and they were in my hair..."

How would you describe your life immediately before you got this role?

Oh God, I was pretty happy living up in Laurel Canyon and living my life simply. You continue to do that, except for the size of your home. Maybe that's gotten a little bigger, but I was gardening and doing lunches and all that sort of stuff that you do when you're 24 and you have time. I think I was at coffee shops pretty regularly, hiking, going to auditions, and hoping that I'd get another show that would take me to the next year. I did shows every year before *Friends*. They would either fail or they'd get picked up for around six episodes. I was the queen of shows that got picked up for six or thirteen episodes. And that was *great*. I got used to it because you pay your rent for the year, and then you move on to the next one. I remember when we found out *Friends* was picked up for a whole season. I was *baffled* by this whole idea that it's going to go on? You mean, it *doesn't* just end after thirteen? **I have to actually play this person more?** But it was also one of those things where you just felt it. You knew something was happening. The energy of these people, they just *wanted* it. You wanted to be around this place. I wanted to be around these people for a long time. Writers, actors, all of them. And clearly that's what happened.

Why does this show connect on so many levels with so many people? After 9/11, viewers came back to the show as if you six were their old friends.

I think we were friends. That's how it feels. I really

you wanted to be

A Date With Destiny: Rachel and Ross on their first official date in "The One Where Ross and Rachel… You Know." According to Executive Producer, Ted Cohen, "Jennifer brings a truth to Rachel that allows her to be funny, even when she and Ross are fighting, breaking up, having a baby, etc., which is incredibly rare."

Girls, Girls, Girls: Cox, Aniston, and Kudrow.

around this place

do feel that way. Besides the fact that New York is my home—where I grew up—there was something especially after 9/11 that clicked for us. It was hard to come back to work and do a sitcom when the world was falling apart. I remember feeling very helpless and not knowing what our place was anymore, and what are we supposed to do? **What can we do? Do we dare go back to work?** It all felt very trite. Then little by little, that first show we did, there was so much energy in the audience, and I realized people just desperately needed that release. And the laughter was harder than ever. It was as if they were crying, but they channeled it through major, extreme laughter. The show provided little pockets of solace for people. People came up to me after 9/11 here, and also in New York, and said thank you for a half hour of escape—it brings me to tears thinking about that time. We looked at each other and we went, "Okay, I guess *this* is what we're doing. I guess we have to go back to work. Let's entertain people and let them laugh for a little bit."

***Friends* has a real emotionality that, say, your old Thursday night homeboys *Seinfeld* explicitly avoided. Is that part of what viewers have connected to?**

I can only compare it to what *I* feel. If *I* wanted to be around these people, then I'm sure that transcends to the other side of the TV screen. It's like what I was saying about how our lives would sort of mimic what was going on with the show, or the show would mimic what was going on in our lives. If *we're* experiencing these growing pains and these experiences in our real life, I'm sure all people in their mid-20s had something to watch and relate to and kind of laugh at themselves.

Besides a pretty decent paycheck, what's been the best part of this job?

The best part of this job is knowing that we give

Boxed Set: The gang watches Chandler chase Kathy after Joey ends his confinement in "The One With Chandler in a Box."

Fun For a Girl or a Boy: Ross attempts to make up with Rachel by giving her a slinky for Christmas in "The One With Phoebe's Dad."

still rea

Lost in Thought: Rachel can't stop thinking about Ross while on a date in "The One Where Ross Finds Out." As Executive Producer Andrew Reich notes, "Jennifer has an ability to make the audience empathize with her that's unprecedented."

"Let's entertain people and let them laugh."

Bad Phone Service: Rachel tells Ross she erased Emily's message about rekindling their relationship in "The One With the Ride-Along."

"When Were You Under Me?": Rachel trying to stop Ross from listening to her drunken message when she tells him she's over him in "The One Where Ross Finds Out."

A Man and a Woman and a Moustache: Ross shows off his artwork on Rachel in "The One in Vegas—Part 1."

The Fall Guy: Joey claims credit for Chandler's misplaced underwear so that Rachel won't find out about Chandler and Monica in "The One With Ross's Sandwich."

this is my family

something to people that they enjoy. That's just the greatest gift of all, and if people aren't enjoying it anymore, then we don't want to do it. That's sort of our philosophy on how and when we want to end the show. **You want to leave when they still really love you.** You don't want to leave when they're going, "Oh, you should have left long ago."

Also, I must say the show has had a pretty good cast.

Every single person in this cast is my family. They feel like a part of my family. And what I appreciate about them is how everybody's work is consistent and everybody's work is committed. What I admire is the evolution of everybody's craft, which has been so much fun to watch unfold as we all learned our comedy chops. We've all learned together how to be better actors. **I learn from these guys every single day I walk on to the set.** Just on our first two days back for this last season, we were laughing—gut-wrenching laughter that gives me such a high. I'm going to miss them. I'm going to miss Matthew Perry making me laugh and then making me cry. I'm going to miss all of them. And I *am* going to see them. There's no way I'm *not*—they're not leaving my life. There's just no way. Hopefully at least, we all say that. The road to hell is paved with good intentions. But I can't tell you how much I love and respect this cast.

Hair, There, and Everywhere: The style seen 'round the world.

What do you suggest the world does with their Thursday nights now that there will be this big gaping hole?

I guess I'm supposed to say watch *Joey*. *[laughs]* I mean, *I* would. I'll be watching *Joey*. **Matt is just heaven.** He has such heart—that's Matt LeBlanc, he's just a big love. I always laugh at our past because I used to be *terrified* of him. He was leather, head to toe—one of *those* guys. And all you're thinking is, "Oh, he's going to try to get me into bed. I can just see it a *mile* away." Then he turned out to be the sweetest, most lovable man. He works really, *really* hard. I just love him. He's a brother. He's like the brother that I have, but here.

As a group, you've been through a lot. For instance, Matthew obviously had a rough patch there. That sort of shared experience must deepen the relationship.

Oh God, when you are faced with the reality that you may lose a friend that way? There was a possibility that we were going to lose him. Forget the show, his *life*. *That* was our main concern. And we were wondering, is everybody doing what we're *supposed* to be doing here? We were *terrified* for him. And yeah, we got pissed. And we got pissed at him for not loving himself, and we got pissed because we were inconvenienced, and it wasn't ending. That's just sort of the human side of it. Then the other part of it is goddamn, you *better* get better, and thank God he did. And he's here, and he's better than ever—*ever*. I mean, truly, and I'm sure one of Matthew's great fears was like the tortured artist: What am I *without* my drugs? Now he's beyond all that. He's tapped into an emotional part of himself that *we* all knew was there, but I don't know if *he* knew was there.

"...we're all just real people doing our jobs."

So none of it's

The Great Hugsy Debate: Joey tries to keep his cool while asking Rachel how his Hugsy ended up in Emma's crib in "The One With the Memorial Service."

Most casts are divided and conquered. How did you manage to stay together as a unit?
Talking a lot. **A lot of talking, and our wanting it to work out.** If we didn't have such a charmed beginning and love for each other from the start, we could easily kind of go, "Oh fuck off, who cares? Let's just go our separate ways. We'll do the work. Come to work, do it, and leave." But there was something here that would not allow that to happen. We *had* to hash it out. We had to talk it out, put it on the table. Some times were easier than others. Our first director who we miss terribly, Jim Burrows, was the one who said, **"Stay together, keep it together as a group." And we just stuck with that.** We took that advice. It was the foundation that we built on, that thought process, that intention, that commitment. You honor your commitments, and that was a commitment we made to each other.

What did you make of it when the same media that put you on their covers slapped you with the backlash for being overexposed?
It's baffling, isn't it? But then you kind of go, well, at least it's not my problem. I'm not sitting there in a cubicle, just trying to figure out what lies and bullshit to make up about celebrities. The media really underestimates the public's intelligence by giving them this crap to read, so that somehow it creates an illusion of how fantastic and fabulous our lives are. People end up thinking, "Oh God, look what amazing lives they have." Then that same media prints a lot of shit about us, which I guess sort of equalizes everybody or something. **So none of it's real.** Not the fabulous part. Not the crap part. It's somewhere in between—we're all just real people doing our jobs.

Birthday Girl: Rachel faces the big 3-O in "The One Where They All Turn Thirty."

A Room With an Excellent View: Rachel singing and dancing naked, doesn't know Ross believes she's putting on a show for him in "The One in Vegas—Part 1."

real

these writers am

Any thoughts on how you want this show to go out and how you'd like it to be remembered?

I can't even think about it. I can't imagine it going out at all. Like I don't know what ending could possibly sum up this show properly. I don't really know how you do that. And thank God that's for our writers to deal with.

Let's talk about the writers for a second. What's their place in this success story?

Oh my God, **these writers amaze me.** Nobody is slacking off. Talk about working hard—the fact that they still have their loved ones in their lives is phenomenal. They work so long, so late, and there's nothing sloppy, there's nothing lazy about what they

Gender Issues: Rachel finds out she's having a girl in "The One Where Chandler Takes a Bath."

Best Face Forward: Aniston gets a touch-up from Robin Siegel on the set of "The One With the Lottery."

do. The writers are so obsessed with making this the best show that it could possibly be. After a couple of years of being on top, you could easily get a little lazy and sit back and just enjoy the ride. They've never given up on making this the best show that it can be.

What would you say Bright Kauffman Crane have done right to make this all happen?

They created a family. You know, Marta and David went to college together. They've had such a history together. Everybody else started so young and fresh, and not having anything to compare it to, and I think Kevin, Marta, and David set the tone for this family. Big group dinners, group watching of the shows, group *this*, group *that*. We did a *lot* of group activities. Also, this is their vision, their lives. I mean, for Marta and David, these are all people in their lives—Monica, Rachel, Ross, and all of these characters. They are people from their personal lives and they set the stage for what's happened here.

In the beginning, you would not read for Monica—is that true?

It is true. They wanted me to read for Monica. And I read Rachel and thought, I'm so much more Rachel than Monica. And I think Court was supposed to read for Rachel, and she said the same thing, I'm *much* more Monica than Rachel. Thankfully.

Rachel could have been a pretty unappealing character, yet she's obviously become one of the most appealing and popular in TV history. What's it been like to mind meld with her?

How we morphed as one? Well, I don't know. I think as Rachel matured, more of myself came into Rachel, maybe as I matured. You know, I was not raised a rich girl, so we were different on that front. There are a lot of things that were *not* similar, but I grew up in Manhattan and saw all the girls from the Upper East Side. So I knew what they were all about.

Turned On: Rachel looking at Monica's "Wedding Album" that she's kept since childhood in "The One With Rachel's Book."

A Real Prinze: Rachel talks with the most sensitive male in TV history, the hysterically nurturing nanny played by Freddie Prinze Jr. in "The One With the Male Nanny." "Jennifer is the sweetest, most sincere person...not to mention she is so damn funny!" reports Prinze. "I completely lost it every time she screamed, 'Damn you, Geller' from off screen while David was firing me as their nanny. I could barely get my lines out or keep a straight face. She is truly an original."

Even when it was the Upper West Side, there were good block and bad block neighborhoods.

Perhaps you knew the rich girls better than themselves because you were watching them so closely?

Oh, I watched them *incessantly*. I was able to go to a private school because my mom was associated with it. We would play volleyball against all of the girls from those fancy private schools, and the people were a trip. They fascinated me. *Fascinated*. They were all beautiful and tall and thin, you know, at 12 it made an impression, obviously a lasting one.

So many great guest stars have worked on *Friends*. Do you think it's a scary place to try and enter?

What was so fascinating to me was how these film actors came in and we're *terrified,* thinking, "Oh God, what are they going to think of this little nutty circus?" And they'd come in and they were all nervous and out of their element. Not everyone was nervous—Julia Roberts just knocked it out of the park. Everybody knocked it out of the park, but I didn't see her as being afraid at all.

May I say I thought your husband really knocked it out of the park?

Ahh, wasn't he great? I couldn't agree more. And boy, let me tell you, he worked *so* hard. We had so much fun doing that show, and it was fun for me to have him come into my world and see what this was all about. And he so admired it, and it was great. But boy, I've never seen anybody so nervous.

Brad Pitt—nervous?

It was one of those things where he was thinking, "I'm *going* to blow my first line, I *know* I am. I'm *going* to blow it." And we're telling him, "*Stop* saying

Moonlighting: Bruce Willis takes on an enviable role as Paul—sweeping Rachel off her feet in "The One Where Paul's The Man." Aniston recalls, "I had a blast with Bruce Willis. Working with him was a fantastic experience."

The Pitts: The gang and some guest actor named Pitt hear Ross's confession of sex with the high school librarian in "The One With the Rumor." Ross explains: "I was working late in the library one afternoon. It was just the two of us. She needed help with her word jumble, and one thing led to another. If you must know, Anita was very gentle and tender...may she rest in peace."

wasn't he great?

“Matt is just heaven.”

that, because you're going to do fine." Sure enough, he did blow it. He *had* to. It was like he had to screw up his first line.

Both your husband and Courteney Cox have surprised me by playing formerly fat people exceedingly well.

Yeah, they're both people who *couldn't* have been fat, and probably don't have that gene anywhere in their body. And yet they sure did nail it.

You're graduating from *Friends* already a movie star. How accommodating has everyone been to make that possible?

Bright Kauffman Crane have been so supportive of us doing other jobs. It feels as if mom and dad *want* their kids to do well, and they've presented us with every opportunity to explore other venues while we're still doing the show. It's amazing they've done this. The fact that I was able to do two movies while I was shooting a show—not that it was fun, nor would I ever do it again. But yes, I could do it. Do I want to? *No.* But they facilitated that for me, and they worked really hard, and this cast really dealt with my pain-in-the-ass schedule, as we do for everybody when they have to leave. I am forever grateful for that flexibility and support, and for the excitement for it all. They really wanted us to do well and have lives beyond this place. And hopefully we will. Maybe we won't. We don't know. We'll have to wait and see, but boy, they've been ultrafantastic. ***Ultra*fantastic.**

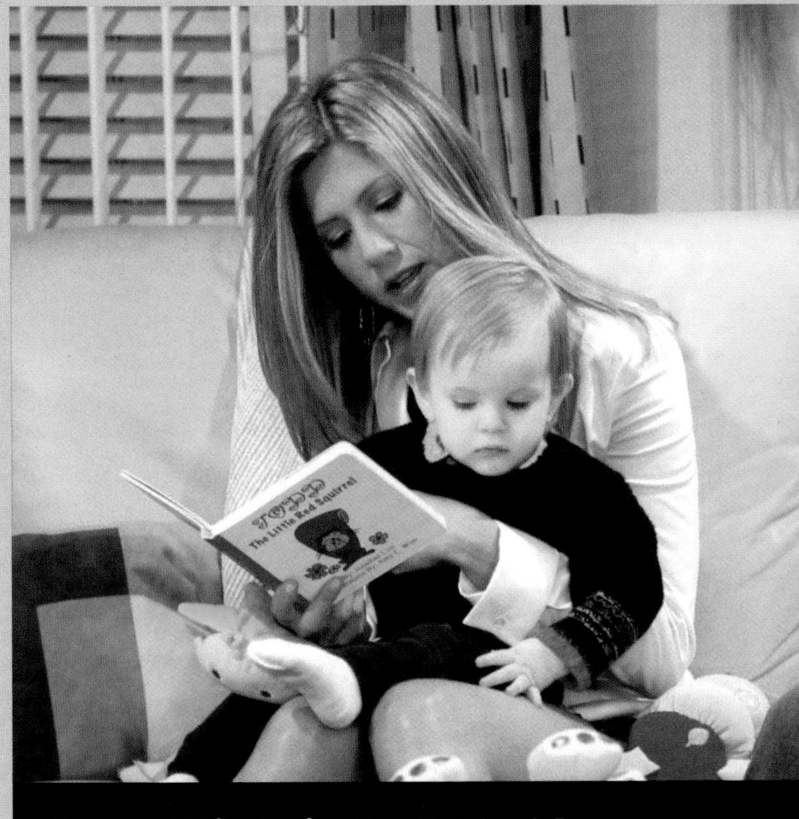

Mother and Child Reunion: Mama Rachel reads Emma a story in "The One With Ross's Grant."

ultrafantastic

Lip Service: Joey rushes back to his hotel room to share a passionate first kiss with Rachel in "The One in Barbados—Part 2." Thoughts of hurting Ross hold Joey back no more after he spots Ross and Joey's ex-girlfriend, Charlie, kissing in the hotel lobby.

SEASON TWO

The Shield: In "The One After the Super Bowl—Part 1," the roommates prepare to protect themselves against Joey's stalker, who turns out to be a perfectly lovely psycho played by Brooke Shields. A fearful Chandler exclaims, "Yes, hitting her with a frying pan is a good idea..." Just a moment later, Joey announces, "This is it. This is how we're going to die!"

IT WAS THE BEST

It was the worst of seasons. The Second Coming of *Friends* saw numerous strong episodes, but also the show's first reckoning with what shall now be known as The Backlash.

Season Two featured the further adventures of Ross and Rachel, including the often unwelcome presence of Julie the paleontologist and the on-and-off couple's first kiss in "The One Where Ross Finds Out," (followed a wholesome eight episodes later by "The One Where Ross and Rachel... You Know"). There was the tragic death of Mr. Heckles, the shocking revelation of Chandler's third nipple, the comeback of Tom Selleck as Monica's older new squeeze, the rise and fall of Joey's soap opera stud Dr. Drake Ramoray, Carol and Susan's lovely lesbian wedding presided over by Newt Gingrich's sister, Phoebe singing "Smelly Cat" and bonding with her half-brother Frank, a curious new roommate for Chandler, as well as the greatest prom video in the history of Western Civilization. *Friends* was clearly the place to be: "The One After the Super Bowl" alone included guest spots from Brooke Shields, Chris Isaak, Fred Willard, Jean-Claude Van Damme, and some actress named Julia Roberts.

Not a bad sophomore year, right?

Still, the second time around, it wasn't all laughs in the world of *Friends*. "I think the second season was pretty scary," says Marta Kauffman. "There was this feeling like, 'We have to try and do that again? And what do you mean everybody is watching what we're doing now?' Although there's a lot in the second season that I'm very proud of, there was a lot of discovery that year. We learned a lot about what does work and what doesn't work, what can you do, what can't you do."

One thing you apparently can't do is get as big as *Friends* did without encountering a law of show business physics: for every TV action, there is an equal and often opposite TV reaction. Suddenly *Friends* wasn't The Little Show That Could. *Friends* was in the media spotlight and the change was palpable—the show was no longer just about six young people you liked. Now it was also about hairstyles, the zeitgeist, and six hot stars you were seeing everywhere. Such was the newfound popularity of the show that in the fall of 1996, numerous new sitcoms seemed like misguided attempts to exploit the *Friends* formula. If imitation is the sincerest form of flattery, few shows have ever been quite so flattered as *Friends* was in Season Two.

Of course, the cast was getting paid more for their trouble. During the summer of 1996 the *Friends* six had made headlines by banding together and collectively renegotiating their contracts, earning a big raise to nearly $100,000 per episode. "The reason we stuck together back then wasn't really about finances," says Lisa Kudrow. "It was about all six of us recognizing that we were selling a show about us being friends. And we were friends. So if any resentment started because someone was making more money than someone else, those feelings would have shown through. So it was all for one and one for all."

Interestingly, some of the same media outlets that were constantly selling images and reports of the *Friends* cast started peddling something far less appealing: the notion that the show's cast was getting overexposed. And in all fairness, for a time during Season Two, the show's young stars were indeed

OF SEASONS.

moving from high profile toward a sort of multimedia omnipresence.

"I think the cast became readily available through a zillion magazine covers, through a commercial, through a theme song, through merchandising, and a couple of movies," says Kevin Bright. "Add it up and it just felt like maybe these people who were so fresh and new in the first season, all of a sudden you were getting to know them a little too much, a little too fast. So while we had the ratings numbers in the second season, I think between Marta, David, and I, you'd probably get a couple votes that the second season is not one of our favorites."

The *Friends* Diet Coke campaign is now seen as the straw that broke the media's back. "We saw that one coming," recalls Jennifer Aniston. "We knew we were doing too much, too soon, but somehow we got talked into it."

When The Backlash hit, it stung Aniston and many in the *Friends* camp: "Did it hurt my feelings? Yeah, but I'm a big wimpy mush, very sensitive. You're going along, doing what you've always done and all of a sudden one day the people who built you up decide they are going to rip you apart. You've got to learn this is part of a game. I guess there's some fascination with the rise and then the fall. It's a bizarre cycle that's just ever-present."

During Season Two, as its success story continued, *Friends* was experiencing a few growing pains. Today it can be seen as part of the show's evolution. Still, not everybody on *Friends* is a big fan of evolution. In "The One Where Heckles Dies," Phoebe memorably notes, "Monkeys, Darwin—you know, it's a nice story. I just think it sounds a little too easy."

A Hairy Moment: As Marcel wrote in his tell-all foreword to *Friends: The Official Companion*, the Season One episode guide, "To the old gang, if you happen to be reading this, there's something this humble chimp has to get off his chest: For what it's worth, after all the fights, all the tense on-set confrontations, and all those unfortunate incidents of cast members slipping on banana peels, I *still* consider each and every one of you to be my true friends."

A Kiss to Remember: In "The One Where Ross Finds Out," Ross storms out of Central Perk after an argument about Rachel having feelings for him now that he's in a relationship with Julie. Before long he returns, and America's favorite couple, at long last, lock lips.

Forward Thinking: Activist Candace Gingrich, who played the minister that married Carol and Susan in "The One With the Lesbian Wedding", today notes on her experience of doing the show, "They all seemed to understand the importance of the message of that episode. Here we are in the midst of fighting for civil marriage for gays and lesbians, and here was the *Friends* cast years ago, already on the bandwagon. We need more shows like that!"

Man and Superman: During "The One With the Lesbian Wedding," Chandler bemoans the fact that there are so many women who are unattainable due to sexual orientation. "I feel like Superman without my powers," Joey adds memorably. "I have a cape, and yet I cannot fly."

Star Struck: In "The One After the Super Bowl—Part 1," Joey meets with Dr. Drake Ramoray's biggest fan and leading stalker, played by Brooke Shields. This appearance would lead to Shields getting a sitcom of her own, *Suddenly Susan*. "I said yes sight unseen to the script because I was just a *Friends* fan," Shields says today. "I thought it was an incredibly hip, wonderful show, and the fact that they wanted me to be in it and not play myself—well, I was thrilled. Having never gone episodic before, I actually really didn't know the world that I was stepping into, and I also had no idea that it would change my life the way it did."

Between the Shots: Matt LeBlanc, Jennifer Aniston, Lisa Kudrow, and Courteney Cox hang out on the set during Season Two.

A Big Hang-Up: Rachel can barely stomach Ross's cutesy phone conversation with Julie, "Let's hang up on three…one, two, three…Well you didn't hang up either!" Rachel eventually hangs up for him in "The One With Ross's New Girlfriend."

Marcel, We Hardly Knew Ye: The dear and departed Marcel's big print ad, from "The One After the Super Bowl—Part 1."

Weapon of Mass Distraction: In "The One Where Joey Moves Out," Rachel finds her bra among Joey's things as he packs. He explains that he and Chandler used it to catapult water balloons out of the window.

Richard the Great: Monica and Richard, played by Tom Selleck, enjoy a dance together in "The One With Barry and Mindy's Wedding." "He was fantastic," says Courteney Cox of Tom Selleck. "I've never met someone so polite and nice, genuine and sweet and talented."

Wicked Duo: On the set of "The One After the Super Bowl—Part 1," Lisa Kudrow poses with rocker/actor Chris Isaak, who would eventually get a fine show of his own. "When I did the show I hadn't seen a whole episode," remembers Chris Isaak. "I have since and really like the show, but back then I didn't know enough to be nervous. I just thought '*Friends*, that sounds like a nice show—bet they're friendly.' I met Lisa Kudrow—who's actually very smart—and tried to teach her a little guitar. Then I met the other girls too, and I thought, 'Wow, the girls on this show are sure good looking. Seems like a pretty good gig hanging around all these pretty girls.' From their behavior, I didn't realize what big stars they were. It's testament

One Shot at a Time: Director Michael Lembeck—an on-screen veteran as Max Horvath on *One Day At A Time*—talks with some of the cast members on the set of "The One After the Super Bowl—Part 1."

Roommate Trouble: Chandler's strange new roommate Eddie (played by Adam Goldberg) has just brought him a goldfish in a tank—actually it's a goldfish cracker—in "The One Where Dr. Ramoray Dies." Says Goldberg, "The impact was wildly disproportionate to the amount of time that has gone by and the amount of time that I worked on the show. I got spotted twice just the other night—once at Bed, Bath & Beyond and shortly thereafter at Radio

Not So Fun Bobby: In "The One With Russ," Monica gets back together with Fun Bobby only to discover that he's not so fun without the booze. Vincent Ventresca, who played Fun Bobby recalls, "The first year it was a show that felt like it had a great cast and an interesting premise and it was building heat. And then the second year I came back and did an episode and it was like singing backup for The Beatles."

One Sip Over the Line: The commerical campaign that some credit with overexposing *Friends* during Season Two.

Scratching an Old Itch: In "The One With the Chicken Pox," Phoebe's former flame Ryan, played by Charlie Sheen, comes back for a visit from the Navy and they both end up with the chicken pox. "I was thrilled to be working with Lisa Kudrow," says Charlie Sheen. "I think she's a real talent and I was just bummed that I was never asked to come back to continue our relationship. I guess my submarine got torpedoed."

Not-So-Secret Agent: After another tough audition, Joey visits his agent, Estelle, to announce that the only way he'll get the part is if he sleeps with the casting agent in "The One With Russ" (above). June Gable—who plays Estelle—with LeBlanc on the set (left). According to Gable, her performance was inspired by three people she has known, but "I can't tell you who, because some of them are still alive." For her, the role of Estelle "was just a small contribution to an enormous hit show, but it was a great way to observe, from a distance, the incredible rush, exhilaration, as well as burden of such overnight fame and fortune. The six *Friends* banded together more, and not less, and there was no fractious infighting, jealousy, backbiting or acting out. It really taught me the value and strength of working together as a group for the good of the ensemble."

EPISODE GUIDE

Episode 25: **"The One With Ross's New Girlfriend"**
Written by Jeffrey Astrof & Mike Sikowitz
Directed by Michael Lembeck
Original Airdate: September 21, 1995

Episode 26: **"The One With the Breast Milk"**
Written by Adam Chase & Ira Ungerleider
Directed by Michael Lembeck
Original Airdate: September 28, 1995

Episode 27: **"The One Where Heckles Dies"**
Written by Michael Curtis & Gregory S. Malins
Directed by Kevin S. Bright
Original Airdate: October 5, 1995

Episode 28: **"The One With Phoebe's Husband"**
Written by Alexa Junge
Directed by Gail Mancuso
Original Airdate: October 12, 1995

Episode 29: **"The One With Five Steaks and an Eggplant"**
Written by Chris Brown
Directed by Ellen Gittelsohn
Original Airdate: October 19, 1995

Episode 30: **"The One With the Baby on the Bus"**
Written by Betsy Borns
Directed by Gail Mancuso
Original Airdate: November 2, 1995

Episode 31: **"The One Where Ross Finds Out"**
Written by Michael Borkow
Directed by Peter Bonerz
Original Airdate: November 9, 1995

Episode 32: **"The One With the List"**
Written by Marta Kauffman & David Crane
Directed by Mary Kay Place
Original Airdate: November 9, 1995

Episode 33: **"The One With Phoebe's Dad"**
Written by Jeffrey Astrof & Mike Sikowitz
Directed by Kevin S. Bright
Original Airdate: December 14, 1995

Episode 34: **"The One With Russ"**
Written by Ira Ungerleider
Directed by Thomas Schlamme
Original Airdate: January 4, 1996

Episode 35: **"The One With the Lesbian Wedding"**
Written by Doty Abrams
Directed by Thomas Schlamme
Original Airdate: January 18, 1996

Episode 36: **"The One After the Super Bowl– Part 1"**
Written by Jeffrey Astrof & Mike Sikowitz
Directed by Michael Lembeck
Original Airdate: January 28, 1996

Episode 37: **"The One After the Super Bowl– Part 2"**
Written by Michael Borkow
Directed by Michael Lembeck
Original Airdate: January 28, 1996

Episode 38: **"The One With the Prom Video"**
Written by Alexa Junge
Directed by James Burrows
Original Airdate: February 1, 1996

Episode 39: **"The One Where Ross and Rachel... you Know"**
Written by Michael Curtis & Gregory S. Malins
Directed by Michael Lembeck
Original Airdate: February 8, 1996

Episode 40: **"The One Where Joey Moves Out"**
Written by Betsy Borns
Directed by Michael Lembeck
Original Airdate: February 15, 1996

Episode 41: **"The One Where Eddie Moves In"**
Written by Adam Chase
Directed by Michael Lembeck
Original Airdate: February 22, 1996

Episode 42: **"The One Where Dr. Ramoray Dies"**
Teleplay by Michael Borkow
Story by Alexa Junge
Directed by Michael Lembeck
Original Airdate: March 21, 1996

Episode 43: **"The One Where Eddie Won't Go"**
Written by Michael Curtis & Gregory S. Malins
Directed by Michael Lembeck
Original Airdate: March 28, 1996

Episode 44: **"The One Where Old Yeller Dies"**
Teleplay by Adam Chase
Story by Michael Curtis & Gregory S. Malins
Directed by Michael Lembeck
Original Airdate: April 4, 1996

Episode 45: **"The One With the Bullies"**
Written by Sebastian Jones & Brian Buckner
Directed by Michael Lembeck
Original Airdate: April 25, 1996

Episode 46: **"The One With the Two Parties"**
Written by Alexa Junge
Directed by Michael Lembeck
Original Airdate: May 2, 1996

Episode 47: **"The One With the Chicken Pox"**
Written by Brown Mandell
Directed by Michael Lembeck
Original Airdate: May 9, 1996

Episode 48: **"The One With Barry and Mindy's Wedding"**
Teleplay by Brown Mandell
Story by Ira Ungerleider
Directed by Michael Lembeck
Original Airdate: May 16, 1996

The F·R·I·E·N·D·S Exit Interview

"Courteney is **amazing,"** says Cox's TV husband Matthew Perry. "She likes to work really hard and she's very into the whole process. She's a brilliantly gifted comedienne and I don't think she knew that at the beginning. But she just grew into it, working with all of us, and bringing her own kind of crazy neurosis to the part. She's an amazing dramatic actress too, and that's what has helped me a great deal in my career and on the show, because we can stop with the joking and have a real moment together."

How does it feel to be so close to *Friends* ending?

It hasn't really hit me that it's going to end.

Let me be the first to break the news to you: it's pretty much over, babe.

Hey, I live in denial.

What do you remember about winning the role of Monica?

Well for one thing, I remember thinking the role was mine. Then I remember being in the ladies room at casting for Warner Bros. and overhearing from the next stall that Nancy McKeon was up for the role too. Suddenly I was less sure. Apparently it was down to the wire. That's probably the thing that stands out in my mind, because it was a surprise and because of where I heard the surprise.

Some of your castmates credit you with helping to establish in no uncertain terms that this show was going to be a true ensemble effort. How do you plead?

I don't know if I deserve any special credit, but I definitely thought that was very important for the show. And I think it turned out pretty well.

Yeah, I would say so. Why do you think it is that this cast has stuck together while so many others have splintered?

I think each time that we negotiated, somebody would spearhead the effort to stay united. We all had our moments.

We Have No Secrets: Chandler and Monica exchange some inside information in "The One With Rachel's Assistant."

Rubber Match: Monica and Rachel fight over the last condom while Richard and Ross's bliss hangs in the balance in "The One Where Dr. Ramoray Dies." Rachel pleads, "I will do your laundry for one month ...I will clean the apartment for two months." Monica challenges, "All right, I'll tell you what—I'll give this to you now if you can tell me where we keep the dustpan."

we all stuck

It was different every single time, but **the most important thing was that we all stuck together.** Everybody felt that was the key from the start. This was, after all, a show about friends. It made a lot of sense. I don't know of any other shows that are like *Friends*, where there truly are six equal characters. In other shows there always seems to be a star, or maybe two stars and a few supporting roles. I think our writers have been really conscious about keeping things equal, and I think it's because of their writing that we felt strong enough to pull this off.

Some members of the cast feel that there was a surprising connection between things going on in the show and things going on in your lives. Did you see it that way?

Sometimes it was surprising, and some of it may have come from overhearing things we were really experiencing. But part of the whole connection is that **the writers were writing about people growing up and living their lives**, and when you come down to it, **that's what we're all doing too,** really.

Suspicious Minds: Chandler gets a call from Joey, who's wrongly worried about Monica cheating in "The One With Rachel's Phone Number."

Originally you were approached to play the part of Rachel, but you chose to play Monica. What was it about her that appealed to you?

I liked the fact that Monica was sarcastic. But the truth is that when you read a pilot, you don't really know. **I felt like I related to her** somehow. She seemed kind of strong, and I thought she would be fun to play. These are all just chances that you take, and in reality I had no idea. I didn't even think about it that much. To me, I thought, "Wow, this is a pretty good pilot and it's a job." And I needed a job.

But when it started, you were the famous one.

In this business, you always need a job. Sure, I may have done things before *Friends*, but trust me, it *wasn't* like I was retiring off my money.

So all the money from your show *Misfits of Science* had dried up?

Well, that bought me a nice little house in Beverly Glen, but it *wasn't* going to support me for the rest of my life. And the same was true for *Family Ties*. Those were all great opportunities and they were fun, but as far as I'm concerned, I'm going to need a job after this job.

How much was Monica defined in the beginning?

When I first read the pilot, **I didn't know that Monica was going to be that obsessive.** I knew that she was neurotic, but I didn't know how high strung or obsessive she would become. I didn't realize she was going to go to that extreme. I thought she was just a girl who wanted to be in a relationship and she wasn't a goody two shoes.

Are you aware that for the pilot, the network expressed concern to the producers that Monica might look like a tramp?

I don't really remember that, but let me say *I* never

together

"She's my friend for life."

we can handle

thought Monica was easy.

Recently you've been producing a home decorating show called *Mix It Up*. Did you learn anything about producing from watching your executive producers on the show, Bright Kauffman Crane?

Of course, I learned so much from observing them. Although I must say that we're doing our show on *such* a small budget. I definitely gained a lot of respect for producing by seeing what they've done. It's hard work. Everyone needs a decision on every single thing, and if you're a control freak like myself, you want to give the answers. And you don't want anyone to make decisions for you. So that can get difficult, but the truth is that I love it. And when I think just how hands on Kevin, Marta, and David have been for these past ten years, I think it's amazing. I have the utmost respect for them.

Did being on a big hit like *Family Ties* prepare you at all for being part of the sort of massive pop culture phenomena that *Friends* became?

No, I don't think so. I mean, *Family Ties* was a great series, but I was definitely not a main character on the show, even though I was there for the last two years. I was so young then. In all honesty, I didn't know what I was doing. **I was *petrified*.** All I can remember—besides the fact that I really enjoyed working with the cast—was that the show's creator, Gary David Goldberg, was one of the nicest and most talented people I'd ever met.

And now on *Friends*, you're working with his daughter Shana, correct?

Yes, Shana Goldberg-Meehan is one of our great writers and producers on the show. But honestly, I don't think I really had to be prepared for this experience. Sure everything happened fast, but the way I see it there's always time to prepare. On any given day, it's amazing what we can prepare for. **We can handle death, so surely we can handle *fame*.**

fame

Training Day: Monica appoints herself Chandler's trainer in "The One Where Ross Finds Out." She goads, "Come on, give me five more. Five more. Five more and I'll flash you!"

Game Face: Monica's still fighting for the football after everyone's gone home in "The One With the Football." She yells, "Let go, I'm a tiny little woman!"

An Electric Moment: Monica obsesses over the electrical plans for the building, searching for the purpose of a seemingly useless wall switch in "The One With All the Rugby." She explains, "I know that switch has got to do something, okay? So, I went down to City Hall and I got these. All I had to do was pay $25 and wait in line for three hours."

In retrospect, what did you learn from the *Friends* backlash after the first season?

I've got to be honest with you, I think that I just missed the whole thing. One time I lived in a haunted house, and everybody said, "Didn't you see that ghost?" Well no, I didn't. I don't know whether I lived in some sort of bubble, but I tend not to get too thrown by these things. Yes, I *heard* there was a terrible backlash in the press but I don't remember getting upset about it. I'm the kind of person who says, **"Please don't send the tabloids to my house, because I don't really care."** I really do care about what people who I know and love think about me, but that's it. I do tend to watch the ratings, but it's not like I lose sleep over them.

Were there moments along the way when it became clear to you just how big a deal *Friends* had become?

When we went to England to film Ross's wedding to Emily, that was a pretty good indication of what was happening. There were so many paparazzi over there that we all said to each other, **"Wow, this really is big."** I preferred shooting on our stage with our crew, but it was a lot of fun. It was a very big working vacation. I shared a hotel room with Jennifer, and we had a ball.

You really were roommates then?

Well, we had two bedrooms, but we shared a suite.

Were there other big moments of realization for you after that?

We'd go shopping and people were following us everywhere. I went to Paris after that, and I do remember realizing, "Boy, this is actually big *everywhere*." After that I'd get copies of tapes with our voice-overs or subtitles in different languages and I realized the scope of the show's success.

Let's talk about the other cast members. What do you like about Matt LeBlanc as an actor?

Matt LeBlanc is probably one of the best-hearted people that I know, besides my husband, David. They run a close race with one another. And that same genuine heartfelt quality is what I also admire so much about his acting. **Matt's able to take this role and make Joey so lovable** and so real, even though he's such a caricature in many other ways. He really commits to that hysterical, doofus part of Joey's character.

How about Lisa Kudrow?

I think Lisa's a brilliant girl, and I admire the way she is so smart and can play a character so innocent and kooky. She is a constant inspiration to me. I look up to her so much. **She is one of my favorite people, period.**

David Schwimmer?

With David Schwimmer, **I love his commitment.** He'll take something and he just commits 100 percent. I have learned so much from him. He is a great actor.

Jennifer Aniston?

Jennifer is an amazing actress, and I love her so much. She is such a real person, and she has so much talent it's unbelievable. Watching her play the dramatic parts on *Friends* and in other roles, and then doing the comedy in such an ethereal way, it's just fantastic. She's like my sister. I adore that girl. **She's my friend for life.**

Do you think you would have played Rachel very differently than Jennifer has?

Oh yes, totally. I don't have the same qualities that

this is

"I have learned so much from him."

Anything But Routine: All the right moves at Dick Clark's New Year's Rockin' Eve in "The One With the Routine." For Executive Producer Andrew Reich, "There's an enthusiasm and a warmth that Courteney projects that's irresistible."

ter Works: Monica reminds Chandler he'll always be the guy who peed her in "The One With the Jellyfish."

really big

"He's like my family."

Outed: Monica says "I love you" to Chandler for the first time after being outed by Phoebe in "The One Where Everybody Finds Out."

Girl Talk: A close reading of *Playboy*, not for the articles, in "The One With the Joke."

Jennifer has. We have the same morals and sense of humor, but we're different in many ways. If I had played Rachel, she would be much more neurotic, whereas I think Jennifer has made her sexy, fun-loving, a little absentminded, and ethereal. I've got to tell you, I love the character of Rachel and I think there's no one better to play her than Jennifer. Rachel's character is actually more fun—Monica is uptight. But everything happens for a reason.

Sweet Stuff: In "The One With All the Candy," a neighbor asks when Monica will have more treats.

Taking Joey To Task: Monica threatens her buddy if he doesn't fix the bathroom floor in "The One With Frank Jr."

You mentioned morals, and some have criticized the morality of the show over the years. From your point of view, do you think *Friends* has had a positive impact on people?
I absolutely think so. I think that people can relate to it. If not all of the characters, at least one of the characters. It has a positive impact because it makes you laugh. If you spend five minutes laughing, it's got to be good for you in some way. We definitely address a lot of issues that people are going through, and I think that can only help. After 9/11, it was amazing to hear people say how we gave them a little dose of escape. I had no idea that we were going to have that impact, but that was really beautiful.

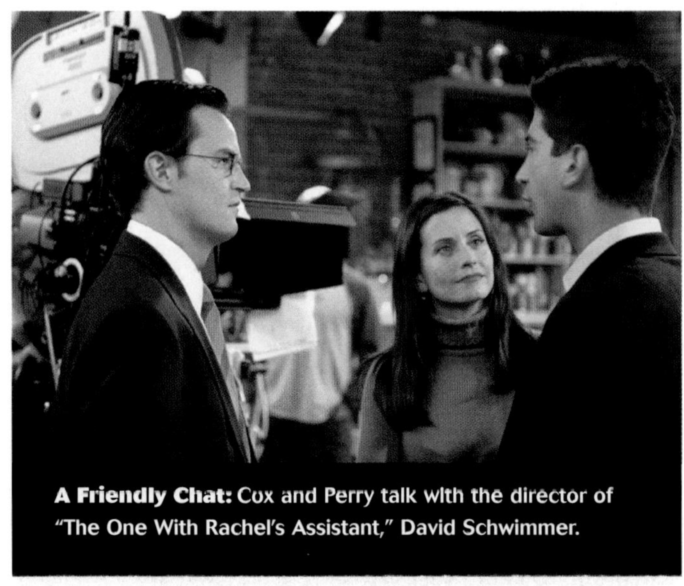

A Friendly Chat: Cox and Perry talk with the director of "The One With Rachel's Assistant," David Schwimmer.

What's it been like for you to spend most of a decade playing one character?
To tell you the truth, I'm the kind of person that really doesn't like to do the same thing over and over again. It's just not my personality. That's why I move all the time. I love change. Clearly this job has been so amazing for me for so many reasons, but it's **not normal for me to enjoy something this long.** It's been great, because I love these people and I love the writing so much. But I'm not looking for another character like Monica after the show, let's put it that way.

We somehow skipped your TV husband. What have you enjoyed about working so closely with Matthew Perry?
Matthew is a comic genius, he really is. He uses inflections that only Matthew Perry can do. I think Matthew is just brilliant at delivering lines, and he is also a great dramatic actor. He's just a one-of-a-kind guy. I've learned a lot from him, and we've been through a lot of ups and downs. He's like my family. I really have worked so closely with him for so many years, and I love him.

Say Cheese: Even medicated, Monica can't get Chandler to look normal in "The One With the Engagement Picture."

"Matthew is a comic genius."

Wide Awake In America: In "The One Where They're Up All Night," Monica and Chandler can't sleep, even after sex. Guess who wants to clean?

a little dose of escape

Location, Location, Location: Monica and Chandler decided to make a baby at the hospital while waiting for Rachel to have hers in "The One Where Rachel Has a Baby–Part 1."

A Request: Monica attempts to get Phoebe to stop playing outside her restaurant in "The One With Rachel's Dream."

On a personal level, are you proud of the way he's turned his life around?

Yes, I'm always proud of Matthew. I'm proud of his growth. I'm proud of his accomplishments. I'm proud of so many things that he's done and that he does. I'm proud to know him, because he's a really good person and he's really grown up.

When you first heard about the romantic relationship between Monica and Chandler, were you excited or nervous?

I was always extremely excited about that plot line, and it made work really fun for me. Work is always fun, but change excites me, and that was a great

Busted: In "The One With the Lottery," it turns out Monica has a secret stash of lottery tickets.

"It changed my life completely."

We made people

change. And I was glad to have an opportunity to have that kind of relationship on the show, because it's fun to play. It's fun to play the comedy *and* the emotion. **I loved the episode where I asked Chandler to marry me.** I hadn't had the chance on this show to play a dramatic, comedic moment quite like that before. I've had other ones, but that episode was really special to me. It's fun to watch, and it's fun to play it too.

When people look back on *Friends*, what would you like its legacy to be?

I want it to be remembered as a show that **made people laugh for ten years,** and a show that grew with the times and stayed relevant. And I'd also like it to be seen as an example of how people really can stick together.

Are you willing to publicly commit now to watching the first episode of *Joey*?

Of course, are you kidding? I love Matt LeBlanc so much I'm going to watch *every* episode. It's a must. Everyone should watch *Joey*. It's going to be hysterical. It is going to be a great, great, great show.

How dramatically do you think *Friends* has changed your life?

Oh God, 100 percent—180 degrees. It changed my life in so many ways. It gave me opportunity. It gave me freedom. It gave me a family of close friends with whom I've grown up. It taught me about comedy. It taught me about relationships. It taught me about everything. **It changed my life completely.** These were important years to all of us, and we came through them all together. It's been an amazing experience to share with people who've actually become your friends.

Supersized: In "The One That Could Have Been—Part 2", Monica cooks up a storm and as you can see, she enjoys every bite.

The first time a lot of us saw you was when you were dancing with an icon—Bruce Springsteen—in his "Dancing In The Dark" video. How does it feel that all these years later, through *Friends*, you have reached iconic status yourself?

Wow, that's weird. I have never thought about that, to tell you the truth. I don't feel like I'm an icon like Bruce Springsteen. He's still an icon to me and I'm still Courteney Cox.

laugh for ten years

The Inside Scoop: Cox reviews her lines on the set of "The One in Barbados—Part 2." According to Courteney's husband, David Arquette, "Courteney has a sensitivity and emotional depth that is so honest that she can't be fake. That is all you could wish for as an actor—to be real and she is to her core. She also has a silly side and sense of humor that I find to be absolutely hilarious."

Sleepless Nights: In "The One With the Princess Leia Fantasy," Monica hasn't slept since her break up with Richard the previous season so her pal Phoebe tries to take Monica to her happy place.

SEASON THREE

IN SEASON THREE,

Ross and Rachel broke up in "The One Where Ross and Rachel Take a Break," while the show kept things together rather well.

"When I think of Season Three, I do think of Ross and Rachel breaking up," says David Crane. "That episode was sort of the lynchpin of the whole season. So it was an emotional season."

Friends was now an established hit—and the best episodes of the third season, including "The One With the Princess Leia Fantasy," "The One With the Flashback," "The One Where Ross and Rachel Take a Break," "The One With the Morning After," "The One With the Screamer," and "The One at the Beach"—show why. Over time, *Friends* was exploring emotional issues with increasing depth. This was evident in Monica's yearning for a child in "The One With the Jam," or Ross's moving sense of loss after Rachel finds out he's slept with Chloe from the copy store in "The One With the Morning After," a standout episode co-written by the show's co-creators Kauffman and Crane. "I really love those episodes," says Kauffman of Ross and Rachel's emotional split. "I like that we always tried to be on both sides, so you can understand both sides of the breakup. You may have an affinity towards Ross or Rachel, but you see there are two sides to that story. In that way, it was sort of like in life."

In the end, this sort of material helped bring an added depth to the *Friends* proceedings—the gang was coming of age before our eyes. And in "The One With the Flashback," we actually got a window into the characters' past. We looked back in laughter. "The audience loved seeing into the *Friends* past. We got to see Rachel's old nose and fat Monica," says Kevin Bright. "It was really a landmark episode of the show. We've gone back and revisited the characters the way they were a few times. Every time, they were always very successful shows." Overall, Bright says, the third season was "a rebound season. I think it was us being able to finally say, let's forget about all the distractions on the outside and we'll just do the show again."

The gang was growing up, onstage and off. Not that growing up is always easy or even fun. There were bumps along the way, including a big one when Matt LeBlanc grossly dislocated his shoulder while jumping on a couch during the filming of "The One With the Jam." Show night was cut short, the audience sent home, and LeBlanc taken to the hospital where he was put in a cast. It was an unforgettable night on the *Friends* set—"though actually, I wouldn't mind forgetting it," Matt LeBlanc says with a laugh. The injury left a big impression on LeBlanc's buddies too. "When Mattie's shoulder popped out of his body—I will never forget that," says Jennifer Aniston. "That was year three of the show and it feels like a minute ago."

Season Three also saw Matthew Perry hurting himself, albeit in a slower, ultimately more life-threatening way. "That was a low point for me, a high point for my addiction," Perry recalls. "But still the show went on—with me and sometimes despite me."

Still, even Perry remembers good times during Season Three. There was "The One With a Chick and a Duck" in which Chandler and Joey spend some quality time with their slightly unorthodox apartment pets. "The thing that comes to mind now is the duck wranglers," Perry recalls. "These two women who had to just constantly clean up duck shit. I always felt somehow a lot of empathy for them. I guess that's just show business."

Captive Audience: In "The One With the Morning After," the gang eavesdrops on Ross and Rachel's big break up—Rachel's just found out that Ross slept with Chloe, the girl at the copy store.

"Commando" Action: In "The One Where No One's Ready," Joey dons all of Chandler's clothes as revenge and announces that he's "going commando." Joey warns Chandler that he better not be forced to do any sudden lunges or he'll end up even hotter and sweatier.

We Have Lift Off: The gang works together to try and get the entertainment center off the ground in "The One With Frank Jr."

Extended Jam: David Arquette—Courteney Cox's future husband—appeared in "The One With the Jam." When asked which cast member made an impression on him, Arquette replied, "Well, let me guess...um...Courteney. But all of my scenes were with Lisa and she was unbelievably wonderful."

A Touch of Blue Velvet: Isabella Rossellini in Central Perk in "The One With Frank Jr.", in which she appears as herself. The daughter of Ingrid Bergman, Rossellini now says, "I was honored to be involved with something as successful as *Friends*. It validated me as a star in America. What happened to me afterwards is that people would stop me in the street and ask me about my appearance as myself on *Friends* with the same frequency as they would stop me to speak about my mother."

rebound season

A Huddle of Friends: Ross and Chandler get stuck with Rachel on their team in the Thanksgiving classic "The One With the Football."

Lot of Love: Lisa Kudrow and David Crane share a moment together on the Warner Bros. lot. "The genius of Lisa is that she can make the most outrageous lines and situations seem truthful," explains David Crane.

Reproduction: In "The One Where Ross and Rachel Take a Break," Ross gets a little too much personal service from Chloe, the girl from the copy store, after Rachel tells Ross she needs some time off from their relationship. Of her experience working on *Friends,* Angela Featherstone, who played Chloe, recalls, "I had a wonderful experience working with fabulous actors."

Male Bonding: In "The One With the Flashback," new roommates Joey and Chandler enjoy a beer over an episode of *Baywatch*, a show Chandler has never seen before.

Comic Relief: Comedy greats Billy Crystal and Robin Williams make a cameo at the beginning of "The One With the Ultimate Fighting Champion." "Robin and I felt like funny uncles who visited the set," recalls Crystal. "We loved the energy and both felt it would have been fun to do more. I got a kick out of it, because Matthew's dad, John, was originally in *Soap*, but was unfortunately recast at the last minute. So to work with his son was very cool to me. I loved the cast, Lisa would later play my wife in *Analyze This* and *That*, and they all were charming and appropriately handsome and beautiful. I'm sorry it's over, I would have loved to do it again."

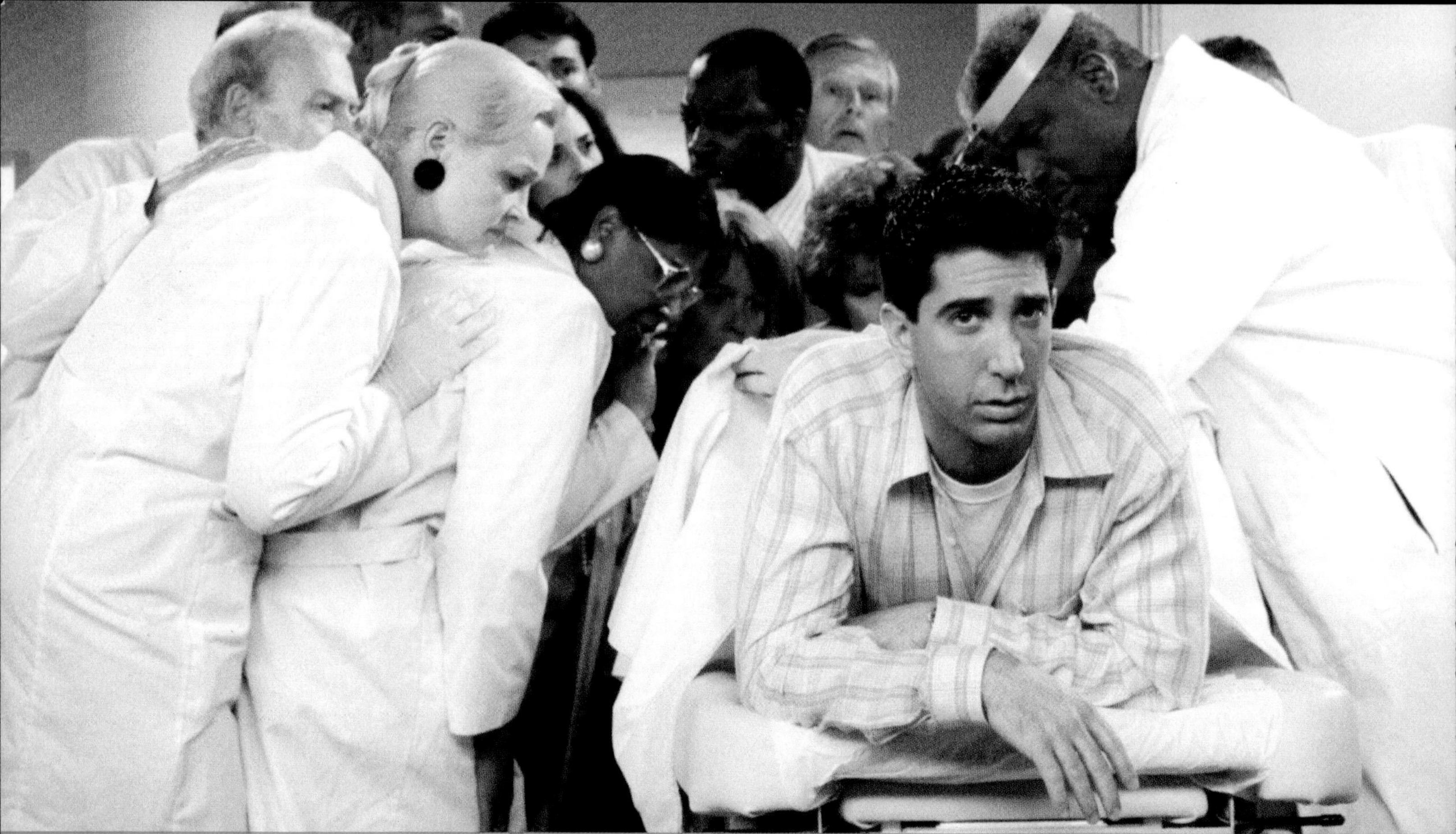

Butt Seriously: The unusual markings on Ross's ass present the modern medical establishment with a compelling mystery in "The One With Ross's Thing." Ross tells his doctor, "You know, I have dinner plans." But the intrigued doctor only addresses his colleagues, "Thank you so much for coming on such short notice. Ladies and gentlemen, I've been practicing medicine for 23 years and I'm stumped."

Stage-Struck: In "The One With the Tiny T-Shirt," Joey meets his new co-star and love interest, Kate. Dina Meyer who played the highly kissable Kate, says of her experience on the show, "I got to kiss Joey. Need I say more? Now my friends think I've really made it."

Ginger Snaps: In "The One With Phoebe's Ex-Partner," Chandler is finally getting comfortable with the idea that Ginger has a fake leg when she finds out he has a third nipple and can't handle it. "It was a wonderfully kind and generous set," recalls Sherilyn Fenn. "I don't think I'll ever play the girl with a prosthetic leg again, but I'd like to!"

Playing With Fire: Ross puts out the fire during his unwanted picnic visit to Rachel's office in "The One Where Ross and Rachel Take a Break." For Schwimmer, "This show has allowed me to do all kinds of physical comedy."

Curling Up With a Good Book: Joey is entranced by *Little Women*, while Chandler tries to get distance from Phoebe's stuff-showing guy Robert in "The One Where Monica and Richard Are Just Friends."

Relax: Rachel and Monica comfort Chandler after he freaks Janice out with his commitment in "The One With the Metaphorical Tunnel." For Matthew Perry, "maturing wasn't easy for Chandler and yes, I *can* relate."

Episode 49: **"The One With the Princess Leia Fantasy"**
Written by Michael Curtis & Gregory S. Malins
Directed by Gail Mancuso
Original Airdate: September 19, 1996

Episode 50: **"The One Where No One's Ready"**
Written by Ira Ungerleider
Directed by Gail Mancuso
Original Airdate: September 26, 1996

Episode 51: **"The One With the Jam"**
Written by Wil Calhoun
Directed by Kevin S. Bright
Original Airdate: October 3, 1996

Episode 52: **"The One With the Metaphorical Tunnel"**
Written by Alexa Junge
Directed by Steve Zuckerman
Original Airdate: October 10, 1996

Episode 53: **"The One With Frank Jr."**
Written by Scott Silveri & Shana Goldberg-Meehan
Directed by Steve Zuckerman
Original Airdate: October 17, 1996

Episode 54: **"The One With the Flashback"**
Written by Marta Kauffman & David Crane
Directed by Peter Bonerz
Original Airdate: October 31, 1996

Episode 55: **"The One With the Race Car Bed"**
Written by Seth Kurland
Directed by Gail Mancuso
Original Airdate: November 7, 1996

Episode 56: **"The One With the Giant Poking Device"**
Written by Adam Chase
Directed by Gail Mancuso
Original Airdate: November 14, 1996

Episode 57: **"The One With the Football"**
Written by Ira Ungerleider
Directed by Kevin S. Bright
Original Airdate: November 21, 1996

Episode 58: **"The One Where Rachel Quits"**
Written by Michael Curtis & Gregory S. Malins
Directed by Terry Hughes
Original Airdate: December 12, 1996

Episode 59: **"The One Where Chandler Can't Remember Which Sister"**
Written by Alexa Junge
Directed by Terry Hughes
Original Airdate: January 9, 1997

Episode 60: **"The One With All the Jealousy"**
Written by Doty Abrams
Directed by Robby Benson
Original Airdate: January 16, 1997

Episode 61: **"The One Where Monica and Richard Are Just Friends"**
Written by Michael Borkow
Directed by Robby Benson
Original Airdate: January 30, 1997

Episode 62: **"The One With Phoebe's Ex-Partner"**
Written by Wil Calhoun
Directed by Robby Benson
Original Airdate: February 6, 1997

Episode 63: **"The One Where Ross and Rachel Take a Break"**
Written by Michael Borkow
Directed by James Burrows
Original Airdate: February 13, 1997

Episode 64: **"The One With the Morning After"**
Written by Marta Kauffman & David Crane
Directed by James Burrows
Original Airdate: February 20, 1997

Episode 65: **"The One Without the Ski Trip"**
Written by Scott Silveri & Shana Goldberg-Meehan
Directed by Sam Simon
Original Airdate: March 6, 1997

Episode 66: **"The One With the Hypnosis Tape"**
Written by Seth Kurland
Directed by Robby Benson
Original Airdate: March 13, 1997

Episode 67: **"The One With the Tiny T-Shirt"**
Written by Adam Chase
Directed by Terry Hughes
Original Airdate: March 27, 1997

Episode 68: **"The One With the Dollhouse"**
Written by Wil Calhoun
Directed by Terry Hughes
Original Airdate: April 10, 1997

Episode 69: **"The One With a Chick and a Duck"**
Written by Chris Brown
Directed by Michael Lembeck
Original Airdate: April 17, 1997

Episode 70: **"The One With the Screamer"**
Written by Scott Silveri & Shana Goldberg-Meehan
Directed by Peter Bonerz
Original Airdate: April 24, 1997

Episode 71: **"The One With Ross's Thing"**
Written by Andrew Reich & Ted Cohen
Directed by Shelley Jensen
Original Airdate: May 1, 1997

Episode 72: **"The One With the Ultimate Fighting Champion"**
Teleplay by Scott Silveri & Shana Goldberg-Meehan
Story by Mark Kunerth & Pang-Ni Landrum
Directed by Robby Benson
Original Airdate: May 8, 1997

Episode 73: **"The One at the Beach"**
Teleplay by Adam Chase
Story by Pang-Ni Landrum & Mark Kunerth
Directed by Pamela Fryman
Original Airdate: May 15, 1997

lisa

KUDROW

The F·R·I·E·N·D·S Exit Interview

"Lisa has this razor-sharp mind," says David Schwimmer. "I don't even know if she knows where her comedy comes from. You don't see it coming. I don't know where it comes from, but suddenly she'll do something that she's never done in rehearsal. When the camera is rolling, there will be bursts of inspiration just springing off of her. **She is literally amazing."**

Describe your life before *Friends*.

Phoebe was all the way there

There was life before *Friends*? Let me think. Oh, I was doing *Mad About You*. I came in one day and I said that I just auditioned for this pilot, and Paul Reiser said, "Oh, what *is* it?" I told him about the show. I remember him saying, "So it's six people sitting on a couch—how is *that* a show?"

So Reiser wasn't mad about you doing another comedy?

No, Paul was just really funny and he was very, very supportive of me. I never took it as anything other than just a joke, and his funny way of saying, "Oh, so we have some *competitio*n for you, huh?"

From your point of view, how much of Phoebe was on the page when you first read the pilot script for *Friends*?

Oh, **all of her.** To me Phoebe was all the way there, because there's a monologue in the pilot where she *very* casually talks about how her mother killed herself and her stepfather went to prison, so *that* was no fun. She lived in a car and she had a junkie boyfriend or something. And I thought, the only way this works is if she's just *really* okay about it. *That's* what makes Phoebe so funny. So to me, Phoebe was already all the way there. For me, that completely defined her—how **amazing things just come out of her mouth like it's no big deal.** It's not *that* noteworthy—just something that happened. In her own way, **she has a lot of perspective, that Phoebe.**

Underground Hero: Phoebe sings in the subway in a scene cut from the pilot but available on DVD. Her immortal love lyrics: "Your love is like a giant pigeon crapping on my heart." For Executive Producer Ted Cohen, "Phoebe is just, plain and simple, a character you have never seen before, and Lisa has such an off-kilter sensibility that she can take lines we (the writers) don't even think of as jokes and make them funny."

NOTARY
SERVICES

Revenge Song: Phoebe sings, "Jingle Bitch screwed me over. Go to hell. Go to hell," after her ex-partner, Leslie, stole "Smelly Cat" for a kitty litter commercial in "The One With Phoebe's Ex-Partner."

Just Friends: Phoebe is both excited and offended to find out Joey was impressed with her body when they first met in "The One Where Ross Finds Out."

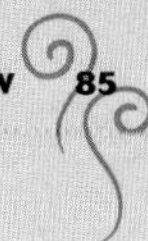

Not that long ago we discovered that Phoebe mugged Ross back before they became friends. How much darker can her past turn out to be?

I hope it doesn't get much darker than it already is, but **I like that she's the kind of person who reinvents herself every day.** It doesn't matter *what* happened before. She's not a mugger *now*. She's not living on the street *now*. Wherever Phoebe lives—and whatever she's doing at any given time—she embraces it. And then the next day it's a whole new deal. I think that's what is so good about her point of view.

How helpful was it to share *Friends*mania with five other people in the same crazy, privileged position?

It helped on a lot of levels. **First off, we had each other.** We could bounce everything that was happening off of each other. We've shared this whole experience—the bad stuff, the good stuff—and we kept each other in check so no one's ego could get *too* inflated. Everyone at different points gets credit for that. In the beginning, Courteney was the one who said, "Look, we've *got* to help each other make this as funny as possible. Because you're all funny, so if any of you see anything that could make it funnier, let me know, and I'll do the same for you." **She kept reminding us that it's an ensemble.** That was crucial because she was the biggest star and had the most celebrity of any of us when we started. Otherwise it might have been easy for people to look at the show as if Courteney was the hub and we're all the *nutty* characters around her. She really drove it home that *no*, this is an ensemble. And that meant we had to all help to make it as funny as possible and not be close-minded about suggestions from one another. That was important. Then when it came to our famous negotiations as a group, *that* was David Schwimmer. He was the first person who said what the truth is—that any one of us or two of us could get more than the others, but that it's more important that there's no resentment and we all make the exact same amount. That also turned out to be important.

Hidden Past: Kudrow and Schwimmer share a laugh between scenes on the set of "The One With the Mugging"—the episode in which Phoebe's criminal past is revealed after one of her old street friends tries to mug them.

What was it like when you all encountered some media backlash starting the second season?

We learned a *lot* from that. That's where I give Jennifer credit, because hers was the voice I remember most clearly when Warner Bros. asked us to do the Diet Coke commercials. She said, "It's too much. We're doing *too* many covers, and it's *too* much." And we could have listened to her. But we didn't. Still, I remember Jennifer was very aware of too much publicity. We're on the cover of everything and people are getting sick of seeing us, and she turned out to be right. **What we did learn eventually was that less is more.** Also, the important thing was that we just kept going as if there *wasn't* a backlash. The only

other

it just

"...everyone's comedic sensibilities just work really well together."

kept going

thing we paid attention to was our decision to stay a little more low-key. Let's just do our work. Let's focus on the show and our work. And people are still watching us, and people still like us. It was really just the press who wanted to have a story. Those are the only people who seemed a little resentful or displeased with anything we were doing. The lesson is to let the media spin its wheels and do their thing. Try not to be affected by it and **just keep your eye on the ball.** Deal with the task at hand. **Focus on your work,** not all this stuff happening out there in the media. That's the only way to win.

Well, the game's not quite over, but I'm willing to say you folks have won big.

With this whole *Friends* phenomena—all the backlashes and the waves of hipness and then all the personal stuff going on like the problems Matthew dealt with—it's *amazing* that this show has been there all along. And it's been *good* all along. Sure, it would go slightly up and slightly down, but **it's amazing that it just kept going.**

You've done some fine films with strong scripts like *The Opposite of Sex, Analyze That,* and *Romy and Michele's High School Reunion,* but what is it you particularly appreciate about the writing on *Friends*?

What I appreciate is the people who are writing the show, an *amazing* group led by David Crane and Marta Kauffman. **I still don't think people understand exactly how hard a *Friends* script is to write.** There are six main characters. There are usually three different stories happening every week, and when you watch reruns, at least one of those stories is impacting the rest of the series. I think that's huge to try and do in a half hour, and that's never been properly appreciated by people outside the show.

A Big Hit: In "The One With the Race Car Bed," Phoebe hits Joey in the nose and doesn't realize she signed for the mistakenly delivered race car bed in all the commotion.

Birth Announcement: Phoebe tells the group she's going to carry Frank Jr. and Alice's offspring in "The One With Phoebe's Uterus." Joey's response: "You're really thinking of having sex with your brother?" Phoebe explains, "Oooooh, no. They want me to be the surrogate. It's her egg and his sperm, and I'm just the oven—it's totally their bun."

In Heat: Having found out about Chandler and Monica, Phoebe plays a trick on them by coming on strong to Chandler in "The One Where Everybody Finds Out."

Friends and Lovers: Phoebe lets Chandler know she's looking forward to their "date" after feeling his bicep in "The One Where Everybody Finds Out." "I love Phoebe's lust for life," says Kudrow.

It must be like a juggling act keeping all those balls in the air.

It's a *big* juggling act. Then on top of that, with our schedules—because they've been so generous allowing us to do films while we're in production—they have to juggle who is not going to be here to rehearse much and then give them a light story. It's so masterfully done. They're unbelievable to have done it so well for so long. They deserve a lot of credit and thanks for pulling that off.

Can I assume you're pretty fond of the *Friends* cast too?

Every one of them is funny, and **everyone's comedic sensibilities just work really well together.** You can really see it when you go off and work on something else. You notice how different it is. With this group, we've all sort of molded into each other somehow, with comedic strengths complementing different comedic strengths. It's really fun to see. For instance, the more crazy you make Monica, the more Courteney embraces it and makes it hilarious. The more sensitive and in touch with his feminine side you make Joey, Matt just embraces it and makes the most of it. That's what makes Joey so interesting.

Over the years, Joey has become a character with a lot of heart.

A *lot* of heart, and I also love his unabashed affection for Chandler and his buddies. And it's great, because he knows *exactly* who he is and he's comfortable hugging or showing some emotion, genuine emotion, to his guy friends too.

Chandler and Joey—a love story for our times?

It's true, it really is a love story for our time. And I think there's something about the relationship that is so true for guys who are friends. They bond very deeply and very strongly, and that's one of the things I *love* about the show. I also love the Monica-Chandler

Fowl Play: Phoebe reprimands the chicken for interrupting the duck in "The One With Chandler's Work Laugh."

"Her love life fits perfectly with who she is."

A Professional Distance: After kissing her massage client, played by Jason Brooks, Phoebe finds out he's married in "The One With the Ballroom Dancing." Of that memorable massage, Brooks says, "Phoebe's an all right masseuse—anyone who bites my ass is a good sport." He continues, "Lisa Kudrow is great. It's no secret she's a brilliant comedienne, but she's really sweet too. Of course, they were all making $2.50 an episode when I was there."

we molded into each other

Two For the Road: Phoebe playing Twenty Questions with Joey who promised her a fun road trip in "The One in Vegas—Part 1."

relationship because no one is bossing the other one around. They're both strong, and they always make up in a very funny way. They blow off whatever the fight was about because their relationship just *works*. I think that's just what you want to see. You want to be able to have faith in a couple that they will be okay. I think that's how you feel about Monica and Chandler.

What makes you most proud about your own achievements on the show?

My own accomplishment is whatever small contribution I could make to the show as one-sixth of the cast. I don't really look at it as *my* accomplishment because I don't write the show. I don't make these stories. So the way I see it I just make my contribution as one-sixth of a cast—a cast that works *really* well together.

Prep Time: Edward St. George (hair) and Robin Siegel (makeup) buff Lisa Kudrow to a polished brilliance on the set of "The One in Vegas—Part 2" while Script Supervisor, Jolie Whitesell, runs Lisa's lines.

Why do you think there was a return to *Friends* in the wake of 9/11?

Obviously this is just a TV show, but I guess there was some value in letting people escape and be entertained whenever it's on. You finally get to lose yourself at least for a half hour in a world that's in a New York that was not affected by 9/11, and I imagine that was very comforting.

How did giving birth on-air compare to the real deal?

I had only given birth about three or four months before we shot "The One With the Birth." I still remember when we were shooting that episode they had written a lot of things in the script and added sounds to try to get across the arc of actually giving birth. But then I remembered that when I had my son, it was just silent. No one could speak. The experience was too awesome.

How would you describe Phoebe's romantic life? Until the last season or two her love life has seemed rather, shall we say, eclectic.

Her love life fits perfectly with who she is. She's this person who takes huge events in her life and stores them away somewhere. I don't know how much she processes or deals with it. And it makes sense that's how she handles relationships too. She believes that she's really going for it, giving the relationship it's best shot, but on some level not really processing it because there's too many *other* things somewhere in her head that she hasn't processed yet.

Yet Pheebs—if I may call her that—seems to have found something almost stable in her relationship with Paul Rudd's Mike.

Oh, and it's just time, isn't it? Marta and David have done a really good job over the years of having Phoebe get a little stronger, a little more mature, a little more cranky, and a little more real. To me it's a

Bull Market: Recovering stock broker Phoebe sings about having two heart attacks after being released from the hospital in "The One That Could Have Been—Part 2."

Gum Would Still Be Perfection: Pheebs looks for gum in her purse in "The One With Rachel's Sister."

natural evolution of someone who is slowly facing reality little by little, season by season. I think Paul—or should I say Mike—is an important part of that evolution. Personally, **I'm really happy for Phoebe that she found a stable, normal guy.** It may sound strange, but that makes me really happy.

***Friends* has always had an unusually open and, to my mind, healthy view of sexuality. Do you agree?**

Well, I think it *is* sexually open. The only problem is that it's on too early, but that's beyond my control. I never felt like *Friends* was an 8:00 p.m. show. With some of that material, I'm still shocked when a seven-year-old girl comes up to me and says, "I *love* your show." I'm like, "Well, *why* have you even seen it?" The answer is because it's on and it's on early.

Phoebe Buffay has been such a pioneer for women in rock. Do you feel her place in rock history has been woefully overlooked?

Doing that stuff was really fun—playing with Chrissie Hynde was pretty cool. The problem with my life as a rock star was I would never commit to actually *learning* the guitar. I don't know if that was part of the reason for just letting the music stuff fall by the wayside, but I imagine it didn't help.

What do you suggest *Friends* fans do with Thursday nights for the rest of their lives?

Gosh. Aren't there other shows? I'll still watch *Will & Grace*. There *are* other shows. And that *Joey* spin-off—I'll watch that one.

When is the last time you frolicked with *Friends* in a fountain?

A couple of years ago. A few years ago we did it again.

Was it as much fun the second time around?

Yeah, it was *just* as agonizing the second time around. No, it wasn't bad. We were all laughing really hard

Revelations: Phoebe confesses to having once mugged Ross outside a comic book store in "The One With the Mugging." Phoebe tells Ross, "You know, if you think about it, it's kind of neat...The rest of you all have these connections that go way back. Now, you and I have a *great* one!"

Lost Gig: Phoebe is replaced at Central Perk by a real pro in "The One With the Baby on the Bus." Chrissie Hynde of the Pretenders reports, "I haven't done a live performance since appearing on the show without someone in the front row shouting out a request for 'Smelly Cat'—more than any Pretenders song it appears now to be my legacy."

Going Corporate: Phoebe does some secret day spa moonlighting in "The One With the Fertility Test." On working with Kudrow, Debra Azar, who played the receptionist, recalls, "Lisa made me feel welcome from our first day together. She's an incredible actress with brilliant comedic timing. Lisa raises the bar of anyone lucky enough to work beside her."

PHOEBE

"... she's the kind of person who reinvents herself every day."

A Modest Proposal: David, played by Hank Azaria, is about to propose in his distinctive, extended fashion in "The One in Barbados—Part 1." According to Kudrow, "Hank falls into that category of *wow*! If he's here, then we've got a good show. I have such a soft spot for Hank. He's so good and so funny, and I've always loved Phoebe and David as a couple." Of working on *Friends*, Azaria reports, "Disneyland and the *Friends* set are the two happiest places on earth."

everyone got to celebrate

because Matthew Perry was cracking us up making so many jokes about how long it was taking. I remember him saying, "I can't remember a time when I *wasn't* wet. I can't remember a time when I *wasn't* cold." We were laughing really hard. **That's what they were shooting—us laughing at Matthew Perry making fun of how uncomfortable it was to be in that fountain.**

You won your own Emmy as Outstanding Supporting Actress in a Comedy in 1998, but what was *Friends* finally winning the Best Comedy Emmy in 2002 like for you?

That was pretty gratifying. Especially for the producers and our writers who just haven't really been acknowledged properly in terms of accolades. It was

Better Late Than Never: Always in touch with her inner child, Phoebe gets the two-wheeler she never had as a kid in "The One With All the Candy."

A Modest Proposal: Mike finally gets to propose to Phoebe in "The One Where Rachel's Sister Babysits." Paul Rudd who played Mike says, "Lisa is a really great actress. I am recognized for playing her love interest much more than anything else I have ever done. 'Yo, *Clueless*' has

I'd like

nice that the whole show won and everyone got to celebrate that. That was good.

How would you like to see *Friends* end?

I'd like it to not be a sad ending, personally. I'd like it to just be a hopeful ending. You've watched these people, you like them a lot, and you hope things always turn out good for them. I'd like to have the show end with a sense that they will. I like the idea that **it's all just going to continue the same way you've been seeing it, except that it's just going to be more private now.**

How late at night—or early in the morning—has a show night taping of *Friends* gone?

It was around 2 a.m.

Is it hard to be funny at that hour?

It's hard, but you can still do it because that's the job—it's all about that moment you're acting. Nothing else is happening then. **Even when you have a cold sometimes, you're just slightly less nasal because your character is not sick.** I'd love to understand the physiology of that, but it's true.

What has it meant to you to be a part of the *Friends* story?

I think it's something I'll know better once we're done because I'm bad at analyzing things when I'm in the thick of it. Maybe exactly one year from now I'll have an answer.

Can you please give me a superficial answer until then?

Okay. On a superficial level it's just cool to have been part of a show that's been unprecedentedly successful since it's inception.

When did you first realize you were part of something massive?

I think I was first aware of *Friends* as a cultural phenomenon when I went on-line and I noticed that

Precious Love: Phoebe accidentally breaks things up with Mike's girlfriend, Precious, in "The One After Joey and Rachel Kiss." Anne Dudek, who played Precious, says, "It was the most fun I've ever had being dumped."

there were all these chat rooms full of people talking about the show. That was during our first season and then through the first summer, and I thought, that's significant. That has to mean something's happening. **This success story wasn't about the critics, it was about the people.**

And what do you think about the people who never jumped on the backlash bandwagon—the fans of the show who have been along for the whole ride? The ones probably reading this book?

Their support is beyond mere appreciation. I appreciate their independent thinking. The real fans of *Friends* don't care what someone's writing about it that week. They don't care what's hip at that particular moment in pop culture. They like the show and they're going to keep watching it. And that's something I *really* value.

hopeful ending

Sitting Pretty: Lisa Kudrow on the set of "The One With Monica and Chandler's Wedding—Part 2."

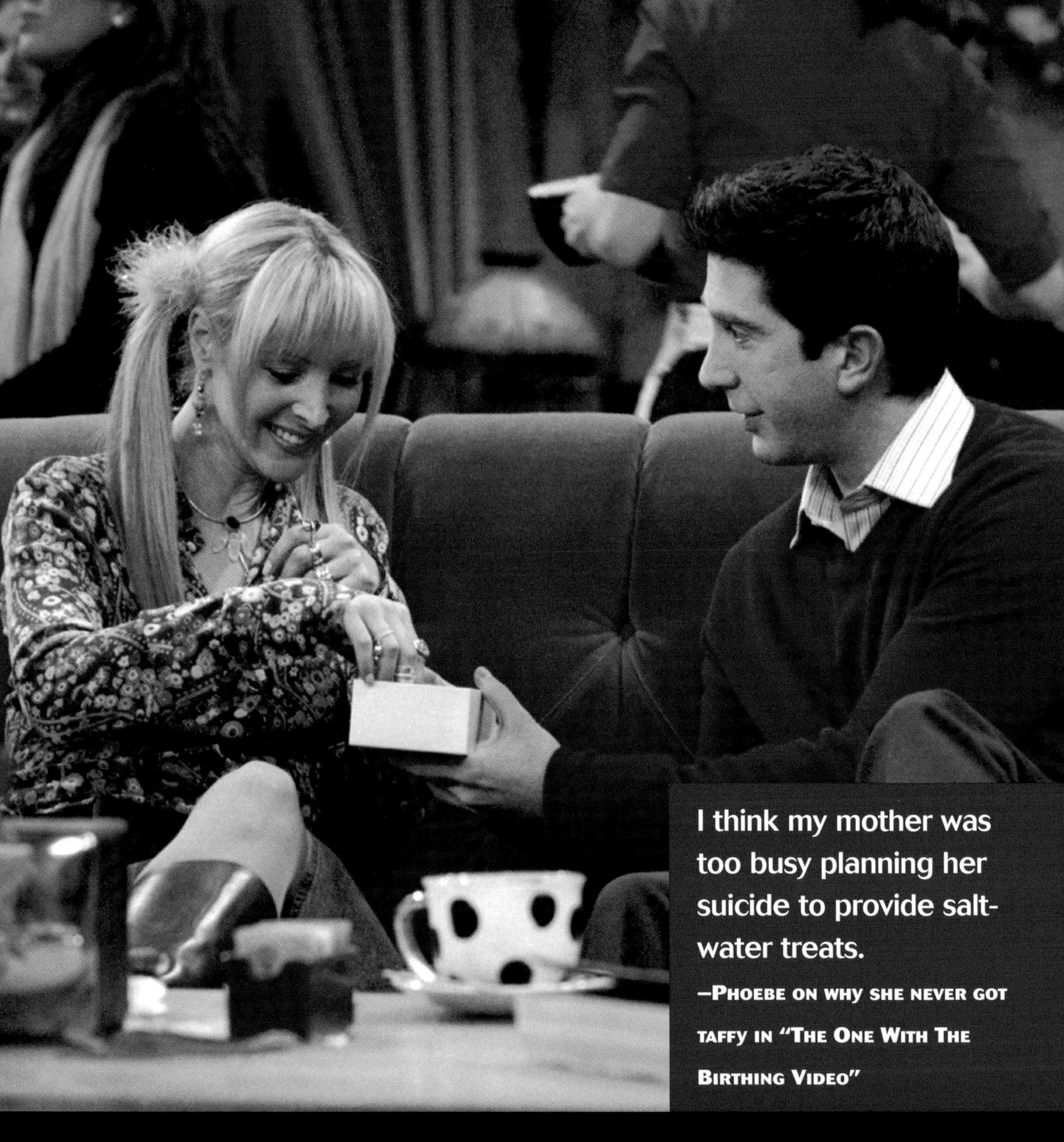

I think my mother was too busy planning her suicide to provide salt-water treats.

—Phoebe on why she never got taffy in "The One With The Birthing Video"

GREAT LINES

MONICA:
Come on. You can't live off your parents your whole life.
RACHEL:
I know that! That's why I was getting married.

—A revealing moment in "The Pilot"

Whenever I see a girl in fishnet stockings, it reminds me of my father.

—Chandler thinking about dear old Dad in "The One With Joey's New Girlfriend"

RACHEL:
Oh God, I can't believe one of us actually has one of these!
CHANDLER:
I know. I still am one of these.

—Rachel in awe of newborn baby Ben in "The One With Birth"

Hi, I'm Phoebe Buffay, and I have babies coming out of me.

—Phoebe's blunt words checking herself into the hospital in "The One Hundredth"

You don't kiss your friend's mom. Sisters are okay. Maybe a hot looking aunt, but not a mom! Never a mom!

—Joey defines a code of conduct in "The One With Mrs. Bing"

Well, I relied on a carefully regimented program of denial and wetting the bed.

—Chandler telling Rachel how he coped with his parents' divorce in "The One With The Two Parties"

We have twins! It's so exciting. Now I have twice as many lives to control!

—Monica delights on the arrival of her babies in "The Last One—Part 1"

Look, just because you played tonsil tennis with my mom doesn't mean you know her.

— Chandler taking mother-kisser Ross to task in "The One with Mrs. Bing"

This is not a marriage. This is the world's worst hangover.

—Rachel reacts to her drunken wedding to Ross in "The One After Vegas"

It seems like yesterday I was talking to you in a little petrie dish.

—Phoebe's welcoming words to the triplets in "The One Hundredth"

SEASON FOUR

London's Calling: Matthew Perry and Matt LeBlanc play two low-profile American tourists, Chandler and Joey, while filming "The One With Ross's Wedding."

/HAT CAN ONE

a season of *Friends* that starts with "The One With the Jellyfish"—in which Chandler pees on Monica to relieve the sting of the title sea creature—and ends with "The One With

Ross's Wedding—Parts 1 and 2" in which it's famously revealed that the same pair of friends have been under the covers together in the Motherland? Well, you can say this: Season Four is definitely one of the *Friends'* greatest ever.

There was so much happening on so many fronts. For instance, this was the season we watched the genesis of Phoebe's surrogate motherhood on behalf of her half-brother Frank Jr. and Alice, a story line that began appropriately with "The One With Phoebe's Uterus." "I guess I'm particularly fond of that episode because that's where we start the whole arc of Phoebe carrying the children," says Marta Kauffman. "What I really liked about it is that it's something that had never been done. I thought it was also a great way to deal with Lisa's actual pregnancy. That was just a really different thing to do, and we feel good any time that we can do something different."

"Phoebe taking on that responsibility was a good thing for her and for that character," says David Crane. "I think it brought Phoebe a new reality, another interesting side. Lisa is always great, but there she amazed even us."

Kevin Bright's favorite episode of Season Four was one of the show's all-time classics—"The One With the Embryos," which he directed. "Giovanni Ribisi and Debra Jo Rupp were great guest actors. Giovanni was probably one of the best things that came out of a show we did called *Family Album*—that's where we first met him. And Lisa was just amazing because of the heart she brought to that story."

There was also some memorable romantic competition between Chandler and Joey for a woman named Kathy, played winningly by Paget Brewster. For the crime of coveting his roommate's girl, Chandler is appropriately sentenced and punished in "The One With Chandler in a Box." Other standout Season Four episodes include "The One With the Dirty Girl," "The One With the Free Porn," and "The One With the Fake Party."

At the end of Season Four came *Friends'* big trip to England for the impending nuptials of Ross and Emily. It was a chance for the show's cast to witness just how global a success *Friends* now was. David Schwimmer recalls "the three guys hung out a lot. That was a good time. But it might have been the first time I had been abroad since the show began, and it was definitely a big realization that we can't really go anywhere—certainly not together. Alone maybe you can sneak by."

On the other hand, the TV groom was somewhat reluctant to take the sitcom plunge. "It's debatable, but I felt the decision to have Ross and Emily get married was a mistake," Schwimmer explains. "When I started the show, I had a very specific idea of who Ross was. I guess I was very married—no pun intended—to Ross. I come from a very strong sense of family and I thought: what if this had happened to me—I married my college sweetheart and she just decided to change one day and become gay and we had a baby together

SAY ABOUT

My whole take on the world would just be shattered. But I never felt Ross was someone who would be divorced again. I just felt that was not giving Ross enough credit."

Indeed, the marital union of Ross and Emily would prove painfully short-lived, but on a happier note, *Friends'* Season Four's numerous triumphs are forever.

Photo Opportunity: Courteney Cox, David Schwimmer, and Helen Baxendale–who plays Ross's second wife Emily–pose for the British press during the filming of "The One With Ross's Wedding."

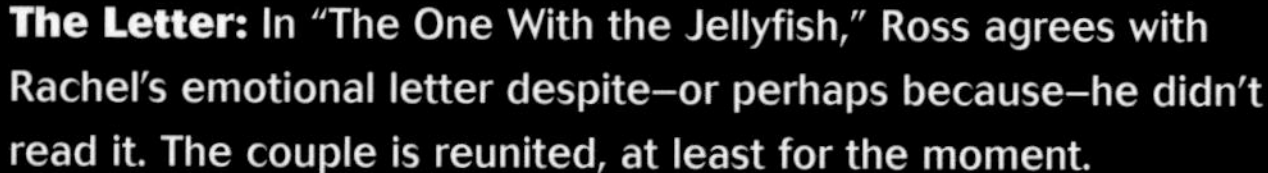

The Letter: In "The One With the Jellyfish," Ross agrees with Rachel's emotional letter despite—or perhaps because—he didn't read it. The couple is reunited, at least for the moment.

Ducking Out: Joey and Chandler challenge each other at the foosball table in a cut scene from "The One With the Jellyfish." No, that's not a jellyfish.

Battle of the Sexes: Joey and Chandler face off with Rachel and Monica in a contest to see who knows the most about each other in "The One With the Embryos." According to Jennifer Aniston, "I love that *Friends* is a show about men and women talking to each other."

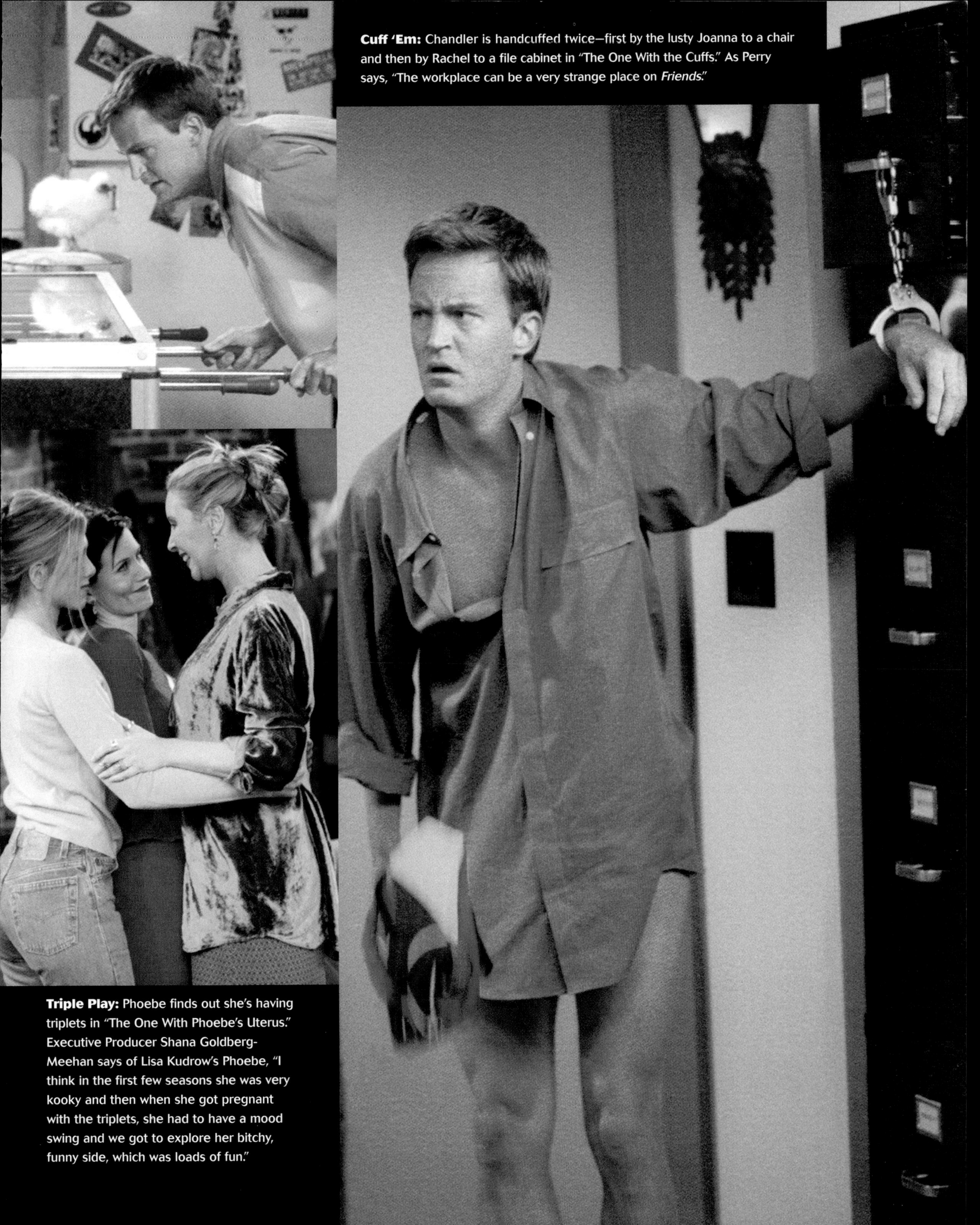

Cuff 'Em: Chandler is handcuffed twice—first by the lusty Joanna to a chair and then by Rachel to a file cabinet in "The One With the Cuffs." As Perry says, "The workplace can be a very strange place on *Friends*."

Triple Play: Phoebe finds out she's having triplets in "The One With Phoebe's Uterus." Executive Producer Shana Goldberg-Meehan says of Lisa Kudrow's Phoebe, "I think in the first few seasons she was very kooky and then when she got pregnant with the triplets, she had to have a mood swing and we got to explore her bitchy, funny side, which was loads of fun."

Free At Last: Joey and Chandler hug after Joey finally opens the box and lets Chandler out in "The One With Chandler in a Box." Joey's forgiven him for hooking up with a girl he liked.

Secret Love: Chandler and Kathy kiss before she leaves the coffee shop in "The One With Phoebe's Uterus." On having created a love triangle with Chandler and Joey, actress Paget Brewster now says, "It was amazing. My only regret is I didn't get a crack at Ross. But I got to kiss Matt and Matthew… Both wonderful kissers, trust me." Paget Brewster—who played Kathy—recalls a real-life situation with Perry involving nudity. "One afternoon Matthew Perry and I had hours of down time between our scenes at rehearsal and he asked if I wanted to go to Universal Studios and go on some rides. Of course I was thrilled, loving both Matthew Perry *and* theme park rides. I figured it was going to be the best non-date of my life and I ran upstairs and grabbed my purse and coat. By the time I got downstairs to his car, I realized this was a terrible idea. 'You can't really go to Universal without being mobbed by fans, can you?' I asked. Matthew was sitting in his green, custom-made Porsche. 'Um, no,' he said, in a really, honest, humble way. So I said I didn't know what to do, we had so much time to kill and he suggested we go to his house and play water basketball in his pool. Sounds good to me! So we drove up to his house and I borrowed a pair of his shorts and wore my bra which was more modest than a bikini, and we jumped in the pool and shot hoops for about an hour. Halfway through the game, Matthew looks over to me to throw the ball and abruptly turns his face away while pointing at me. I don't know what he's doing. While looking away from me he keeps saying 'There's… aaahhhhh… um, you might want to… ahhhhhh, Paget? Ahhh… ' and he's pointing at my chest. Remember this was actually before all of the Victoria's Secret Miracle Bra inventions. My push-up pad was sticking out of the top of my waterlogged bra ALONG WITH MY NIPPLE. Easily the most embarrassing moment of my life… But I will never forget how he was trying to alert me to this in the most charming, gentlemanly way. I think I still have a crush on him."

Landlocked: Joey and Chandler sit canoe-dling in the boat they traded for Joey's hand-built entertainment center in "The One With the Cat." "It's a great love story," says Matt LeBlanc of the largely platonic relationship of Joey and Chandler.

Shower the People: Following a long fishing trip, Joey—so close to serving as Al Pacino's butt double—takes the liberty of using Charlton Heston's private shower on the set of the TV show that they are shooting. As you can see, Heston catches him. On working with Charlton Heston, Matt LeBlanc recollects, "He said the coolest thing to me. I go, 'Can I ask you a question?' He goes 'Sure, what is it?' I go, 'You played a lot of amazing roles. What was your favorite role you've ever played?' He goes, 'I don't know kid, it ain't over yet.'"

Puppy Love: Phoebe visits her mother to discuss whether she should carry her brother's baby in "The One With Phoebe's Uterus." Mom loans her a puppy to show her how hard it might be to give the baby up. "Having Teri Garr play my mother was great," recalls Lisa Kudrow. "That was just one of those perfect things."

Altar State: Ross and Emily together during their ill-fated nuptials in "The One With Ross's Wedding—Part 2."

Overseas Friends: Perry and LeBlanc on the set of "The One With Ross's Wedding."

Get Me to the Church on Time: Monica, Emily, and Ross are shocked to find out that the chapel where Emily and Ross are to be wed is being demolished in "The One With Ross's Wedding."

A Royal Pleasure: Matt LeBlanc and Sarah Ferguson, Duchess of York, on the set of "The One With Ross's Wedding." Today, Ferguson gives the experience a rave review: "Being on *Friends* was exciting and fun and importantly it gave me some street cred with my teenage daughters and their friends. I especially love the fact that the episode I'm in was filmed all those years ago and for some reason my happening goddaughter has only just seen it. Suddenly she's treating me with renewed respect. At a time when Fergie-bashing had become a national pastime, *Friends* was a welcome relief. It always helps to have *Friends*." Of her American co-stars, "The cast was fantastic and I adored them all. They were kind and supportive to a rookie like me, all greeting me in unison with 'It's Fergie' as I arrived on set. I'll never forget Joey rather firmly plonking his hat on me. We had a lot of fun and many laughs. I even managed to muster a few lines without too much of a delay to the filming schedule."

Over There: Chandler, Rachel, Ross, Emily, Monica, and Joey in London for "The One With Ross's Wedding."

A Messy Situation: Ross tries to keep his eyes on the prize, but ultimately he's freaked out by the sloppy apartment of his dirty new girlfriend played by Rebecca Romijn-Stamos in "The One With the Dirty Girl." As Schwimmer says, "It's not the first mess Ross got into."

Egging Her On: Phoebe visits Dr. Zane, played by Cindy Katz, for her insemination as Frank Jr. and Alice look on in "The One With the Two Embryos." Debra Jo Rupp (*That '70s Show*), who played Alice, recalls, "Working on *Friends*, I got an idea of how sitcoms work well—and how much it makes a huge difference when people really like and respect each other. I still remember when I first got to the *Friends* set, I met Giovanni Ribisi—who looked 12—and found out all I was going to do was make out with him—it was a bit horrifying. He said, 'You know what I'm thinking?' I said 'What?' He said, 'I'm thinking we just go for it.' I went 'Okay.' And that's what we did. He made me so comfortable and you can see that in our scenes. I just adore Giovanni."

Episode 74: **"The One With the Jellyfish"**
Written by Wil Calhoun
Directed by Shelley Jensen
Original Airdate: September 25, 1997

Episode 75: **"The One With the Cat"**
Written by Jill Condon & Amy Toomin
Directed by Shelley Jensen
Original Airdate: October 2, 1997

Episode 76: **"The One With the Cuffs"**
Written by Seth Kurland
Directed by Peter Bonerz
Original Airdate: October 9, 1997

Episode 77: **"The One With the Ballroom Dancing"**
Written by Andrew Reich & Ted Cohen
Directed by Gail Mancuso
Original Airdate: October 16, 1997

Episode 78: **"The One With Joey's New Girlfriend"**
Written by Michael Curtis & Gregory S. Malins
Directed by Gail Mancuso
Original Airdate: October 30, 1997

Episode 79: **"The One With the Dirty Girl"**
Written by Scott Silveri & Shana Goldberg-Meehan
Directed by Shelley Jensen
Original Airdate: November 6, 1997

Episode 80: **"The One Where Chandler Crosses the Line"**
Written by Adam Chase
Directed by Kevin S. Bright
Original Airdate: November 13, 1997

Episode 81: **"The One With Chandler in a Box"**

Episode 83: **"The One With the Girl From Poughkeepsie"**
Written by Scott Silveri
Directed by Gary Halvorson
Original Airdate: December 18, 1997

Episode 84: **"The One With Phoebe's Uterus"**
Written by Seth Kurland
Directed by David Steinberg
Original Airdate: January 8, 1998

Episode 85: **"The One With the Embryos"**
Written by Jill Condon & Amy Toomin
Directed by Kevin S. Bright
Original Airdate: January 15, 1998

Episode 86: **"The One With Rachel's Crush"**
Written by Shana Goldberg-Meehan
Directed by Dana J. DeVally
Original Airdate: January 29, 1998

Episode 87: **"The One With Joey's Dirty Day"**
Written by Wil Calhoun
Directed by Peter Bonerz
Original Airdate: February 5, 1998

Episode 88: **"The One With All the Rugby"**
Teleplay by Wil Calhoun
Story by Andrew Reich & Ted Cohen
Directed by James Burrows
Original Airdate: February 26, 1998

Episode 89: **"The One With the Fake Party"**
Teleplay by Shana Goldberg-Meehan & Scott Silveri
Story by Alicia Sky Varinaitis
Directed by Michael Lembeck
Original Airdate: March 19, 1998

Episode 92: **"The One With All the Haste"**
Written by Wil Calhoun & Scott Silveri
Directed by Kevin S. Bright
Original Airdate: April 9, 1998

Episode 93: **"The One With the Wedding Dresses"**
Teleplay by Michael Curtis & Gregory S. Malins
Story by Adam Chase
Directed by Gail Mancuso
Original Airdate: April 16, 1998

Episode 94: **"The One With the Invitation"**
Written by Seth Kurland
Directed by Peter Bonerz
Original Airdate: April 23, 1998

Episode 95: **"The One With the Worst Best Man Ever"**
Teleplay by Michael Curtis & Gregory S. Malins
Story by Seth Kurland
Directed by Peter Bonerz
Original Airdate: April 30, 1998

Episode 96: **"The One With Ross's Wedding–Part 1"**
Written by Michael Borkow
Directed by Kevin S. Bright
Original Airdate: May 7, 1998

Episode 97: **"The One With Ross's Wedding–Part 2"**
Teleplay by Shana Goldberg-Meehan & Scott Silveri
Story by Jill Condon & Amy Toomin
Directed by Kevin S. Bright
Original Airdate: May 7, 1998

matt

LEBLANC

The F·R·I·E·N·D·S Exit Interview

"To me, Matt was the biggest and most pleasant surprise about *Friends*," says Jennifer Aniston. "He is as brilliant an actor as Joey is a questionable one. It takes a *very talented* man to play a bad actor. **Today, when I think about Matt, I think about his heart.** In the beginning, he scared me. He had that *look*. And all you're thinking is, 'Oh, he's going to try to get me into bed. I can just see it a mile away.' Then he turned out to be the sweetest, most lovable man."

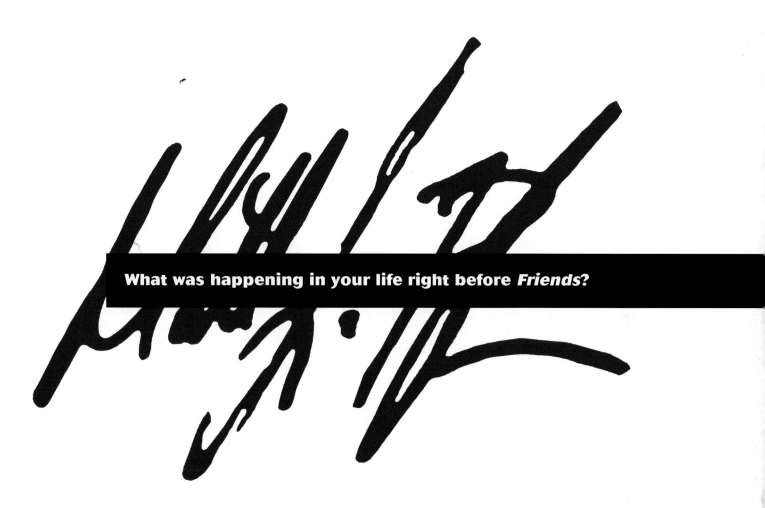

What was happening in your life right before *Friends*?

I was at a crossroads. I had no money, but I was in denial about the fact that I was facing the big question: **"Okay, do I have to get a regular job? Who am I kidding now?"** I had some money in the bank at one point from some Fox shows that I did—*Top of the Heap* and *Vinny and Bobby*. They went nowhere, but I got paid. But I burned through all of it over time. I stretched it out pretty good, but I had no work. I was right at that point of thinking, what am I going to do? I hope *something* goes. It's like the kiss of death to bring that desperate energy into the audition situation with you, because it's as if **you want to say please after the big speech. *Please.***

Is it fair to say Joey is the character on *Friends* who's gone through the most growth?

Absolutely. My character in the beginning wasn't fleshed out much at all. Fortunately, the last series that I did two years prior to that was this Italian, kind of dim character. I thought Joey was similar to that guy, but the jokes are funnier. I had a structure in my head of who the guy was, so we went with that. Then it started to become evident that the show was going to be an out-of-control hit and I wanted to stick around, so I decided, **let's really figure this guy out.** For one thing, I didn't buy that the girls on the show would be friends with Joey. Both Ross and Chandler had a sensitivity with the girls that justified their friendship. My character did not.

I had no work

Bracelet Buddies: Joey gives Chandler a golden friendship bracelet in "The One With the Prom Video." Joey asks, "Do you have any idea what this will do for your sex life?" Chandler replies, "It will probably slow it down at first, but once I get used to the extra weight, I'll be back on track."

Career Opportunities: Joey tells Rachel about a job at Fortunata Fashions in "The One Where Rachel Quits."

What did you do?

I went to Marta and David and I said, **could it be that Joey thinks of these three girls as little sisters and wants to go to bed with every other girl but these three?** *Then* I buy that they're friends. Otherwise, I just don't think they'd even *talk* to him if he hits on them every single time. That's unless he's going to get lucky. Right away it was like lights went off. They were immediately receptive to it. It made sense to them too.

Did you personally have a hands-off attitude towards women on the show?

Oh, yeah. Now I had a little crush on Jen in the very beginning, but I think the whole world did too, so what are you going to do? That didn't last very long because they did become like sisters. Jen became like a little sister and Courteney and Lisa became like big sisters. With Courteney, if you had a problem, she would say, "Okay, *here's* what you're gonna do. Let's roll up our sleeves." **She has your life absolutely sorted out in a half hour.** And you go, "Fine, I'm going to talk to you once a week for the rest of my life."

The Naked and the Dead?: Joey tries to see if Ugly Naked Guy is asleep or deceased in "The One With the Giant Poking Device."

What's life like on the *Friends* soundstage?

At times it's like working on an assembly line. At times it's like being at a party. At times it's like being in class. Really it's a lot of different things at different times.

What was your first impression of Bright Kauffman Crane when you met them?

I had never really seen *Dream On*. My first impression of Marta was that she had a great sense of humor, because when I showed up at the audition, I had a big ugly cut on my nose that was fresh from that morning. Here's the story: The night before, I'm thinking, I've got this big audition for a pilot called *Friends Like Us*. It's a big deal because it's going on the air and Jim Burrows is directing. So I'm nervous because it sounds *perfect* for me. And my buddy goes, "Let's go out—because that's what friends do."

How profoundly logical.

Yes, and I said, you're right, let's do it. I was prepared. I just needed to forget about it a little bit. I ended up sleeping on his couch that night and when I woke up, I tripped in his bathroom and fell face first into the toilet. I cut my nose on the seat of the toilet. Big cut on my nose, and I couldn't believe it. So at the audition, Marta asks, **"What *happened* to your nose?"** That's the first thing she said to me, and I said, "It's a *long* story, you don't want to hear about it, trust me." She laughed, and that kind of set the mood for a willingness to laugh. **You *are* telling jokes that *they* wrote, so they're gonna laugh.**

When you think back to the pilot, what stands out for you?

I had this incredible fever and flu. It was *awful*. I was on Occicillin and Echinacea and Golden Seal and everyone was giving me different remedies. I took *everything*. I was pouring medications into my body because the day before the pilot I had a 102° fever. I was falling apart. But it was amazing. I know it

a bunch

sounds corny but you could just feel, **there was something magical going on that night.** We were at the Warner Ranch, and there was something really, really special happening. The chemistry, the timing, everything. Right from the start, this was a real team effort. It was amazing. We had a great crowd. It didn't feel like a pilot. It felt like Season Three, any given episode. It just felt *right*.

Do you think it helped that everyone had been on shows that didn't feel as good?

Our acknowledgement and understanding of each other happened during rehearsal. Before we went to shoot, during the week of rehearsal everybody worked hard at getting along. **It was like starting a bunch of marriages.** Everybody was courteous to one another's feelings and we all worked really, really hard to truly and ultimately love one another.

You've played this character for ten years, and perhaps will do so for ten more after that. What's it been like growing up with Joey?

Without a doubt, it's changed my life. It's weird how you always have those kinds of profound moments where art imitates life, absolutely coincidentally. Joey's grown as a character quite a bit, and I've grown as a person quite a bit. But the fame thing is an uncomfortable suit for me. Yeah, it's nice to get a great table in a restaurant. It's nice to be able to get a backstage pass to a concert or a lap around a race-track in a pace car. That stuff is *great*. But there are times when it's not so great. I remember I was living in an apartment thinking, "I need to be in a place where it's more private. I've got to move because people are knocking on the door all the time." In the supermarket I was being followed. **I was followed *everywhere*.**

Did you like it at first?

It's *great* in the beginning because what's the down-

Watching Joey Grow: The gang looks toward Joey for wisdom in a cut scene from the Thanksgiving episode, "The One With Chandler in a Box."

Best Man?: Joey throws Ross a bachelor party before his wedding to Emily in "The One With the Worst Best Man Ever." The party lasts longer than the marriage.

A Real Pro: Thanks to Monica, a hooker's just shown up for Chandler's fake bachelor party in "The One With the Fake Party."

# of marriages

side when you're initially famous? It's *awesome*. Everybody wanted to be my friend. And it's not like you're famous for being a *bad* guy. I remember when I did *Lost in Space* with Gary Oldman. When people saw him on the street they would be a little intimidated. With me, **they would grab me and hug me.** The power of the TV.

People feel you are their friend.

You're in their bedroom. You're in their living room and their bathroom. Wherever they have a TV, you're there. A movie is an event. You get dressed up, you go out, you buy your popcorn, and you get a babysitter or whatever. It's bigger than life. It's different with television in the sense that you're in their home. Fans feel like they have a relationship with you. You're part of their family. Your voice is in the background of family discussions. They can turn the TV louder because they've got to go to the bathroom, and they're craning their neck looking at it through the mirror. All these weird things go along with TV. As a result of all that, there is this relationship. That's why people feel that connection.

It's almost a chemical reaction between the six of you playing those six characters.

The strongest episodes are when there's no guest cast, and **all six of us are in a room together**

Spitting Distance: Actors playing actors, Matt LeBlanc and Gary Oldman exchange saliva fire as they pronounce their "P's" in "The One With Monica and Chandler's Wedding—Part 1." According to Oldman, "Being on *Friends* was the event of the century—just beating out World War II."

The Wall of Fame: Joey's dry cleaner won't put his 8" x 10" photo on the wall in "The One Where Paul's the Man."

The Cover Up: Joey takes the fall again for Chandler and Monica in "The One With Ross's Sandwich."

driving each other bananas. *That's* what people want to see because there's no pipe to lay. There's no new character introduced. It's nothing but fun—22 minutes of fun. With just the main six, you already care about the characters. You already know the history. You already love them. So it's all about what they're going to say to each other.

How would you describe the way this cast works together?

We have a kind of group therapy. We critique each other and **we push each other to be the best we can be.** We cover each other's backs. I have five other people who *absolutely* know what I'm talking about when I say I'm having difficulty about something going on in my life. Because a lot of people would say, "Oh, cry me a river. Is that your mansion? What do you have to complain about?" But what I've heard said is true: **Fame is just a different set of problems.**

What was it like to see your contract negotiations become a subject of international significance and debate?

Unbelievable. That was the next bit of anonymity to go. Every aspect of my life has been written about. Anyone who is in a position to get a raise—no matter *what* the job is, no matter *what* the tax bracket is—and doesn't go for it is stupid. So it's not a question of are they *worth* it? It's about *can* they get it? And *did* they get it? And they *did,* so good for them. That's what *I* say. It's that simple. Am I *worth* a million dollars a week? *No,* I'm not. I'm not finding a cure for cancer. I'm maybe finding a cure for some sadness or boredom for a little while.

How were you able to stick together during the negotiations?

When we first tried to do it, everyone said, "Well that will *never* work." People have tried in the past and it

Captain, My Captain: New sailboat owner Joey tries to set the record straight about Chandler's views on marriage in "The One With the Proposal—Part 2." Executive Producer Andrew Reich calls LeBlanc, "Just a master of delivery and facial expressions."

didn't work, but we made a pact with each other to stick together. "If they come to *you* behind my back, you tell me. If they come to *me* behind your back, I will tell you. **Everyone in? Everyone's in."** And it worked because we had the power to take the show away. If we *all* walk, they've got *nothing*. If they want to fire you, the other five will *all* walk, and that's a promise. That's a good feeling. And we meant it. We all walked a couple of times.

Like Elvis, the *Friends* actually left the building?

There were a couple of times when everyone left the building. One particular time there was a big issue, and one person felt so strongly about it, that she left. And everybody said, "Okay, let's go." It was during one of the middle seasons. We were back the next day. It got resolved *very* quickly.

In retrospect, how do you view the *Friends* backlash that happened after that first dream season?

It was the epitome of "Prop you up to knock you down" idea. **"Press Backlash" was *not* in my vocabulary** at that time. It was surreal—we did the magazine covers. They all *begged* us to be on the covers. We said, "Sure." We were just trying to promote the show. We were prepared for a longer battle to get the ratings.

You didn't know you had already won the war.

We didn't know we only needed to do *one* cover. Lesson learned. Be careful how exposed you get. In case you were wondering, *that's* why it's harder to get us to do covers these days.

Do you think critics went after some of your early movies as part of the backlash?

Well, speaking for myself, my first movie was with a monkey who played third baseman. I *knew* I had to choose a little more wisely. Matt Perry has a really funny story about that. I beat him out for that horrible

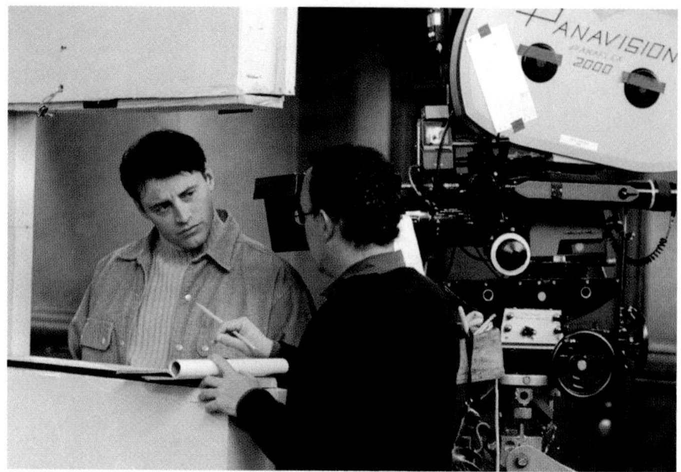

Script Conference: Executive Producer David Crane consults with Matt LeBlanc while rehearsing for "The One With All the Cheesecakes."

Evolution of the Species: Joey's congratulated for even thinking about having a meaningful relationship in "The One With Ross's Library Book."

Everyone in?

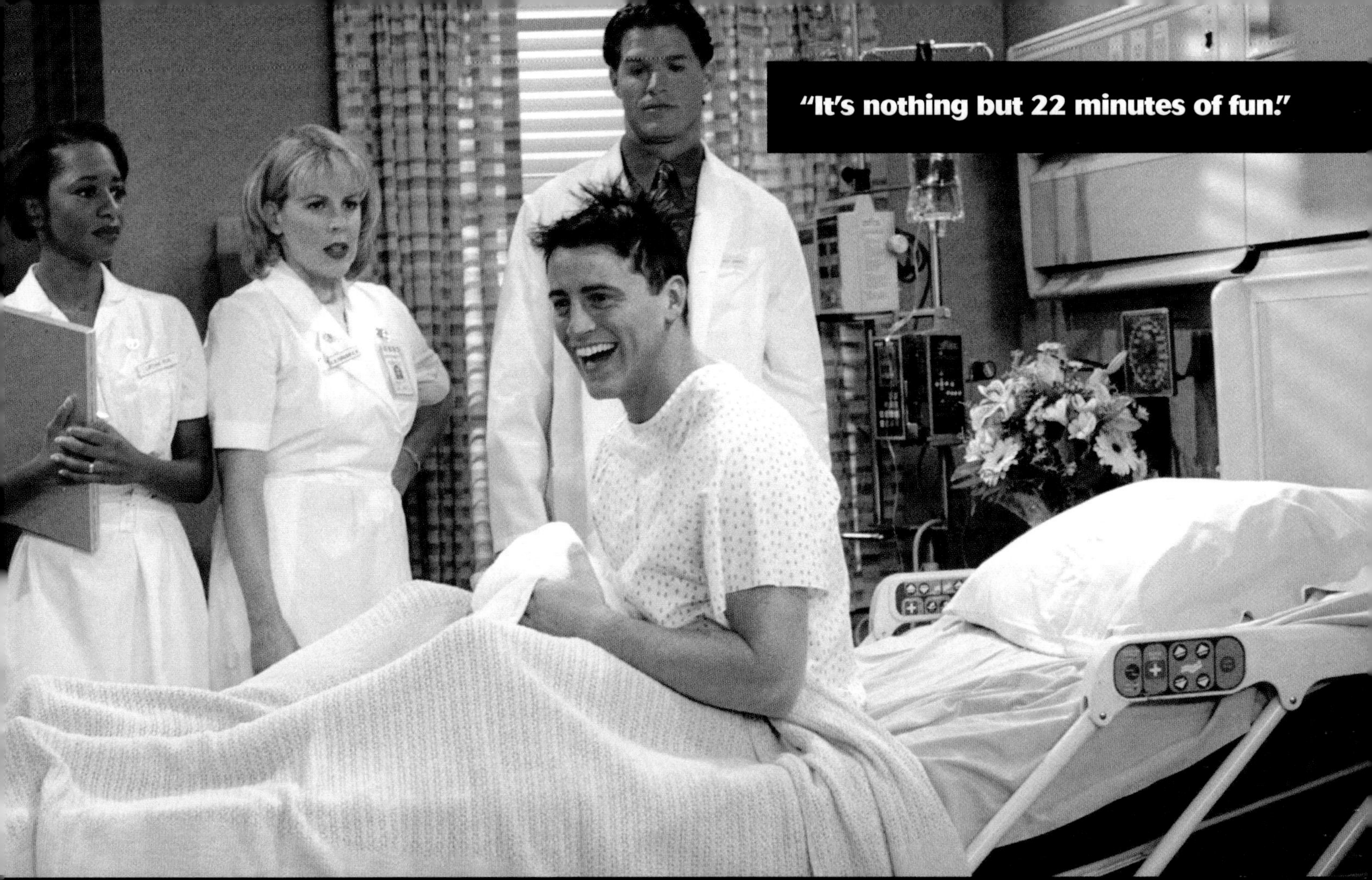

"It's nothing but 22 minutes of fun."

Comatose but Never Better: Joey's back as Dr. Drake Ramoray in "The One With Rachel's Assistant." On working with Matt LeBlanc, Executive Producer Scott Silveri reveals, "The great thing about Matt is no matter what we throw at him, no matter how silly it might be, he will try—he will commit to it."

Everyone's in?

"I had a crush on Jen in the very beginning..."

movie. Hey, it was for kids. I saw little kids enjoy it with my own eyes, for whatever that's worth.

Would you agree that the Joey-Chandler relationship is one of TV's greatest love stories?

I think it was groundbreaking for buddy comedy. In the past, when it was two best friends, there was always a moment when there's something borderline gay—like exposed caring—it was always, "Whoa, *hey*. How about that *game* last night?" I always played it differently. **I played Joey as *so* secure with his sexuality that stuff never bothered him.** He could sleep in Chandler's bed and hug him all night—which *wouldn't* be a problem. He could even do it naked. We did that one episode where he and I are on the fold out couch. We were sleeping in the same bed and I'll never forget, Chandler goes, "Hey *squirmy*" or "Hey *kicky*, what are you doing?" I say, "I can't sleep with my underwear on." He says, "Well, you're *gonna*." When Monica and Chandler got married, I missed that relationship. It hurts a little.

Talking about getting hurt, what do you remember of the episode when you got injured during a taping?

Sure, I have a *great* scar to remember it by. I dislocated my shoulder—*grossly* dislocated my shoulder diving on the couch. I've jumped out of planes; I've jumped on motorcycles. I snowboarded on glaciers in Alaska and yet I get hurt in a controlled environment on a soundstage in Burbank. Go figure.

Did you know right away?

Oh *yeah*. I looked down, and I had no shoulder. It's the weirdest thing to look down, and go where the *hell* is my shoulder? Then the shock set in. Then I got nauseous. I turned white and they had to cut the scene.

So there was an audience watching?

The Diet Coke contest winners no less, flown in from

The Perfect Kiss: Joey's just given Phoebe something she wanted to experience before turning 30—the perfect kiss—in "The One Where They All Turn Thirty." Kudrow praises LeBlanc as, "*So* funny and *so* adorable."

Big Night: Chandler's fallen asleep at Joey's premiere after being chosen as the lucky one in the group to nab the only extra ticket in "The One Where Rachel's Late."

True Confession: Joey tells Rachel that he's in love with her in "The One Where Joey Tells Rachel."

writers a

all over the place. And during the second scene we had to shut down.

What do you think of your writers over the years?

Well first of all, I think they're highly, highly, highly underrated. I think **our writing is right up there, some of the best writing on TV.** We have this really fun thing that we do with David Crane. He's super, super smart, but he's also ultraconservative in that he doesn't like toilet jokes. So Perry and me, just to egg him on, will pitch toilet humor to him. And we'll pitch it with a straight face in front of everyone. He doesn't have any idea we do it on purpose.

To embarrass him?

Yeah. I'll say, "What if Joey just goes in the bathroom here?" We tried one time; I'll never forget it. It's a classic. Since I didn't say anything for three pages, I suggested that I go to the bathroom door and say, "I've gotta go," and shut the door. Then I'm gone. I don't come back for the rest of the scene.

Classy stuff.

That's how we pitched it. So I said, "David, what do you think of that pitch?" He goes, "I've got to say, I don't like it." I go, "Why?" And he goes, "I couldn't think about the rest of the scene. I didn't care what they were saying. I was thinking, so Joey is just in there shitting." **But our writers are the funny ones and sometimes we get the credit.** Being one of the actors on *Friends*, you're considered by the community as an authority on what's funny.

Is there anything the writers came up with for you which you thought wouldn't work?

Everyone was really skeptical about the Joey-Rachel thing and it worked great.

Bamboozled: Some game show fun playing "Bamboozle"—for which Joey is about to audition—in "The One With the Baby Shower."

Air Quotes: Joey pleads ignorance about understanding the meaning of Ross's finger quotes in "The One Where Emma Cries."

Your Cheating Heart: Joey thinks Monica is cheating on Chandler in "The One With Rachel's Phone Number." Actually, Chandler was hiding from Joey to get out of seeing a Knicks game so he could hang out with Monica.

re the funny ones

How was the big kiss for you?
It was nice. Twenty takes. I kept messing up, I don't know why.
Is that true?
No... 15.
How well did the production adjust to all the movies you and your pals were making?
It's been an interesting schedule at times, but Todd Stevens, (Co-Executive Producer) God bless him, has always been able to work it out. He's one of the true greats, that guy. He's so on it.
I remember you were crisscrossing the world constantly while shooting *Lost in Space*?
I was traveling a lot for that other movie I did too, called *All the Queen's Men,* which opened on 12 screens across the country.
You've been in the *Charlie's Angels* movies as well as *Friends*. I sense a trend emerging–you seem to work well with three hot women.
I *like* that theme. You know how some cultures have rice as a staple in the diet. I'd like to keep that as a staple of mine.
Joey's had many relationships on the show, but few significant ones.
Joey's relationships are always off camera, always discussed, which I think is clever because you never have a face to feel badly for. It can just be jokes and the tallest tales ever, and because it's Joey, of course

Not a Breast Man: Joey doesn't handle Rachel's breast-feeding Emma very well in "The One Where No One Proposes."

"...it was groundbreaking for buddy comedy."

Practice Makes Perfect: Joey practices all the right moves on Chandler before his first real date with Rachel in "The One With Ross's Tan."

Waxing and Waning: Dealing with eyebrow issues in "The One Where Monica Sings." Joey had one waxed but couldn't go through the pain of the second, so Chandler tries to fill them in.

it's true. But there were not that many *on* camera relationships—Ross has probably had more on camera—if they were off camera, you wouldn't believe them. [*laughs*]

What's it been like being a really good actor playing a really bad actor?

It's been interesting. When we first started we would go to the *Days of Our Lives* set and shoot over there. That was fun until we realized that we're making fun of all these people. We decided we probably should do this on our own stage so we don't get jumped. Then last season, Joey had the roof top party for all the soap people and I was talking to them. I didn't realize how hard they work. Their workload is *unbelievable*. Thirty pages a day of dialogue—now that's hard to remember. Really well written dialogue flows right off your tongue. Mediocre writing is harder, and poor writing is almost impossible to memorize because there's no thread through it. Fortunately I get great writing.

Is Joey getting better as an actor?

I don't think so. **I think it's better for him to stink because if he's successful, he's not the underdog anymore.** The underdog is the funny guy—the guy that just can't catch a break. Well, he can catch a little bit of a break, but then fucks it up.

How would you like *Friends* to be remembered? Maybe as the show that led to *Joey*?

I could say that. I guess as a piece of history. To me, I remember all the people that have been really important to me. I kind of wish there were a few years left so that I could get ready. **It will be *really* sad when it ends. Really sad.**

really sad

The Honeymoon is Over: In "The One After Ross Says Rachel," Chandler and Monica discuss ditching Ross so they can have sex in the honeymoon suite he was supposed to share with Emily. "Marriage is a blast—on *Friends* and in real life," says Courteney Cox

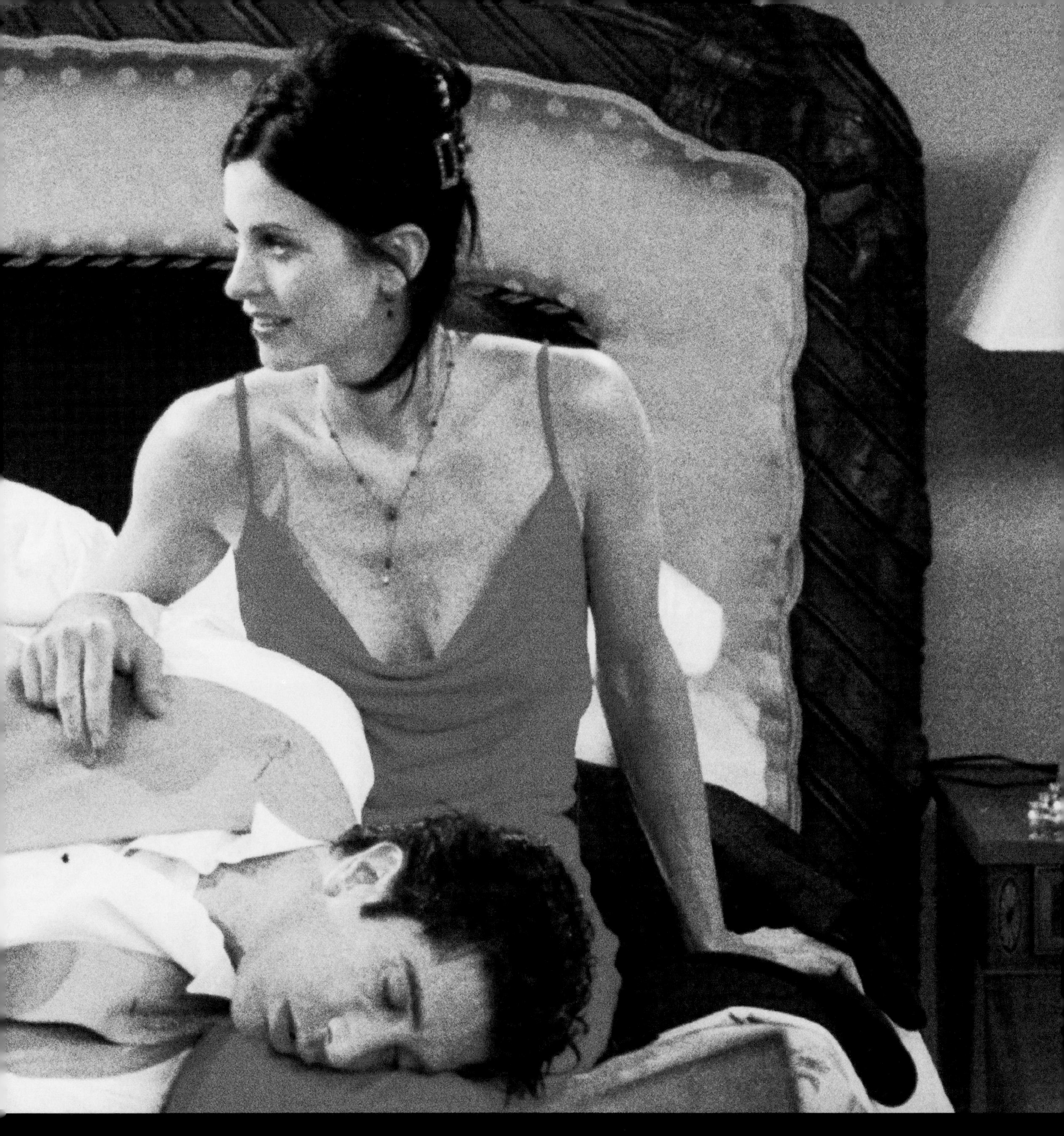

SEASON FIVE

EARLY IN SEASON

***Friends* arrived in television's biggest winning circle with its 100th episode.**

In television, reaching one hundred episodes means that a show now has enough of a backlog to provide many, many years of profitable syndicated fun. For *Friends*, "The One Hundredth" episode also marked another significant passage when Phoebe gave birth to the triplets she had been carrying for her half-brother and his wife since Season Four. "Hi, I'm Phoebe Buffay, and I have babies coming out of me," the multiple mother-to-be offered by way of a hospital introduction.

"Getting the hundredth episode done felt like a big deal—of course, getting every episode done felt like a pretty big deal," says David Crane.

After "The One Hundredth" wrapped around midnight, new TV surrogate mom Lisa Kudrow—who had already given birth a few months earlier off-screen—and her castmates celebrated at a big on-set party where many friends, including Pee Wee Herman, joined the cast and crew, as "That's What Friends Are For" played over the sound system.

Phoebe wasn't the only one being fruitful and multiplying in Season Five—the Bright Kauffman Crane partnership suddenly had three shows in production. Their series *Veronica's Closet,* starring Kirstie Alley, had opened the previous year, and in the fall of 1998 they were also overseeing another new NBC sitcom called *Jesse,* starring Christina Applegate. At the start of the season, after filming the first post-pilot episode of *Jesse,* Bright Kauffman Crane were aware of how much they'd taken on their shoulders. Speaking to me for my book *The Showrunners,* Kevin Bright told me, "It's funny, when we finished last night I said to Marta and David, 'Well, the great news is one down, *sixty-seven* to go.' "

With that unusual workload, it would be a long season for Bright Kauffman Crane, but for *Friends* another quite good one. "The One After Ross Says Rachel" got things off to an excellent start, far better than Ross and Emily's marriage. Other strong episodes included "The One With the Kissing," "The One With Chandler's Work Laugh," the two part "The One In Vegas," and "The One With the Cop," which introduced Michael Rapaport as Gary, a man in blue who was for a time on Phoebe's odd romantic beat. "Michael was wonderful," Kudrow recalls. "I thought, this show is *so* good if Michael Rapaport wants to do it."

Much fun was had with Monica and Chandler attempting to keep their budding relationship secret. This story line climaxed with perhaps Season Five's finest episode, "The One Where Everybody Finds Out."

"I *love* that episode," says Marta Kauffman. "I think what I appreciate about it is that we actually got to be emotional as well. That is something that David and I always enjoy doing, when we can do something more emotional than just another TV show. It was a big moment for the show."

Once again, the relationship between Chandler and Monica took on a life of its own. "It was not meant to be a really long-term thing," Matthew Perry reveals. "It was just going to be a few episodes of them trying to have sex without everybody knowing it. But the reaction was so huge—and the chemistry was so great

FIVE,

between the two most neurotic members of the show—that it's ended up going all the way."

Going all the way—that's what *Friends* are for.

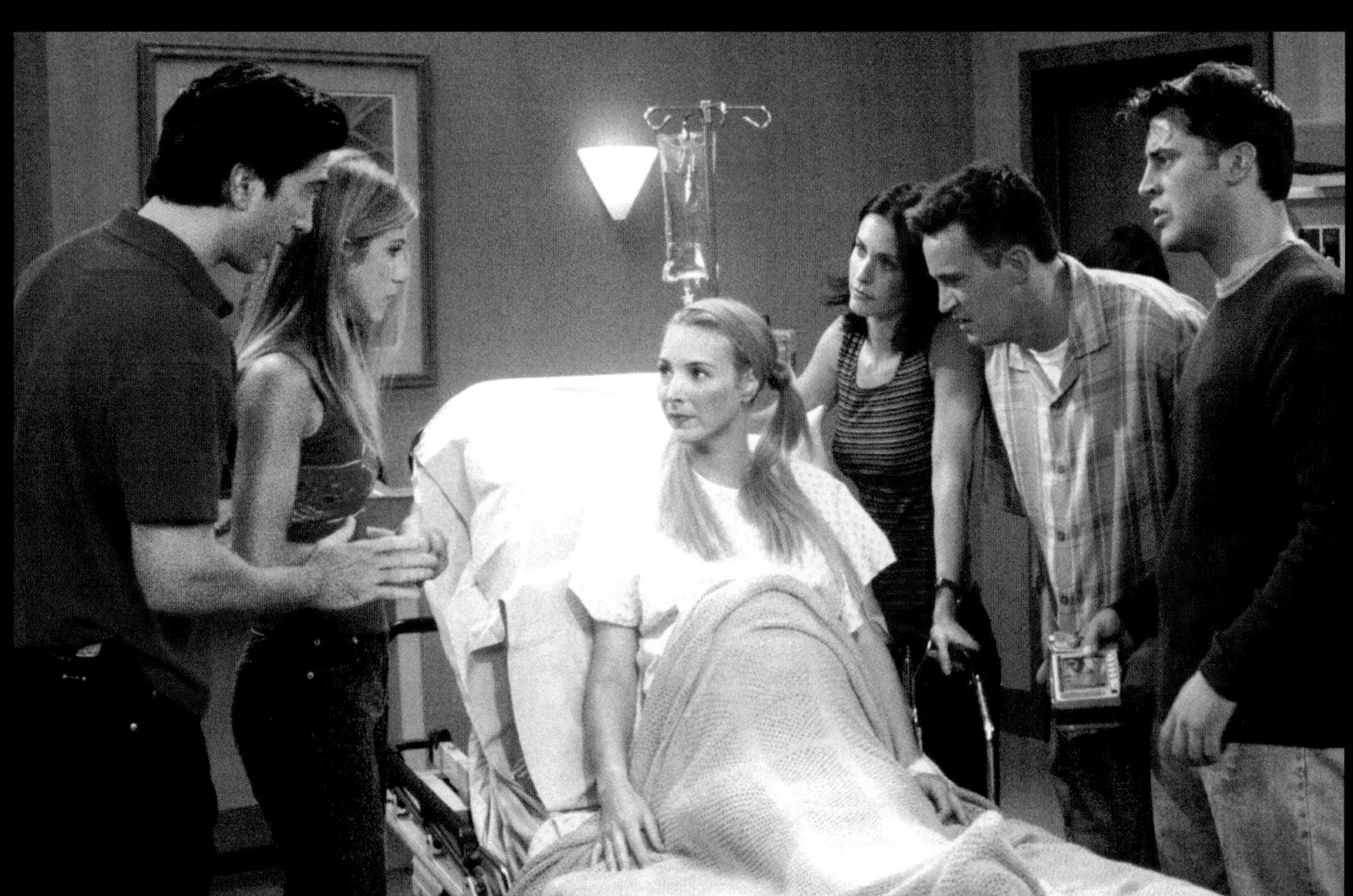

Celebrate Good Times: Images from the festivities surrounding "The One Hundredth." At a celebration on the set, Kevin Bright said, "Contrary to popular opinion, it doesn't feel bad to hit one hundred." Crane saluted the writers, and Kauffman told the cast, "You are the *Friends*, and you are our friends."

Do Not Disturb: Joey wants Chandler to let him into their hotel room because he's got a girl with him. Chandler's goal is to keep Joey out because he's got a girl too—Monica—in "The One After Ross Says Rachel."

An Ugly Memory: Chandler, Rachel, Ross, and Monica in all their glory at the Geller's 1987 Thanksgiving dinner in "The One With All the Thanksgivings." As Courteney Cox points out, "Acting is not always glamorous."

Payback Time: Once upon a scary fashion time, Monica tried to seduce Chandler so she could humiliate him later for having called her fat the year before in "The One With All the Thanksgivings."

going all the way

Job Satisfaction: Rachel accidentally kisses Mr. Zelner, her job interviewer at Ralph Lauren in "The One With Rachel's Inadvertent Kiss." Steve Ireland, who played Mr. Zelner, reports, "I had to do most of my scenes with Jennifer Aniston. Am I a lucky guy or what? When we were doing 'The One With Rachel's Inadvertent Kiss', I left my script out on the table at home and my wife flipped through it during breakfast. I come in and she says 'Wait, what is this? Jennifer Aniston touches your crotch?' I said 'Oh no honey, it's uh, all camera angles and special effects.' (I don't think she bought it.)"

Animal Magnetism: Joey's attempt to scare Chandler by putting a turkey on his head goes perhaps predictably wrong in "The One With All the Thanksgivings." Phoebe helps Joey escape Monica's wrath by garnishing the bird and offers him a few comforting words, "Of course it smells bad [in there] you've got your head up a dead animal's ass!"

Exposed: When a naked picture of Monica slips out of one of Chandler's magazines, Joey refuses to be a part of the cover-up anymore in "The One With Ross's Sandwich." "We got a lot of comedy mileage out of people keeping Monica and Chandler's relationship a secret," says Marta Kauffman.

Lovin', Touchin', Squeezin': Monica gives Chandler a very painful massage in "The One With Joey's Bag." Meanwhile, she's sure he's lovin' it and tells him, "You know, I don't like to brag about it but I give like the best massages."

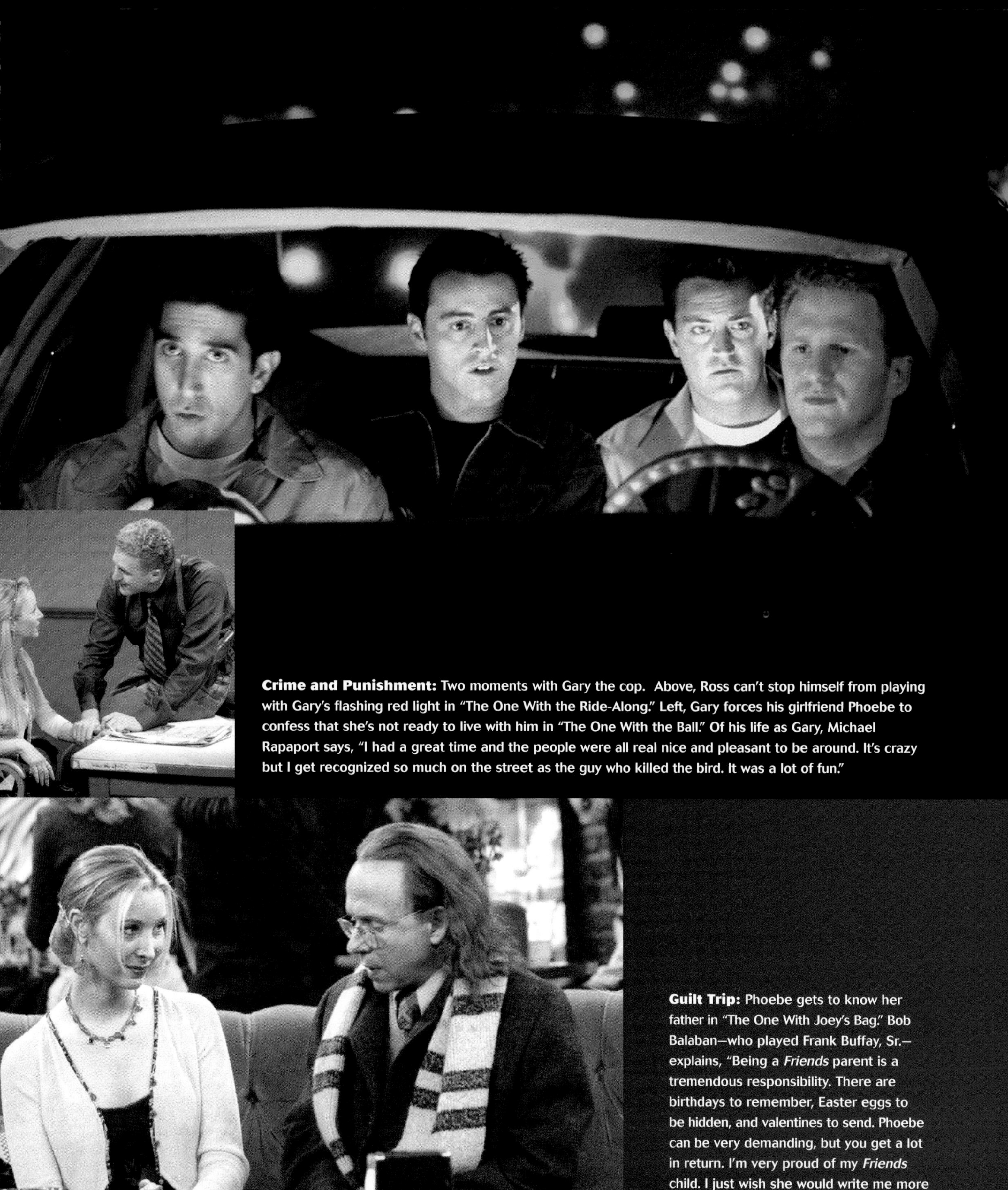

Crime and Punishment: Two moments with Gary the cop. Above, Ross can't stop himself from playing with Gary's flashing red light in "The One With the Ride-Along." Left, Gary forces his girlfriend Phoebe to confess that she's not ready to live with him in "The One With the Ball." Of his life as Gary, Michael Rapaport says, "I had a great time and the people were all real nice and pleasant to be around. It's crazy but I get recognized so much on the street as the guy who killed the bird. It was a lot of fun."

Guilt Trip: Phoebe gets to know her father in "The One With Joey's Bag." Bob Balaban—who played Frank Buffay, Sr.—explains, "Being a *Friends* parent is a tremendous responsibility. There are birthdays to remember, Easter eggs to be hidden, and valentines to send. Phoebe can be very demanding, but you get a lot in return. I'm very proud of my *Friends* child. I just wish she would write me more often. She never initiates phone calls. I occasionally get cards on Purim, but that's about it."

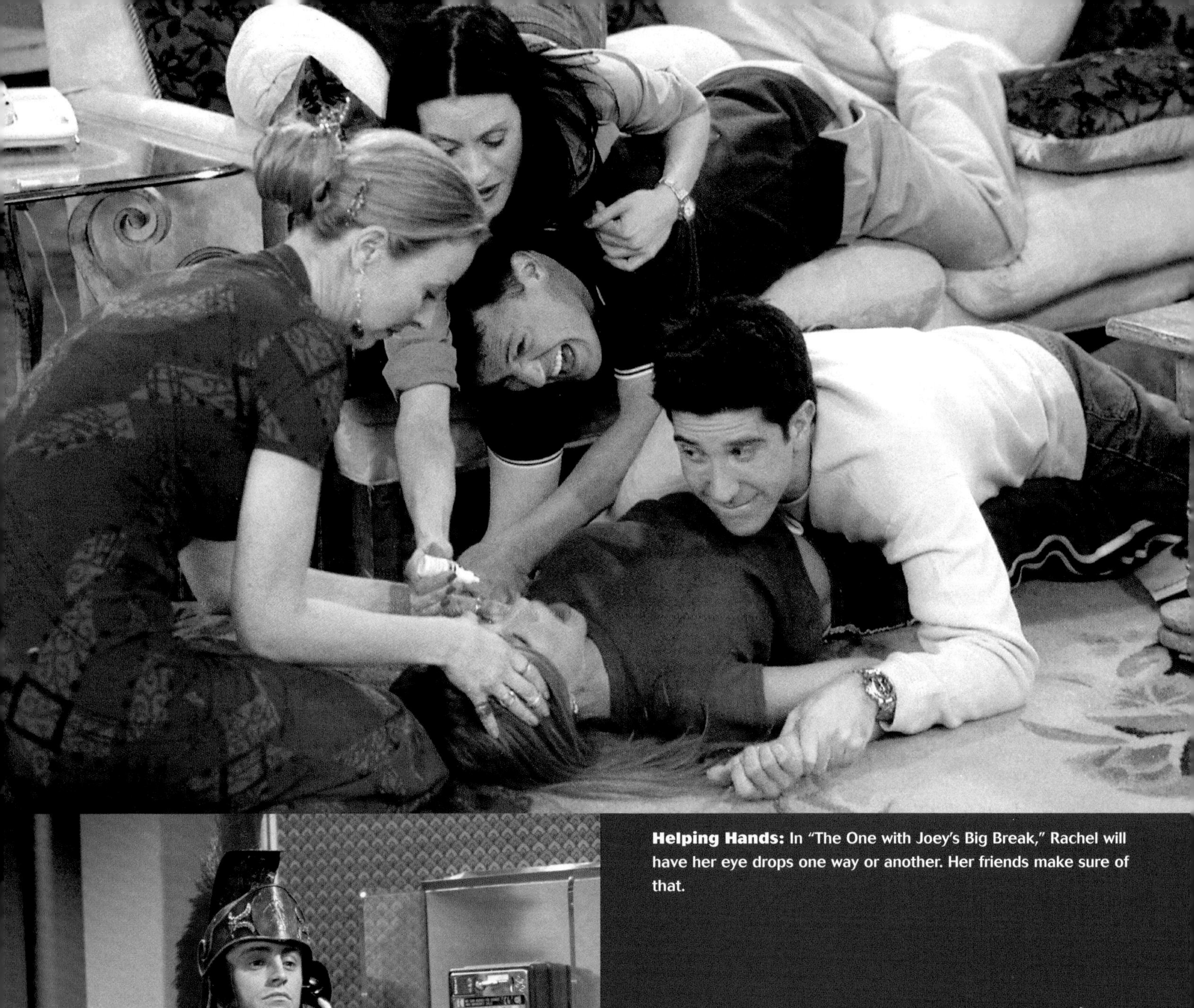

Helping Hands: In "The One with Joey's Big Break," Rachel will have her eye drops one way or another. Her friends make sure of that.

That's the Breaks: A disappointed Joey hides the fact from his friends that his big gig in Vegas turned into a big bust after production shut down in "The One With Joey's Big Break." "Being an actor playing an actor can get a little strange," says Matt LeBlanc.

EPISODE GUIDE

Episode 98: **"The One After Ross Says Rachel"**
Written by Seth Kurland
Directed by Kevin S. Bright
Original Airdate: September 24, 1998

Episode 99: **"The One With All the Kissing"**
Written by Wil Calhoun
Directed by Gary Halvorson
Original Airdate: October 1, 1998

Episode 100: **"The One Hundredth"**
Written by Marta Kauffman & David Crane
Directed by Kevin S. Bright
Original Airdate: October 8, 1998

Episode 101: **"The One Where Phoebe Hates PBS"**
Written by Michael Curtis
Directed by Shelley Jensen
Original Airdate: October 15, 1998

Episode 102: **"The One With the Kips"**
Written by Scott Silveri
Directed by Dana DeVally Piazza
Original Airdate: October 29, 1998

Episode 103: **"The One With the Yeti"**
Written by Alexa Junge
Directed by Gary Halvorson
Original Airdate: November 5, 1998

Episode 104: **"The One Where Ross Moves In"**
Written by Perry Rein & Gigi McCreery
Directed by Gary Halvorson
Original Airdate: November 12, 1998

Episode 105: **"The One With All the Thanksgivings"**
Written by Gregory S. Malins
Directed by Kevin S. Bright
Original Airdate: November 19, 1998

Episode 106: **"The One With Ross's Sandwich"**
Written by Andrew Reich & Ted Cohen
Directed by Gary Halvorson
Original Airdate: December 10, 1998

Episode 107: **"The One With the Inappropriate Sister"**
Written by Shana Goldberg-Meehan
Directed by Dana DeVally Piazza
Original Airdate: December 17, 1998

Episode 108: **"The One With All the Resolutions"**
Teleplay by Suzie Villandry
Story by Brian Boyle
Directed by Joe Regalbuto
Original Airdate: January 7, 1999

Episode 109: **"The One With Chandler's Work Laugh"**
Written by Alicia Sky Varinaitis
Directed by Kevin S. Bright
Original Airdate: January 21, 1999

Episode 110: **"The One With Joey's Bag"**
Teleplay by Seth Kurland
Story by Michael Curtis
Directed by Gail Mancuso
Original Airdate: February 4, 1999

Episode 111: **"The One Where Everybody Finds Out"**
Written by Alexa Junge
Directed by Michael Lembeck
Original Airdate: February 11, 1999

Episode 112: **"The One With the Girl Who Hits Joey"**
Written by Adam Chase
Directed by Kevin S. Bright
Original Airdate: February 18, 1999

Episode 113: **"The One With the Cop"**
Teleplay by Gigi McCreery & Perry Rein
Story by Alicia Sky Varinaitis
Directed by Andrew Tsao
Original Airdate: February 25, 1999

Episode 114: **"The One With Rachel's Inadvertent Kiss"**
Written by Andrew Reich & Ted Cohen
Directed by Shelley Jensen
Original Airdate: March 18, 1999

Episode 115: **"The One Where Rachel Smokes"**
Written by Michael Curtis
Directed by Todd Holland
Original Airdate: April 8, 1999

Episode 116: **"The One Where Ross Can't Flirt"**
Written by Doty Abrams
Directed by Gail Mancuso
Original Airdate: April 22, 1999

Episode 117: **"The One With the Ride-Along"**
Written by Shana Goldberg-Meehan & Seth Kurland
Directed by Gary Halvorson
Original Airdate: April 29, 1999

Episode 118: **"The One With the Ball"**
Teleplay by Gregory S. Malins
Story by Scott Silveri
Directed by Gary Halvorson
Original Airdate: May 6, 1999

Episode 119: **"The One With Joey's Big Break"**
Teleplay by Wil Calhoun
Story by Shana Goldberg-Meehan
Directed by Gary Halvorson
Original Airdate: May 13, 1999

Episode 120: **"The One In Vegas—Part 1"**
Written by Andrew Reich & Ted Cohen
Directed by Kevin S. Bright
Original Airdate: May 20, 1999

Episode 121: **"The One In Vegas—Part 2"**
Written by Gregory S. Malins & Scott Silveri
Directed by Kevin S. Bright
Original Airdate: May 20, 1999

his is me.

So is it true you helped some other people audition for Chandler?

A bunch of actor buddies of mine said, "This character is very much like you. Could you help me with the audition?" So I got to know the part in that way for a period of about three weeks while they were trying to cast it. Some of my friends got *really* close to becoming Chandler. They went into the final audition with me helping them, as well as their own talent, of course. But I'd try to show them the whole Chandler thing of putting the accents on the wrong words—the way Chandler talks. Thankfully, what ended up happening was that NBC and Warner Bros. finally *watched LAX 2194* and smartly realized that this probably wasn't going to get picked up. So they auditioned me in second position for the show, assuming rightly the other show would bite the dust.

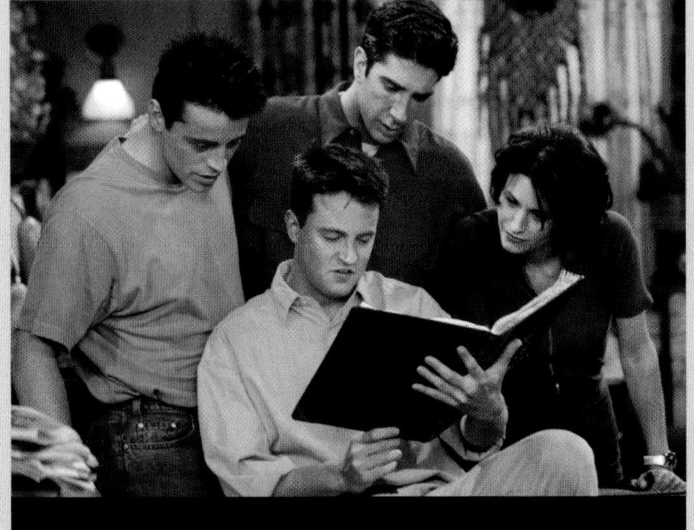

Raising Heckles: The gang discovers the late great Mr. Heckles was a class clown in "The One Where Heckles Dies"

And by this time you were already well prepared to play Chandler?

I knew the whole thing. I didn't even bring sides—the script pages—to the audition with me. I just walked in and said, "What would you like me to do?" I had helped everybody else so I knew the whole script, frontwards and backwards. **As soon as I found out I had a chance to get in the room, I *knew* I was going to get the part.** I read for Marta Kauffman on Wednesday. I read for Warner Bros. on Thursday. I read for the network on Friday, and then we started on Monday. And in case you hadn't heard, we're still going.

You had already worked with Bright Kauffman Crane on *Dream On*, correct?

Yes. At the time, I was more proud of that episode of *Dream On* than anything else I'd ever done. I had been watching *Dream On* and liked the show. This was back in 1992, and I believe that was actually the first episode that Kevin Bright was going to direct, and I met Marta and David that way too, just as a guest star on their show. They remembered me and obviously liked the work a little, so that helped my chances.

How much of Chandler do you think was on the page in the *Friends* pilot?

Well, that's really interesting. The one-liners were already there. I may have thought of a couple when we were shooting the pilot, but all the really funny observations about life were already there on the page. And that's who I really was—**I had just spent my early 20s not living a life and making fun of other people. And strangely, that's what Chandler was at the beginning of *Friends*.** Originally Chandler seemed like a character who was simply supposed to be an observer of other people's lives. He existed to say the funny thing at the end of scenes in which other people were doing things. That all came out of how smart Marta Kauffman and David Crane were about

I knew I was goin

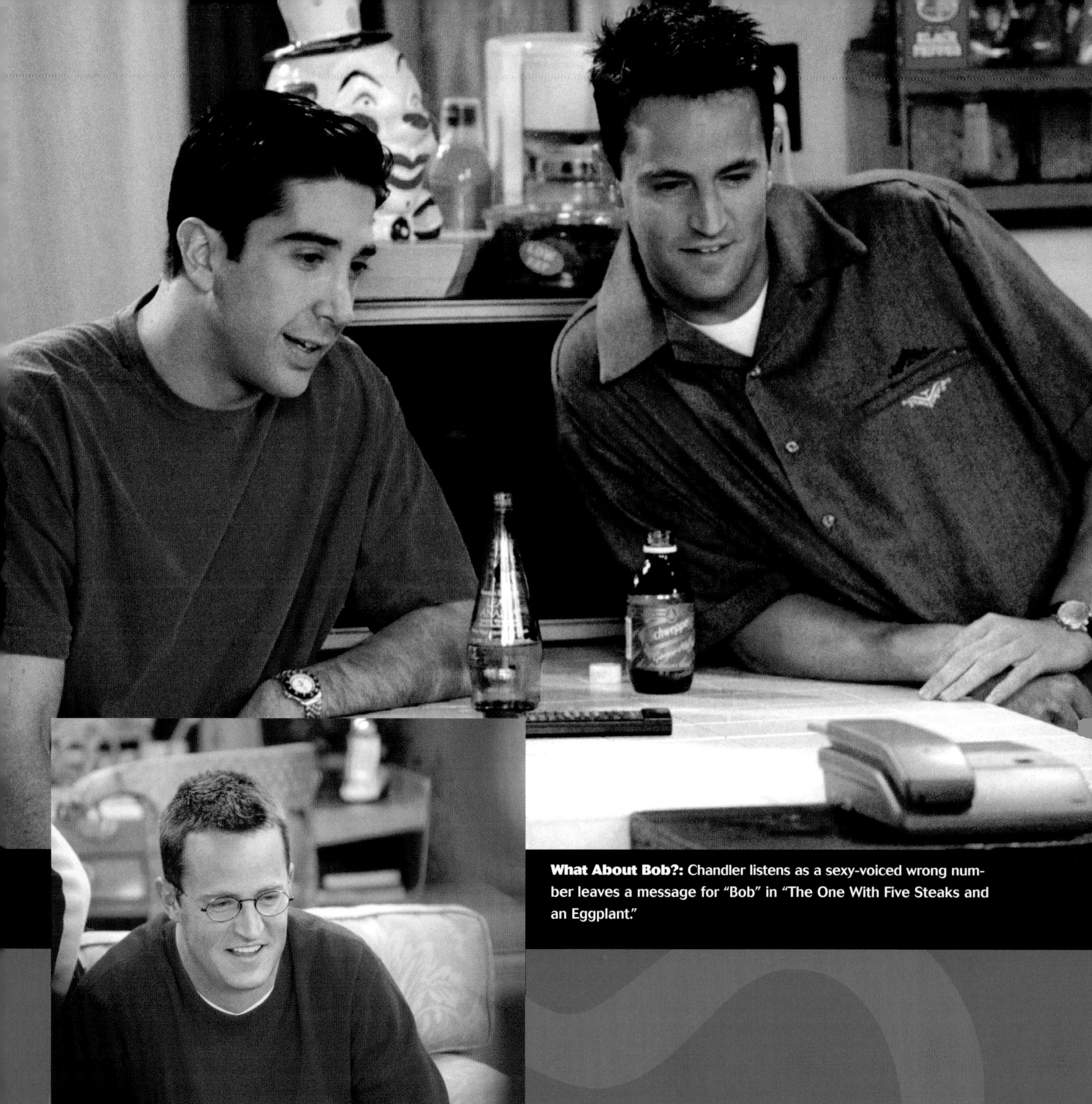

What About Bob?: Chandler listens as a sexy-voiced wrong number leaves a message for "Bob" in "The One With Five Steaks and an Eggplant."

Quick Study: Matthew Perry on the set of "The One With the Memorial Service."

g to get the part

observing everybody. They took everybody separately out to lunch in between the pilot and the first episode, and found out what made us tick. They discovered who we were and what our lives were about. They said, "Tell us something interesting about you, so maybe we can incorporate it into the show."

So what did they learn about your life?

Well, I remember I wasn't doing very well dating at the time.

Come now, Matthew.

No, *definitely* true. And I remember telling them, "I'm not an *ugly* man, but I don't do very well with women." They also saw how I tend to break up emotional or serious moments with a joke whenever I can, because I'm not comfortable in serious moments. And you know, *that's* Chandler. That's what ended up being Chandler. I remember telling them I had just been on a date the previous night. I got home, I called my friend and he said, "How did the date go?" And I said, **"I'm going to *die* alone."** So then four episodes into *Friends*, *Chandler* said that, and then we just kept going that way.

What has it been like for you growing up in public?

Well, on the personal side it's been quite difficult at times, and then ultimately very rewarding. On the show it's been very interesting because the character of Chandler, he really *has* grown up. Who would have guessed from the first couple of years that Chandler and Monica would be a couple and that Chandler would be the first one to get married on the show—other than *Ross*, of course? In my own personal life, it's been interesting, because I don't really feel that need anymore to deflect real moments in life with trying to be funny. And Chandler has dropped that a little bit too. Chandler and Monica have certainly had a lot of real heartfelt moments on the show. That said,

Crane Shot: Perry and Cox talk with Executive Producer David Crane on the set of "The One With the Lottery."

Runaway Non-Bride: Guest star Julia Roberts leaves Chandler stranded wearing only *her* underwear in "The One After the Super Bowl—Part 2."

Blackouts are Perfection: Chandler finds himself stuck in an ATM vestibule with Jill Goodacre in "The One With the Blackout." Perry recalls, "That is one of my favorite episodes of the show. It was exactly the perfect dream/nightmare for my character—he's thrilled about it, then he gets nervous and screws it up." Of that memorable scene in the vestibule, Goodacre recalls, "Matthew Perry and I had such a great time. He was a joy to work with. We ad libbed a lot, including the pencil thing, I started doing it and we just messed around and had fun."

he really

has grown up

Having His Say: Perry makes an announcement to Executive Producer Kevin Bright during the filming of "The One With Ross's Wedding—Part 1."

Thy Roommate's Date: Chandler covets Joey's girlfriend Kathy, played by Paget Brewster, in "The One Where Chandler Crosses the Line." "Matthew Perry will always hold a special place in my heart as my first on-air kiss. And he teased me about it for two weeks—all that tension paid off. My knees buckled." To this day, Brewster says, "I am almost exclusively recognized as being Kathy from *Friends*, even after having done three other series—albeit short-lived ones—and twelve movies. It has been six years and I am still getting *Friends* checks from New Guinea. But I am always amazed when someone recognizes me from the show since my hair was cut so short."

we could really le

Chandler has always been to me the perfect character for a sitcom—a guy who just *has* to make a joke about everything. So he's got a built-in reason to be joking all the time.

But clearly for you growing up hasn't all been a laugh riot.

Well, I was 24 when I got on the show. I'll be 34 when it's over, and those are *really* important years in somebody's life. So to do it all in public for me—for Matthew Perry—as opposed to Chandler *was* difficult. At first you have the wave of **"I'm famous and this is *exactly* what I've wanted my whole life."** And I was the kid who wanted to be on TV—wanted to be on the NBC lineup. But then you go through the whole recluse stage where you think, **"I wish everybody would stop *staring* at me."** And then you eventually, hopefully, get through all that. And you realize that all that attention isn't *really* real, and it's sort of like ether, it can go away at any moment. So you find things in your life that are grounding like your family and good friends…and other things that I've done along the way.

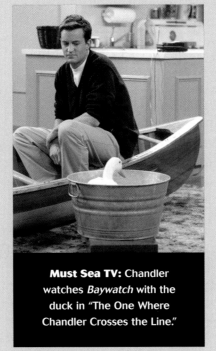

Must Sea TV: Chandler watches *Baywatch* with the duck in "The One Where Chandler Crosses the Line."

Did your fellow *Friends* offer you some much needed grounding?

Certainly they did at first, because **we were six people—or nine if you include the producers—who had our lives changed suddenly in a very bizarre way.** For all six of us, it changed in the *exact* same way, so we could really lean on each other. We could always keep each other in check. That way no big egos could ever come out. And I don't believe that they ever have. If somebody comes in and thinks they're the most important person in the world for a second, the other five of us are there to say, "Shut up, what *are* you doing?"

You've kept each other in check?

Yeah, that's right. It really started on the third day of the pilot with Courteney Cox, who was pretty much the only name going in. She was the one who said, "There's no Jerry Seinfeld on this show so let's all work together. This is a true ensemble." That's what she said, and we all held to that. And it's been very interesting the way it's worked out through the years. I guess the first year everybody was only talking about David Schwimmer. Last year most people were talking about Jennifer, and in between we've all had our moments when we were the one who was garnering the most attention. And clearly sometimes I was getting attention I didn't particularly want. But it didn't really matter who was in the spotlight, because that's just the nature of the show and of celebrity. **The important thing is the six of us have been able to stay close-knit.** We've always been a very, very loving group of people. And that's made it a lot easier.

When you watch the show, does it take you back to what you were going through? Because at times you were going through some personal problems that weren't remotely funny.

I've gone through a couple of very dark periods in my life during this show, and that tends to affect your weight and how you look. So it's tough for me when the really thin episodes come on. I don't watch them

an on each other

"The more serious material has been some of the most rewarding."

a well-oiled mac

that often. I just remember how sad I was during that time and how difficult it must have been to work with me. But thankfully, in my life, I've come to terms with it and made peace with all of that. Still, to answer your question, it can get kind of tough. **Imagine your darkest moment, except you're being watched by 32 million people.** The third season was *very* difficult for me, and I made things *very* difficult for other people with my addiction problems and my behavior.

Are you amazed that the shows all got done—that ultimately the show went on despite all the trouble?

Well, that is my ultimate thank you to everybody who worked on the show—for putting up with me and never raising an eyebrow. People understood that I was in trouble, that it had nothing to do with anything that I had planned. I was into something that was bigger than me, and I had to go and change my life and fix all these things. Finally, that was my only responsibility. I just *had* to do that. **The *Friends* production is a very well-oiled machine**, and I had to do a vast amount of work to make up for the time that I was away, but we all got through it, and now those days are over.

How did you handle the first wave of *Friends* backlash?

Well, it was bizarre at the time, because we didn't understand. Now in retrospect, I look at it and I don't even care, but at the time it was very difficult because we didn't know *what* was going on. **We were doing the *exact* same things, and the press was all of a sudden *hating* us.** Now, having been through it for ten years, you realize that's the story. That's what happens with *everyone*. If somebody gets a phenomenal success, they're going to be praised and written about, and then their next move is *really* going to be difficult. Because they can't write anything better so they go in *completely* the opposite direction,

Enter Laughter: Monica discovers the horror of Chandler's fake laugh in "The One With Chandler's Work Laugh."

Getting in the Zone: Taking care of oily T-zones in "The One With the Cheap Wedding Dress." As Matthew Perry says, "What a great group of guys we've got on this show."

Home Maintenance: In "The One With the Joke," Chandler tries to convince Monica—who's worried that she's too high maintenance—that he likes "maintaining" her. On working with Perry, Executive Producer Shana Goldberg-Meehan, says, "He has such good instincts. I feel like so many times when he delivers a line, it may not be how you thought it was, but it's better."

Blessed Bath Time News: Ross and Rachel share the news that they're expecting a baby girl while Chandler's bath becomes a shared moment in "The One Where Chandler Takes a Bath."

and that's when there's a backlash. It really did bother us. I wish I had the knowledge then that I do now about that, so I could just tell everybody, "Calm down. In about a year we're going to be the best thing again."

On a happier topic, any fond memories of frolicking in the fountain?

We had to do it twice. What I remember most about that was the first time, **you've got six people in a fountain at 4:00 in the morning who are about to embark on a journey and they just have *no* idea what is in store for them—** other than it's going to be fun and *maybe* it will work. It was *freezing* cold and we were out there for hours and hours and *hours*. Then seven years later, we did

Sex Machine: Chandler smokes to deter an oversexed and ovulating Monica in "The One With Phoebe's Birthday Dinner."

an episode where we had to get in the fountain again, and we made sure that it was a half hour. We made sure the water was heated and we made sure we did it ***exactly* the way we wanted to do it.** We weren't going to agree to just do anything anymore. But it was fun. I remember both times we were just laughing hysterically. We were all supposed to dance in the fountain, and I *can't* dance. But I remember a really warm kind of nice feeling about shooting the second one, because it was like going back to exactly where we had started. But my memory of the first time is powerful to me—we're six people moving around in a fountain while there's music playing and we have *no* idea what's in store for us.

How often do you run into that *Friends* theme song in your day-to-day life?

One of the worst things is when I go to sporting events. Sometimes they will put the camera on me and play the song in its entirety up on the big board, and there's *nothing* you can do. You can do a stupid smile for the first five seconds and then... then you're just an idiot. A couple of times like I've been driving in my convertible or something, back when the song was on the radio all the time, I'll hear the first couple of bars of the song, and I reach to turn it down *so* fast. Like almost as fast as when you're listening to a song that you think you like, and then it turns out to be a song you can't stand and you change the channel right away.

From your point of view, what's the role of Bright Kauffman Crane in this story?

Well, they've done just about *everything* right. One of the best things—and it doesn't get talked about anywhere nearly enough—is the writing staff. As soon as some writers are able, they leave to go do their own shows. So they have to be replaced, and one of the things that's kept the show fresh was that the writers have changed throughout the years. Where Marta and Kevin and David really show a lot of

Making the Upgrade: Monica demands the same first-class treatment that the other honeymooners ahead of them received in "The One Where Rachel Tells Ross."

The Out-Of-Towners: Chandler announces that he and Monica will be moving to Tulsa in "The One With the Pediatrician."

everything right

Class Act: Chandler supplements Ross's alumni class update page—"I've cloned a dinosaur who's now my girlfriend and it's the best sex ever"—in "The One With the Memorial Service."

Wedding Bell Blues: Chandler's parents, played by Morgan Fairchild and Kathleen Turner, continue their Cold War during their son's wedding in "The One With Monica and Chandler's Wedding—Part 1." On playing Chandler's transvestite father, Turner explains, "It was a rather irresistible role. When they came to me and offered me the job, I thought, O.K., a woman playing a man playing a woman. I don't believe I've done that before. The bitchfest that Morgan and I had was great fun and Matthew still calls me dad."

talent, that's not expressed often enough, is year to year they hire the most genius writers. Then they lose some of their star players and they replace them with the star players of the next year. They just have this brilliant eye for it. **They also *always* protect the characters.** They never take the characters into areas that are not believable. They also have an amazing gift for finding new ways to put these characters into new situations.

What did you make of the *Friends* ratings going up after 9/11?

I've heard people say that watching *Friends* was like having a really great grilled cheese sandwich. It's a classic, it's comforting, and it's always going to be there for you. The characters have emotion and, of course, they're funny. As far as I'm concerned, **it's always been the nicest place to be.** You can count on 22 minutes when you're going to sit there and laugh unexpectedly every week. Basically, they're just nice people that you want to be around. And every group seems to have a Ross or a Chandler in them, and people really relate to the show on a great many levels. It's amazing that the show skews demographically all over the place, you know. People over 50 watch it, and obviously, the 18 to 49 demographic watch it. It is an unpretentious crowd pleaser. It really *is* like eating a great grilled cheese sandwich, but you don't get fat watching it.

What sort of Freudian nightmare—or a wet dream—has it been to have Morgan Fairchild play your mother?

It's been very bizarre because I had watched *Flamingo Road* and liked all those shows that she did. It's just very bizarre, but **Chandler's whole family is insane. Don't forget, Kathleen Turner is my *dad*.**

What's your recommended Thursday night activity for the world post *Friends*?

Well, hopefully the fine people at NBC will find *some*

nicest

"We certainly are the new *Brady Bunch*."

The Mother of All Babysitters: An ovulating and overheating Monica demands to be serviced while she and Chandler babysit Emma in "The One With the Blind Date." As Executive Producer Ted Cohen says, "Matthew has some of the most impeccable timing of anyone I have seen. He just hits it out of the park, every time."

abso

thing that can help it—like, say, *Joey*. But I think the smartest answer would be going to see one of our movies.

What's your fondest memory of *Friends* finally winning the Best Comedy Emmy?

Jay Leno didn't say *Friends*, he just turned the envelope over that said *Friends*, and we all were just in sheer shock. **We were so giddy and happy because we were absolutely stunned.** Even though people were saying this was the year *Friends* was going to win. But people have said "*This* is the year that they're going to win" *every* year. Especially the first few years, we felt like this show is so *stupidly* good, we've *got* to win *some* of these awards. But we never did. I had just lost for Best Actor that night, and when you're nominated for that after so many years, it was a weird kind of downer. Then to see that the show won by Jay Leno just turning over the envelope, it was amazing. We all leapt to our feet. We couldn't believe it. Just to look over and see David Crane holding an Emmy was an *awesome* feeling.

How would you like the show to be remembered? The end is here, though syndication is forever.

We certainly are the new *Brady Bunch*. I would like it to be remembered the way I remember it—as being the nicest place to be for ten years.

And what's it meant to you to be a part of the *Friends* story?

It's meant the world to me. **It's meant so much to be a part of something *so* good and *so* successful, but also to be part of such a loving environment,** with all its ups and downs. Obviously for many of those ups and especially downs, I was right at the center of them. But the best part of it all is the feeling of leaning towards your windshield when you're driving to work as opposed to complaining about where you're going. You almost want to run red lights to get to work. To have that experience for ten years is *insane* and will never happen again. We've always made sure to remember these moments because it's just the best our lives are ever going to be work-wise.

Do you have a favorite line from the show?

One of my favorite lines is one of my first lines in the pilot, when my character said—"I wish I was a lesbian" and then he said, "Did I say that out *loud*?" Also all the Joey put-downs, after Joey says something *really* stupid. Then the camera cuts to me and people laugh already, because they *know* I'm going to say something to make fun of him. One of the best of those was, "Joey, you have to *stop* the Q-tip when there's resistance."

Beyond the jokes, *Friends* has gone to some surprisingly emotional places for a sitcom, hasn't it?

There's real stuff going on, but the producers and writers are so great at not pushing the line, never going into melodrama or soap opera-type things and always being able to break it with a joke. The more emotional and serious material has been some of the most rewarding, and it's certainly the direction I'm heading for my career in the *next* ten years. Believe it or not, I learned I like doing dramatic stuff by doing a sitcom. I think that's what differentiates us from, say, *Seinfeld*, which was a brilliant show, but prided itself on no emotion. Whereas at *Friends*, we really pull at heartstrings too, and I think that's why **the finale of *Friends*—I said it here first—might be the most watched show ever.**

***Seinfeld* was always said to be a show about nothing. For you, what's *Friends* about?**

Friends is a show about lovable losers who, in the end, become winners by leaning on each other. At least *that's* what I think.

All Hail the Bing: Perry strikes a dapper pose in "The One With Ross's Inappropriate Song."

I'm going to get one of those...job things.

—The formerly spoiled Rachel gets in touch with her newfound professional ambition in "The Pilot"

It's like the mother ship is calling you home.

—Phoebe responds to Rachel getting a job interview at Saks Fifth Avenue in "The One With All the Poker"

Who's FICA? Why is he getting all my money?

—Rachel finds out about paycheck taxes in "The One With George Stephanopoulos"

All right, kids, I gotta get to work. If I don't input those numbers...it doesn't make much of a difference.

—Chandler confesses to his vague professional life, or offers a subtle attack on capitalism, in "The pilot"

GREAT LINES

ROSS:
No, no, no, *Homo habilus* was erect, *Australopithecus* was never fully erect.

CHANDLER:
Well maybe he was nervous.

—SOME HARD PALEONTOLOGICAL-PENILE TALK IN "THE ONE WHERE ROSS AND RACHEL… YOU KNOW"

Put some pants on kid, so I can kick your butt.

—CHARLTON HESTON MAKES A POINT TO BOND WITH YOUNG ACTOR JOEY IN "THE ONE WITH JOEY'S DIRTY DAY"

After all your years of struggling, you've finally been able to crack your way into show business.

—CHANDLER CONGRATULATES JOEY ON HIS ASS STAND-IN ROLE IN "THE ONE WITH THE BUTT"

ROSS:
Joey, *Homo sapiens* are people.

JOEY:
Hey, I'm not judging.

—ANOTHER SCHOLARLY CONVERSATION IN "THE ONE WITH THE GIANT POKING DEVICE"

Everybody lies on their resume, okay? I wasn't one of the *Zoom* kids either.

—JOEY CONFESSES TO FAKING HAVING BEEN A SUCCESSFUL CHILD ACTOR IN "THE ONE WITH ALL THE JEALOUSY"

SEASON SIX

Alternate Lifestyles: A group shot of the gang if their lives had turned out differently in "The One That Could Have Been—Part 1." For Matt LeBlanc, "The magic is when all six of us are together."

SEASON SIX WAS

of maturation on *Friends*—for the characters and the show itself.

Monica and Chandler were growing more and more serious as they worked their way towards Monica's season-ending proposal. Meanwhile, Courteney Cox had already gotten married during the summer break to her *Scream* co-star David Arquette—a former guest star in Season Three's "The One With the Jam." And so it was that for the season opening "The One After Vegas," the entire cast added Arquette to their last names.

Such was the place of the show in pop culture that numerous guest stars now made their way onto the *Friends* set, including Reese Witherspoon in "The One With Rachel's Sister" and "The One Where Chandler Can't Cry" and Ralph Lauren as himself in "The One With Ross's Teeth." Arguably, the most notable visit came from Matthew Perry's co-star in the hit film *The Whole Nine Yards*, Bruce Willis. Starting with "The One Where Ross Meets Elizabeth's Dad," Willis appeared for an extended run as the father of Ross's young love interest Elizabeth. Almost immediately Elizabeth's dad took a special interest in Rachel. Not for the first time on *Friends*, age difference became an issue. "Looks like I'm not the only one interested in fossils," Ross told Rachel.

"It was really fun to have Bruce come on the show, because we had just done the movie," Perry remembers. "He was so terrific on the show. And the fact that Bruce Willis was nervous about doing our show was pretty stunning to us. To us, this is just what we do. To see that these major, major film stars get nervous was really fascinating."

Like other guest spots before and since, the Willis visit came about organically. "Bruce had told Matthew that his kids were huge fans of *Friends*, and that he'd love to be on the show," Kevin Bright recalls. "It wasn't a difficult negotiation and he donated all of his *Friends* salary to charity. We were afraid though, about having this big movie star come to our set and not feeling like we were up to snuff. But Bruce was very gung ho about everything. He never complained about anything. And the thing that was great was seeing that twinkle in Bruce that I don't think audiences had seen since *Moonlighting*. He didn't have to save the world—he didn't have to save *anything*. He just had to be a dad—a dad who luckily gets in bed with Rachel."

"Bruce came in and had great ideas," Matt LeBlanc recalls. "You see the performance he gave. Standing there with his shirt off, flexing like a goober in the mirror. Huge laugh. *Huge*. Bruce blew the roof off the place."

"He was mind-blowingly good in the part," says David Schwimmer.

Still, the emotional high point of the season came very much from the inside in *Friends'* inspired season-ending double-header, "The One With the Proposal—Parts 1 & 2." Monica's actual proposal to Chandler is one of the most emotional in the history of the show. "Our instinct is generally to keep the laughs coming," says David Crane, "but there are some moments that you don't want to undercut."

A TIME

For all the emotion, Perry still gets to deliver one of Chandler's best lines ever to that marrying man Ross. "If you're not careful," Chandler tells him, "you may not get married at all this year."

Love and Marriage: After Monica proves too emotional to finish her proposal, Chandler asks her to marry him in "The One With the Proposal—Part 2." As Courteney Cox puts it, "For all the jokes, there's something very romantic about Monica and Chandler's relationship." For Executive Producer Andrew Reich, "I think that the proposal scene was some of Matthew and Courteney's best work."

The Night Before: In "The One After Vegas," Rachel and Ross express shock as they suddenly realize what they did the night before—got married. Ross recalls, "Wait, wait, wait, I remember being in a chapel. They would *not* let us get married when we were *that* drunk?" Joey astutely points out, "They let you get married when you're drunk. Most people who get married in Vegas *are* drunk."

Court Date: Ross and Rache demand that the judge grant them an annulment after she denied them one because she found out they had slept together in "The One With Joey's Porsche." As Jennifer Aniston says, "People have always just loved Ross and Rachel, no matter what situations they get themselves into."

Boys Don't Cry: In "The One Where Chandler Can't Cry," Monica tries to reduce Chandler to tears—apparently she's unaware of the title of the episode. She tells him, "If I die from a long illness and you're writing my eulogy and you open the desk drawer and find a note from me that says, 'I will always be with you' and you still can't shed one tiny tear—I know you'll be crying a river inside."

Family Secrets: Exposed for inhaling, Ross busts Monica by telling the Gellers that she and Chandler are living together in "The One Where Ross Got High." On Elliott Gould and Christina Pickles' Mr. & Mrs. Geller, Executive Producer Kevin Bright says, "Elliott embodies Jack Geller and he's so wonderful. He connects with the audience because he really feels like your dad. He says those things that are hurtful even though they're not meant to be. He makes it all real and loveable. And Christina has been his perfect soul mate, because she's that mother who walks the line of being the person you dread when the door opens up and she's there, and also being somebody who really does love her children—she just has a hard time expressing it in a way that they can understand." As Elliott Gould points out, "Christina is such a fine artist, so seriously funny. She makes Judy Geller such a hysterical character, which of course helps to make Jack Geller as perplexing as he is."

Repellent Behavior: Joey tries "repelling" his new roommate, Janine, played by Elle MacPherson, and finds it has worked too well in "The One Where Phoebe Runs." "Working on the *Friends* set was one of the most rewarding experiences I have had," recalls Elle MacPherson. "It was a huge challenge working with an ensemble in front of a live audience. I remember having difficulties with comic timing and line delivery with Americanisms that were unfamiliar to me—the whole team from *Friends* was really patient and encouraging. They helped me to relax and do the best I could, showing support and friendship. Watching them work and interact together was awe-inspiring. It was a magical time!"

It's a Laugh: Colleagues Aniston and Schwimmer share a laugh on the set of "The One Where Chandler Can't Cry." As David Schwimmer points out, "The show wouldn't be as much fun if we weren't having so much fun making it."

Pinned: Rachel and Phoebe show Ross they are prepared for danger—at least from him—in "The One With Unagi."

Boss Lady: Go-getter stock broker Phoebe fires her assistant for making one mistake in "The One That Could Have Been—Part 1."

The Pad: A married Rachel visits her favorite soap stud in "The One That Could Have Been—Part 2," and finds him sprawled in his leather chair when she arrives.

High-Pressure Problems: In "The One That Could Have Been—Part 1," Ross, Chandler, and Monica visit high powered bitch Phoebe in the hospital after her heart attack. Ross comforts her, "Come on Pheebs. It's not that bad. You know most people would be excited if they didn't have to work for a couple of weeks. Phoebe the workhorse replies, "Most people don't like their jobs. I love my job. I've been not working for three hours and I'm already going crazy."

A Friendly Tip: Joey tells Chandler that Monica went to Richard's apartment and that Richard wants to marry her in "The One With the Proposal–Part 2." "I've called *Friends* one of the joys of my professional life and I've meant it," says Tom Selleck, who played Richard. "Before *Magnum P.I.*, I guested on a bunch of shows and it wasn't always that pleasant. I was nervous before my first *Friends* episode because even though I'd done a lot of TV, I was the new guy—but they were always a pleasure. For me, *Friends* hit a home run because plain and simple it could make you cry and make you laugh. Courteney's strength is that she is able to put heart into her comedy—which takes an awful lot of skill. That's why the relationship between Monica and Richard worked—the laughs came out of the characters. And it wasn't all about the laughs. For all their success, they're still the same people they were going into this. That's a major accomplishment in this town. As gifted as they all are, I think they're still grateful to have been part of something so special."

A Friends Hug: Matt LeBlanc and Jennifer Aniston on the set of "The One Where Ross Dates a Student." LeBlanc, who confesses to having had a little crush on Aniston in the beginning of the show, now calls her his "little sister."

All Wet: The gang revisits the scene of an earlier comedy crime. Says Matt LeBlanc, "It wasn't easy, but somehow they got us back in the fountain."

Split Decision: Monica and Rachel fight over candlesticks as Rachel packs to move out of their apartment in "The One Where Joey Loses His Insurance." Rachel believes they are hers but Monica thinks otherwise. Finally, they each decide to take one.

growing up

EPISODE GUIDE

Episode 122: **"The One After Vegas"**
Written by Adam Chase
Directed by Kevin S. Bright
Original Airdate: September 23, 1999

Episode 123: **"The One Where Ross Hugs Rachel"**
Written by Shana Goldberg-Meehan
Directed by Gail Mancuso
Original Airdate: September 30, 1999

Episode 124: **"The One With Ross's Denial"**
Written by Seth Kurland
Directed by Gary Halvorson
Original Airdate: October 7, 1999

Episode 125: **"The One Where Joey Loses His Insurance"**
Written by Andrew Reich & Ted Cohen
Directed by Gary Halvorson
Original Airdate: October 14, 1999

Episode 126: **"The One With Joey's Porsche"**
Written by Perry Rein & Gigi McCreery
Directed by Gary Halvorson
Original Airdate: October 21, 1999

Episode 127: **"The One On the Last Night"**
Written by Scott Silveri
Directed by David Schwimmer
Original Airdate: November 4, 1999

Episode 128: **"The One Where Phoebe Runs"**
Written by Sherry Bilsing-Graham & Ellen Plummer
Directed by Gary Halvorson
Original Airdate: November 11, 1999

Episode 129: **"The One With Ross's Teeth"**
Teleplay by Perry Rein & Gigi McCreery
Story by Andrew Reich & Ted Cohen
Directed by Gary Halvorson
Original Airdate: November 18, 1999

Episode 130: **"The One Where Ross Got High"**
Written by Gregory S. Malins
Directed by Kevin S. Bright
Original Airdate: November 25, 1999

Episode 131: **"The One With the Routine"**
Written by Brian Boyle
Directed by Kevin S. Bright
Original Airdate: December 16, 1999

Episode 132: **"The One With the Apothecary Table"**
Teleplay by Brian Boyle
Story by Zachary Rosenblatt
Directed by Kevin S. Bright
Original Airdate: January 6, 2000

Episode 133: **"The One With the Joke"**
Teleplay by Andrew Reich & Ted Cohen
Story by Shana Goldberg-Meehan
Directed by Gary Halvorson
Original Airdate: January 13, 2000

Episode 134: **"The One With Rachel's Sister "**
Teleplay by Sherry Bilsing-Graham & Ellen Plummer
Story by Seth Kurland
Directed by Gary Halvorson
Original Airdate: February 3, 2000

Episode 135: **"The One Where Chandler Can't Cry "**
Written by Andrew Reich & Ted Cohen
Directed by Kevin S. Bright
Original Airdate: February 10, 2000

Episode 136: **"The One That Could Have Been—Part 1"**
Written by Gregory S. Malins & Adam Chase
Directed by Michael Lembeck
Original Airdate: February 17, 2000

Episode 137: **"The One That Could Have Been—Part 2"**
Written by Marta Kauffman & David Crane
Directed by Michael Lembeck
Original Airdate: February 17, 2000

Episode 138: **"The One With Unagi"**
Teleplay by Adam Chase
Story by Zachary Rosenblatt
Directed by Gary Halvorson
Original Airdate: February 24, 2000

Episode 139: **"The One Where Ross Dates a Student"**
Written by Seth Kurland
Directed by Gary Halvorson
Original Airdate: March 9, 2000

Episode 140: **"The One With Joey's Fridge"**
Teleplay by Gigi McCreery & Perry Rein
Story by Seth Kurland
Directed by Ben Weiss
Original Airdate: March 23, 2000

Episode 141: **"The One With the Mac and C.H.E.E.S.E."**
Written by Doty Abrams
Directed by Kevin S. Bright
Original Airdate: April 13, 2000

Episode 142: **"The One Where Ross Meets Elizabeth's Dad"**
Teleplay by Scott Silveri
Story by David J. Lagana
Directed by Michael Lembeck
Original Airdate: April 27, 2000

Episode 143: **"The One Where Paul's the Man"**
Teleplay by Sherry Bilsing-Graham & Ellen Plummer
Story by Brian Caldirola
Directed by Gary Halvorson
Original Airdate: May 4, 2000

Episode 144: **"The One With the Ring"**
Written by Andrew Reich & Ted Cohen
Directed by Gary Halvorson
Original Airdate: May 11, 2000

Episode 145: **"The One With the Proposal—Part 1"**
Written by Shana Goldberg-Meehan & Scott Silveri
Directed by Kevin S. Bright
Original Airdate: May 18, 2000

Episode 146: **"The One With the Proposal—Part 2 "**
Written by Andrew Reich & Ted Cohen
Directed by Kevin S. Bright
Original Airdate: May 18, 2000

david

SCHWIMMER

The F·R·I·E·N·D·S Exit Interview

"Schwimmer plays a teacher on the show, and the truth is you can learn a lot from the guy," says Matt LeBlanc. "David's got an actor's eye, but also a director's eye. When I met him, I thought, **'Okay, class is in. Let's pay attention.'** He's a really good director, partly because he speaks an actor's language. There needs to be a freshness for everybody on the set—a collaborative kind of energy that goes into every single idea—and Schwimmer has that. From the beginning, he knew so much, including how important it was for all of us to stick together."

It's an

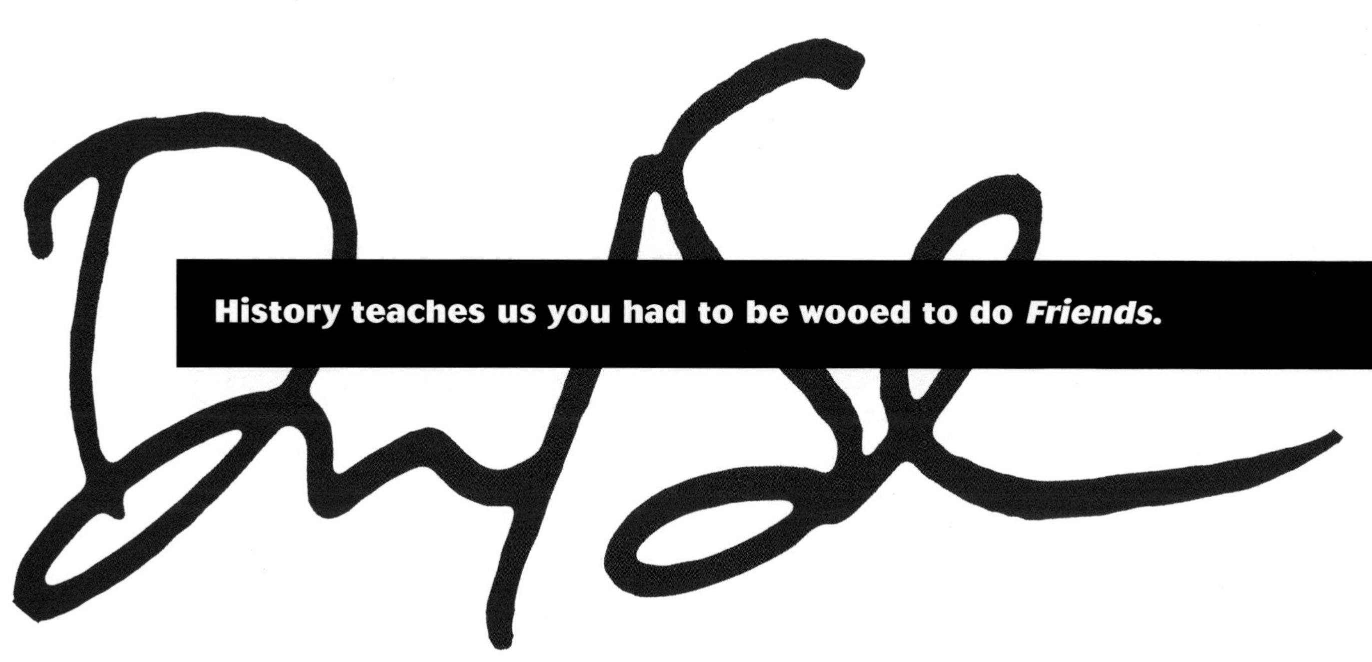

History teaches us you had to be wooed to do *Friends*.

I remember hearing about the show. I was in Chicago doing a play with my company there—the play was *Master and Margarita*. I was crashing at my buddy Joey Slotnick's place while doing this play. Leslie, my agent, called me. I had *sworn* not to do television again because I didn't have a very empowering experience my last time around, which was on a show called *Monty* with Henry Winkler.

If memory serves, *Monty* was not Henry Winkler's best TV show either.

No, *no*. And to his credit, he was great, but the environment was such that I had *no* voice. I would try to speak up and give notes and they'd say, "Yeah, yeah." Then they would completely do whatever they wanted. So I just didn't like that atmosphere and I thought I'd never do that again. I think it also had to do with the fact that it was a TV show built around a star. So my agent called and said the magic words to me. She said, "Look, I *know* you don't want to do television, but please just look at this. **It's an *ensemble* show." That was the magic word for me,** and I said, "Well, send the script." It was *really* funny. But I was still reluctant. I had auditioned for the producers a year previously for another pilot that I didn't get. I tested against my friend Johnny Silverman who got it. But I guess they had remembered my voice or the character I created, so they wrote Ross with that in mind. I didn't know all this until *much* later. Then I get a phone call from Robby Benson of all people.

ensemble show

Some people might not know that the former teen heartthrob has directed several episodes of *Friends*.

Yes, and he's good friends with the producers. He calls me and says "Hi," and I'm thinking, "My God, it's Robby Benson." *Cool*. He says, "Listen, I know you're thinking of not doing this. I just want to say these guys are *great*." And I was so blown away they were going to all this trouble to get me to come and meet with them that I said I definitely would come and talk. So we squeezed a meeting in between performances of the play. I came out and met the producers, and of course, they were awesome. I also met with Jim Burrows and that was it. I said, "Okay, let's give this a shot."

Hot Pants: Ross confronts the downside of leather pants in "The One With All the Resolutions." "I think David is brilliant at physical comedy and he can take pratfalls and punches like nobody I've ever seen before. I'm always just in awe of the sort of craft he has," explains Executive Producer Shana Goldberg-Meehan.

From the start, this cast pulled together and really stayed together for the common good of all. How the hell did you pull off that neat and rather profitable trick?

It's a combination of things. One of the elements is definitely just chance. **The six of us actually liked each other. That's rare.** I didn't know the other five people when we started working together. I felt they were all really cool, really funny, and really nice. I go into any kind of job or whatever I do assuming the best of the person until proven otherwise.

That could be a dangerous assumption in this business.

I know, I know. It is and I've been hurt a lot of times in other situations. But the second thing would be that what happened to us the first year was jarring, in terms of our place in the world. That sudden celebrity was so scary for all of us. Everyone handled it differently, but the only other people you could really talk to about it were the other five. **We grabbed onto each other and clung for dear life on this ride.** Really it was like suddenly being launched on a roller coaster. So I think that experience helped a lot in terms of bonding the six of us together. We had nowhere else to turn.

Some other cast members credit you as being a force early on to encourage unity.

Well, my experience from my ensemble theater company is that of a truly democratic decision-making process where everyone has a voice. Everyone is really listened to and heard. There's debate, there are arguments, there's a lot of passion, but it's always done with a certain amount of respect. I will listen to you and hear your point, and I will counter it with my point, and ultimately the majority vote wins out. I was just urging the group to work in that fashion. I was trying to model how we behaved, how we functioned as a cast, on my theater company in Chicago. So if some idea came down from NBC or Warner Bros., like "Will you guys do this one thing?", then, as a group we would go in a room, privately talk about it, debate the pros and cons, and then decide. Luckily, that stuck. It's

Cuddle Lessons: Ross explains to Chandler how to cuddle with Janice and still have his sleeping space in "The One With the Jam." Ross describes the steps, "You're in bed. She's over on your side cuddling. Now you wait for her to drift off and then you hug her and roll her over to the other side of the bed. And then you...roll away. Hug for her, roll for you." Chandler responds, "Okay, the old hug and roll! One question—you're pretending the pillow's a girl, right?"

clung for dear life

"Matt Perry is just the funny."

Another Wife Bites the Dust: Ross is comforted after breaking up with Emily in "The One With the Yeti." Rachels asks, "Is there anything we can do?" Ross replies, "Yeah, you can help me get my furniture back from Gunther."

"The producers have done a *lot* right."

A Friendly Gesture: Ross gives Rachel the finger without actually giving her the finger in "The One With Joey's New Girlfriend."

hard to do that over a ten-year period.

Yet it worked?

Things have slipped through the cracks several times, but by and large I think we have functioned successfully that way. I knew the power of that process from the success of my theater company in Chicago. **But I didn't realize the power it would eventually wield us in terms of our negotiations.** That wasn't a big ploy on our part. The cards just fell that way.

On many shows, the cast is divided and to some extent conquered.

That's what happens on most shows. I hear even the *Seinfeld* cast—the supporting characters, the three of them couldn't decide in a unified way what they would come back for. It's not easy. Because people have their own lives and families and over time we all change. Everyone changes as human beings.

Did coming from a family of lawyers help educate you about such matters?

Well, my grandfather was a lawyer, my parents are lawyers, and my sister is a lawyer. I think it definitely helps, because I grew up in an atmosphere of understanding argumentation and also an atmosphere of understanding techniques of negotiation. I didn't realize I'd be employing those skills years later or that all those dinner table conversations would pay off.

Now that *Friends* is over, I know you're going to be working as a director/producer and behind the scenes in addition to what you do as an actor. So producer to producer, what do you see that Bright Kauffman Crane has done right in this success story?

Well, obviously they've done a *lot* right. And they've made their share of missteps, but not so many in terms of our show. We are all flawed. We've had some mis-

Moving Experience: Ross and Rachel try to get his new couch up the stairwell in "The One With the Cop." According to Executive Producer Andrew Reich, "David has a rare ability to push things pretty far but still keep them grounded and funny."

Social Climbing: Ross and Joey shimmy down each other after getting stuck on the roof in "The One Where They're Up All Night." A horrified Ross lets go after Joey reveals his pants are falling down and he's not wearing any underwear.

a part of

steps along the way in our careers. But to their credit, first of all, their being present is *huge*. There were some times when they *weren't* as present—when they were working on other shows in addition to *Friends,* and I think we really felt that. The show suffered from it because they are just plain geniuses. I mean, they're *really* good at what they do. But there's such a thing as burnout. Everyone in the cast—and everyone on the show—has probably experienced it at some point. Thank God not at the *same* points. But I'm sure there was a time when they themselves personally hit walls creatively, or just in terms of exhaustion, and they needed to detach. They too have families and other lives. And to their credit they've always surrounded themselves with excellent people—other writers who infuse the show with new life and new energy and new funny.

With the negotiations and all the entities involved—Warner Bros., NBC—how much tension has there been?

It was never a hostile workplace. At times—during one of the big renegotiations a while ago—it was definitely tense. It was hard and sometimes uncomfortable because our job is to come in and—with the writers and producers—find funny. You *can't* do that when you're in the midst of someone calling and giving us an ultimatum—"You have 'til 6:00 p.m. to respond, take it or leave it." You can't then go out, get into makeup, and be funny. I mean, you *can*, and we *did*, but it's not the greatest way to work. When all that was happening, you feel like you're kind of living a lie. Some of the timing of certain tactics and negotiations or deadlines that we had to meet were delivered in such a way that was just the *worst* timing ever—like on a Friday night in the middle of a show. My attitude was, you know what, at *least* have the respect that we're creating something. We're in

Delayed Reaction: Ross finds out about Emily's call to start things up again on the eve of her wedding in "The One With the Ride-Along."

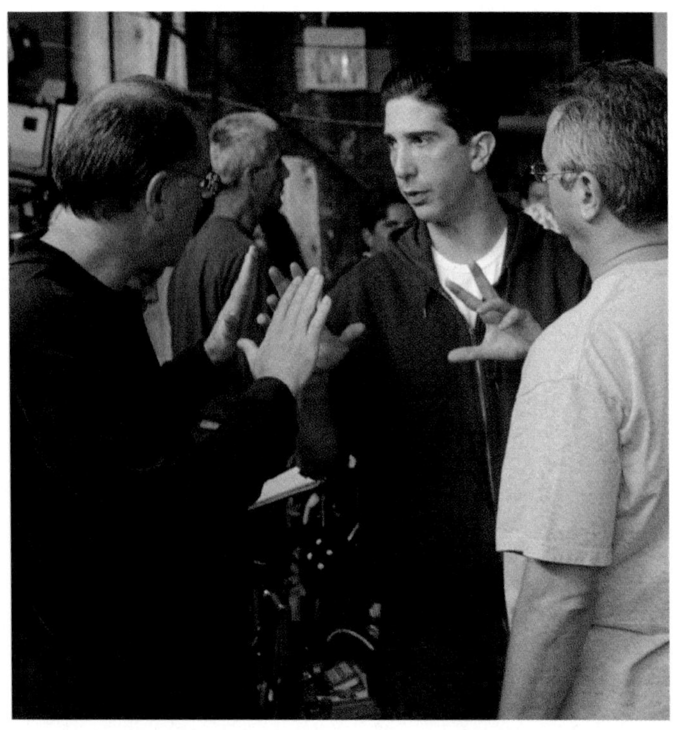

The Right Direction: Sometime *Friends* director Schwimmer confers with Roger Christiansen and Kevin Bright on the set of "The One With Rachel's Assistant."

the middle of filming a show for you. I think there was one time we actually had to make the audience wait an hour while we were all talking. I was so angry about that. But to everyone's credit, no one ever really took it personally. That was the biggest challenge. I hope the producers never really took it personally. And I know I didn't with them.

Big business is big business.

Because I come from a family of lawyers, I can look at stuff like that as just business. I don't get as emotionally involved as others do. I look at it as *this* is what you want, *this* is what we want. These are *your* tactics, these are *our* tactics. It's business and it's not personal. The advantage that the studios have over actors is usually their job is impersonal. It's *never* personal for them. But for actors or writers or directors, it *is* personal. But that's enough about the negotiations.

When did you first become aware you were part of something bigger than just another hit show?

It wasn't until probably three or four years into *Friends* that it dawned on me. A professor of mine from Northwestern said, **"You do realize you're now a part of pop culture."** I think that was the fourth year. I did the math. It hit me that what *Happy Days* was to one generation, or *All in the Family* was to my generation and me, *this* could be for another generation. And that was pretty cool.

Class Act: Ross is confronted with the fact that he and Rachel are still married in "The One Where Joey Loses His Insurance." Rachel barges into Ross's class while he's trying to impress his students and yells, "Ross, are you crazy? I am still your wife? What were you just never going to tell me? What the hell is wrong with you? I could just kill you!"

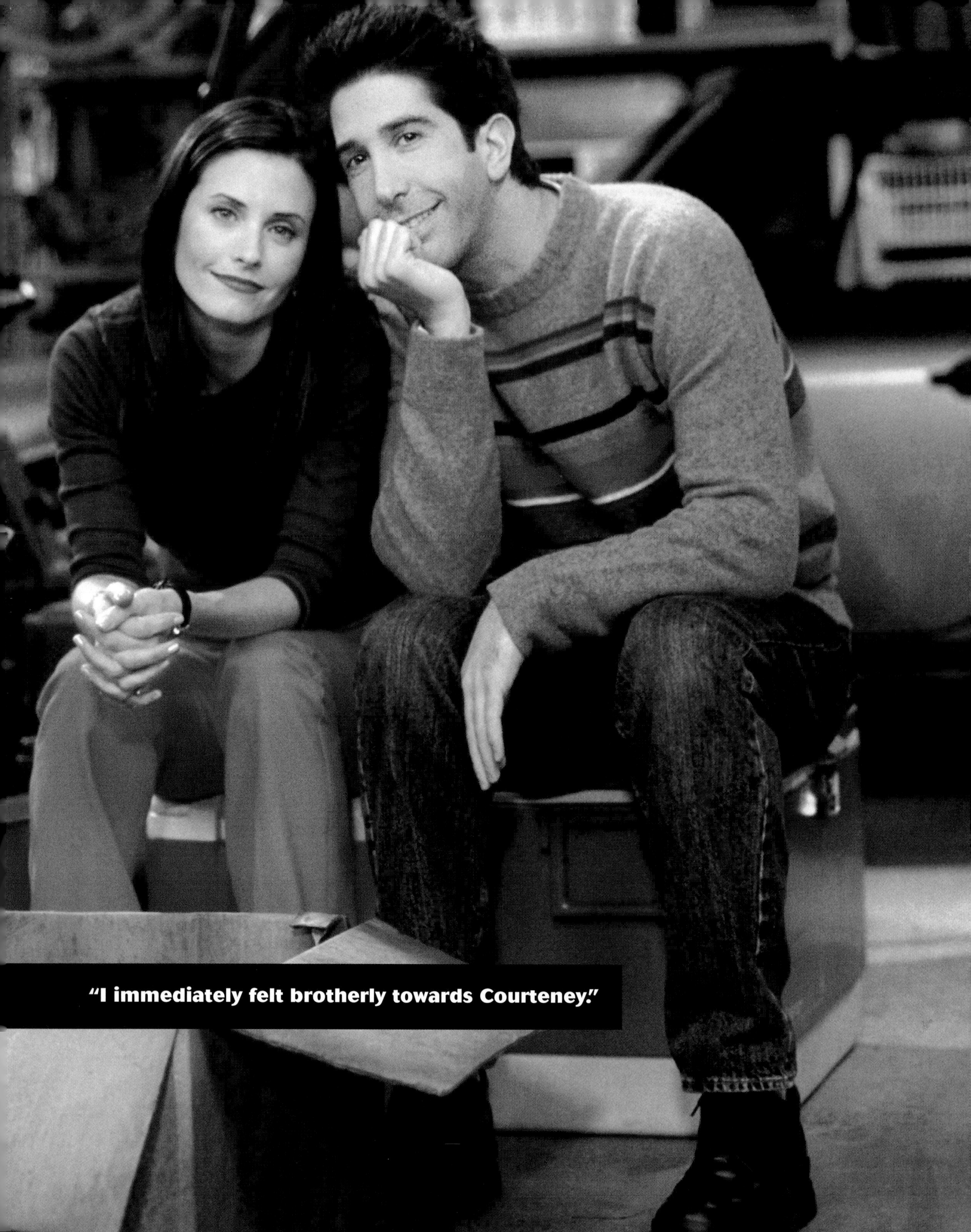

"I immediately felt brotherly towards Courteney."

What—besides all the funny—accounts for the connection viewers have with this show?

I firmly believe **the success of *Friends* is not just that it was funny, but that there was some real heart to these characters**—the love between them and how they looked out for each other like a family. There's a lot of love on the show, from the romances, real love, to Ross and Rachel's high school kind of love lasting as long as it does. It's very different from *All in the Family* in that it's not an issue-oriented show. That was never the writers' intention. But I think it can be just as emotional as a show like that.

You've run a theater company. With the *Friends* players, what do you see as their particular strengths?

You know when you ask me that, it's hard for me to separate the actor from the person, it really is.

It's hard for the fans to separate as well.

I'm sure it is. With Courteney, for example, the first thing that comes to mind is **her extraordinary generosity and her big heart.** Both as an actor and a person, she's *so* generous. And it shows in her acting too. With Courteney, there's a real sweetness about her—both personally and through her character—that is beneath everything. She's also not neurotic but always on top of things. This comes out every time she gets together the next house that she's designing. She is the most organized person. She can juggle so many things, and delegate responsibility and knows *exactly* what she wants. She has really taken that part of her personality and infused it into Monica. Combine that with her extraordinary generosity and you've got this wonderful walking contradiction in both Courteney and in Monica.

And she walks so well.

And she *does* walk so well. She's not bad on the eyes.

In Quite a Spot: Ross's red car gets stuck in "The One Where They All Turn Thirty."

Those Who Do Not Remember the Eighties are Doomed to Repeat Them: Ross and Chandler home from college in all their dated glory in "The One With All the Thanksgivings."

Misty-Colored Memories: Reminiscing about childhood in the Geller garage in "The One Where Rosita Dies."

some real heart

you work hard

Was it hard for you to initially go to a sisterly place with her because she is obviously extremely attractive?

No. I don't know why. Maybe because there's part of her that reminded me of my own sister, but I immediately felt comfortable in that way. I immediately felt brotherly towards Courteney. So no, that was really easy.

Okay, so what does Lisa bring to the party?

Lisa has this razor-sharp mind. Her instincts are impeccable, and I don't even know if she knows just how funny she is. She's hilarious and might I add, sexy too.

Okay, how about Matt LeBlanc?

I always look at LeBlanc as one of those guys who you always want around. He's got the mind-set of a construction guy. That's what he is, he's a blue-collar worker and I *really* like that. I feel that even though I grew up middle class, with my theater company in Chicago I always feel that I'm a blue-collar worker too. We build our own sets, we paint, make our costumes, rig the theater—we actually built our own theater. I really saw that in LeBlanc. He's a guy that's always on time. First one there, last one to go home. He's there to do his job and he gives it 100 percent, and if you misstep on the ladder, he's the one that's going to grab you by the tool belt and catch you. He's just there. Matt's *so* solid. I also think he's the most improved actor on the show. He's found so many layers and so many nuances to that character, which was originally written as a one-dimensional, go-to-joke kind of thing. Matt has so much heart and such sweetness that I'm glad, finally in the last year or two, he's getting the acting credit he deserves, because he's a fine actor.

Punch and Joey: Ross ends up with a broken thumb after aiming for Joey but connecting with an iron pole instead. Another blow for Ross after learning that Joey let Rachel mistakenly think he was proposing to her in "The One Where Emma Cries."

Next—Matthew Perry?

Matt Perry is just the funny. He's got a nonstop mouth and 85 to 90 percent of what comes out is funny.

That's a very high batting average.

Yeah, he really keeps the atmosphere up on the set. He's just one of those guys whether you're out with him or on the set, he will say something funny. So when some joke falls flat during the filming, Matthew usually has a suggestion whether the writers use it or not. I'd say 50 percent of the time they will. **His mind is *constantly* looking for the funny.**

He's a heat-seeking comedy missile.

Yes, that's exactly right. His work ethic is excellent, really excellent. He works *hard*. And to me it's so important that when **you come to work, you work hard.** I think we owe that, first of all because of the money we're being paid and to the fans of the show. It's not easy to find new and fresh stuff. We need to work harder so we don't repeat ourselves.

You haven't told me what strikes you about Jennifer Aniston.

I was kind of saving her for last. She's amazing. I **really compare her to Lucille Ball—one of the best comediennes of all time.**

How about you and Ross? What's it been like playing this guy for a decade?

I have a love-hate relationship with it. But it's interesting, because **in order for me to survive in the regular world I actually kind of forget that I'm**

"She's amazing."

Love at First Sight: Ross helps Rachel finally spot their child during her first sonogram in "The One Where Rachel Tells Ross."

Games People Play: Ross and Ben walk in as Phoebe colorfully expresses her displeasure with the Ms. PacMan game in "The One Where Joey Dates Rachel." "They were a little bit like big kids," Cole Mitchell Sprouse—who played Ross's son, Ben—says of the *Friends* cast members. "They weren't my age, but it was fun. I liked working with everyone there, but most of my scenes were with David Schwimmer and Jennifer Aniston, so I spent a lot of time with them. David was cool. One time I went into his dressing room and he had video games and stuff there and he let me play with them."

Big Winners: The group's Powerball number proves a small $3 payoff in "The One With the Lottery."

on a TV show. It's not until someone comes up to me or calls me "Ross" or something that I remember. Oh yeah, I'm on TV. Luckily I am able to wake up every morning and I completely forget. I don't know how others deal with it or handle it, but for me I don't even think about it until I step on that soundstage. Then I put on the coat and I become the guy. The challenge is a creative one; it's trying to find the funny. Trying to do stuff I've never done before and remember the essence of why that character is funny, and what my function is in the group of six.

How did you react to the initial *Friends* backlash that hit during the second season?

Personally, I took it very hard. I also happened to suffer directly from it because I was trying to open a movie at the time, my first movie.

***The Pallbearer*?**

Yeah. It came out in the middle of this backlash and really suffered from that. We were suddenly opening in the midst of a lot of bad press, and that was rough. But more than that, I think I was just completely shocked and hurt by it. I took it personally. I took it really hard, because we were just doing our jobs. We were kids. I mean, we were in our 20s—we didn't know what the hell we were doing. We were just doing what we were told—like photo shoots to promote the show. Promote, promote, promote, that's what we were doing. That was our job. We didn't know any better, and then suddenly before we knew it, it was like a slap in the face. We're sick of *Friends*. Enough *Friends*. We're thinking, "Wow. What the *hell* happened here? What did we do? What is our crime? That we're funny?" But now, of course, I *completely* get it. I mean, there came a time when the six of us were personally feeling the *exact* same way as the press and the public—which was, *I* was sick of us. The theme song was everywhere and you're seeing

Free Preview: Ross listening to the mourners who showed up for his "memorial service" in, what else, "The One With the Memorial Service."

I forget that

Bummed Out: Rachel is not impressed that Ross has gotten an asinine laugh out of Emma with "Baby Got Back" in "The One With Ross's Inappropriate Song."

Dinosaur Act: Determined to be chosen as keynote speaker at an upcoming paleontology conference, Ross so enthralls Professor Sherman with his gripping topic that he promptly falls asleep in "The One With the Donor."

I'm on TV

us everywhere, and there were so many products that they were pushing for us to do.

What's been the most positive part of this experience for you? We all know it will pay a few bills.

I guess being part, a small part, a tiny slice, if you will, of history—what will become American history or at least pop culture history. And really the most meaningful part is when the everyday person comes to me and says, "My daughter's sick in the hospital. She watches your show. That's the one thing that's making her happy. That will get her through this." That's *huge*, do you know what I mean? To know that you're influencing and perhaps making so many people that you'll never meet or hear of, feel a little better. That's the most positive part—that you're really helping them in some way get through something. If we offer one half hour that takes their mind off things, then that feels good.

Did the return of viewers in the aftermath of 9/11 mean something to you?

Yes, and it seriously influenced the entire cast in terms of giving meaning to what we were doing again. It made us feel good about the work we were doing, and good about the idea of continuing to do it.

And what would you suggest the world do with their Thursday nights after *Friends*?

Since LeBlanc's a friend of mine, I would encourage them to watch *Joey*. I sincerely hope it does well because he deserves it and he's a great guy. I just hope they'll protect him with good writers, and Kevin Bright is going to be involved, so I know he will. More than that, I think my little humble opinion would be to surround him with a really good supporting cast so it's not all on his shoulders. I really wish him the best of luck with it. Maybe I'll come on.

Season's Greetings: In "The One With the Holiday Armadillo," Ross promised his son Ben that Santa would visit, but the store was out of Santa costumes, so he appears as "The Holiday Armadillo," Santa's representative with a bagful of presents.

Archie Bunker's chair ended up in the Smithsonian. Are you ready for the Central Perk couch to achieve similar immortality?

I'm reminded of that when I have people visit the set for the first time. Especially kids, when they see it, they gasp, "Oh my *God*." They're amazed that they can sit on the couch and that the sets are right next to each other. The Smithsonian would be pretty cool.

Have you thought about how you would like to see *Friends* end?

I guess I'd like to see it end with us all sitting around laughing and eating ice cream. I'll let the writers decide which flavors.

Baby Love: In "The One Where No One Proposes," Rachel finally gets Emma to breast feed, and she and Ross decide to start "talking about us again."

# of history

SEASON SEVEN

EVERYBODY LOVES

right? First and foremost, Season Seven was a long drive to the altar for Monica and Chandle

The season opening, "The One With Monica's Thunder," found the gang reacting to news of the impending nuptials, with Phoebe pitching to provide the wedding music and Rachel acting out. Throughout the season, wedding bells rang, thanks in large part to the planning of control freak Monica. Assorted wedding issues were hashed out in episodes like "The One With Rachel's Book," "The One With the Engagement Picture," "The One With the Nap Partners," "The One With the Truth About London," and "The One With the Cheap Wedding Dress."

"Hey, who can blame her?" asks Courteney Cox. "Come on, what woman *doesn't* like to plan her TV wedding?"

"It was a lovely affair, and good TV," says David Crane.

So perhaps it's only fitting that Season Seven—which ended with "The One With Monica and Chandler's Wedding—Parts 1 & 2"—featured many notable guests along the way. Among them was Kathleen Turner, who made quite an impression as Chandler's dad. "What young man *doesn't* grow up wishing Kathleen Turner would play his father?" asks Matthew Perry. Hank Azaria—last seen on *Friends* in Season One—returned as Phoebe's scientist flame in "The One With All the Cheesecakes." Kristin Davis of *Sex & The City*—another show about friends in New York City—checked out the *Friends* scene in "The One With Ross's Library Book." *Seinfeld* alum Jason Alexander—who Marta Kauffman and David Crane knew from their New York theater days—brought added comedic life to "The One Where Rosita Dies." Gary Oldman acted up a storm opposite Matt LeBlanc just before the wedding. "I've been a huge fan of his dramatic work, but his physical comedy is just beautiful," says Schwimmer. *Felicity*'s Eddie Cahill made a big impression, particularly on the ladies, as Rachel's boy toy assistant Tag starting in "The One With Rachel's Assistant"—one of the season's best episodes and one of two in Season Seven directed by none other than David Schwimmer. "David's a terrific director," says Kevin Bright. "He has so many great ideas and the actors obviously respect him."

A number of the season's guest stars seemed nervous at first but then came through with flying colors, like Susan Sarandon who played *Days of Our Lives* soap opera diva Cecilia Monroe. "I had been a fan of Susan Sarandon ever since *The Rocky Horror Picture Show*—forget Rocky Horror, since *Joe*," says Kevin Bright. "Then there's *Atlantic City*, *Thelma and Louise*, *Dead Man Walking*, I mean, we were in *awe* of this woman. And then there's the realization that the guest actors are far more scared of us than we are of them. She was very nervous about the live audience, but one of the things that gave her peace of mind was her daughter had a small part in the show too. Having her daughter around, I think, made it more comfortable for her. She was just so great."

Similarly, Winona Ryder in "The One With Rachel's

A WEDDING,

Big Kiss" turned out to be a sleeper hit," recalls Matt LeBlanc. "At first, she looked like a deer in the headlights, like she was *really* nervous. Then when the cameras were rolling, what a *pro*. Every little tiny nuance was just so. She was just perfect, and I was so impressed with her. It's amazing to watch how good some of these people are up close."

Matthew Perry recalls the end of Season Seven as a rough time for him personally, but somehow it all came out well in the end. "I was lucky to marry Courteney Cox," says Perry, "even on TV."

Let Them Eat Cake: The cast and Bright Kauffman Crane gather onstage to celebrate another landmark episode of *Friends*.

Busted: In "The One With Ross's Library Book," Ross is caught making out with a lovely woman at the library in the section with his thesis. He had gone there to stop others from making out, but ends up making out pretty well himself with another reader played by Sarah O'Hare. "Working on *Friends* was a fantastic experience, actually more like an out-of-body experience," recalls Sarah O'Hare. "I had watched and loved the show for years and to suddenly be there on the set was so strange! David Schwimmer directed my episode and was fantastic to work with—as were the rest of the cast. One thing that blew me away was that the cast knew all their lines and I never saw them once reading the script."

Always a Bridesmaid?: Monica takes Rachel and Phoebe to brunch to discuss who will be her maid of honor in "The One With the Nap Partners."

I Saw Monica Kissing Santa Claus: In "The One With the Holiday Armadillo," Monica gets the lusty kind of Christmas spirit when Chandler dons this merry suit.

A Call For Help: Phoebe's first call as a telemarketer is to a despondent office manager, played by Jason Alexander, who plans to kill himself. Phoebe tracks him down and tries to stop him from suicide in "The One Where Rosita Dies."

Tag, You're It: Tag has just found out Rachel has a crush on him in "The One Where Chandler Doesn't Like Dogs." Eddie Cahill, who played Tag, remembers, "When I was hired, I knew that there was the possibility that Tag and Rachel would become a couple, but it wasn't a sure thing. That being said, the possibility alone was incredibly exciting."

Hannukah Rocks: Ross tries to interest Ben in the holiday of his faith with little luck in "The One With the Holiday Armadillo." Cole Mitchell Sprouse, who played Ben, recalls that of all the episodes he worked on, this was his favorite. "I like how everybody got dressed up in costumes," Sprouse explains.

The Best Soap Opera Actress in History: Susan Sarandon (left) appeared in "The One With Joey's New Brain" as soap opera actress Cecilia Monroe, with her daughter Eva Amurri (above). "Guesting on any TV weekly show is a real challenge because of the time frame of the learning curve," Sarandon said recently. "I can honestly say I had more fun doing the taping of *Friends* than during any other experience. It's not that there was any more time to get over one's fear, there just was such a supportive, playful atmosphere. Right before the taping, David Schwimmer came over to Eva, who at the time was 15, and I, and told us to watch the segments before ours—everyone watches and seems to genuinely enjoy watching the other segments they're not in. Jennifer and Courteney kept cracking up and starting over, and by our turn I felt much braver and less self-conscious. Eva had been watching *Friends* since she was little and said it was the reason she wanted to act. All the cast really knows their territory and they bring out the best in each other. The respect and love they have for each other is genuine and palpable."

Emotional Water Damage: David Crane talks things through with Schwimmer, Cox, and Elliott Gould on the set of "The One Where Rosita Dies" when Monica discovers her father has used her boxes to stop the floodwaters in the Geller garage. Don't cry for her—she got a Porsche for her emotional trauma. Elliott Gould explains, "Jack Geller is purely the creation of the writers and all I actually do is just interpret it."

Thirtynothing: The gang confronts adulthood in "The One Where They All Turn Thirty." They discover just how unexcited Rachel is about her big birthday but she decides she can deal with getting older as long she has "a plan"—one that apparently involves Prada coming out with a line of maternity clothes.

to the altar

Battle of the Brides: In "The One With the Cheap Wedding Dress," Monica and Megan—played by Andrea Bendewald—fight the good fight for the perfect wedding dress in the discount bridal shop that Monica has told her about. Says Bendewald, "Jennifer Aniston and I are best friends and have been since we were 14, so the greatest part of doing the show personally was working with Jen. And also I had just gotten engaged a week before when I got a call to come to the part. I said, 'I'll do anything. I'll carry a tea cup.' I called Jen, and she had no idea. So we got to spend a week at work, talking about being engaged, looking at wedding dresses together, so I was through the roof. And it was a trip professionally, because I know the cast really well but to be acting with them in front of an audience really was kind of like a dream."

A Loving Moment: Executive Producer David Crane with Courteney Cox on the set of "The One With Rachel's Big Kiss." For Crane, "This cast is a writer's dream."

Father Figure: Chandler goes to Vegas to ask his father—with unusual paternal presence by Kathleen Turner—to attend his impending nuptials in "The One With Chandler's Dad." "When we rehearsed 'It's Raining Men,' in the nightclub scene, you should have seen Matthew's face, I thought he was going to die!" recalls Turner.

Family Affair: Ross copes with unpure thoughts regarding his lovely cousin Cassie—played by Denise Richards in "The One With Ross and Monica's Cousin." Richards looks back on her *Friends* experience with the fondest of memories and says, "I loved working on the show and I must admit I was a bit star struck. I've been a huge fan since the pilot. I'm really going to miss watching *Friends*, I wish it could go on another ten years!!!"

A Large Joey Sandwich: Executive Producers Kevin Bright and Marta Kauffman get hands on with Matt LeBlanc on the set of "The One With the Truth About London." Marta Kauffman says, "It means a lot to me that people realize how amazing Matt is." Kevin Bright calls him, "A great guy and a really big talent."

It's All Greek to Them: In "The One With Monica and Chandler's Wedding—Part 2," just as the Greek Orthodox priest (played by Steve Susskind) begins the service, Joey runs in and says "That's my line." Steve Susskind recalls that, "All in all, with the exception of my unwarranted concern following a casual remark when I arrived on the set—that I looked more like a Rabbi—the whole experience, stem to stern with everyone, including the cast, the producers, and the director, was delightful. They say there are no small parts, just short days. Well, the shoot day was quite long—but I for one, was sorry to see it end."

Runaway Groom?: Ross looks for Chandler in "The One With Monica and Chandler's Wedding—Part 2." "I always cry at weddings," says Christina Pickles—who played Judy Geller—of Monica and Chandler's nuptials. "Even TV weddings."

EPISODE GUIDE

Episode 147: **"The One With Monica's Thunder"**
Teleplay by Marta Kauffman & David Crane
Story by Wil Calhoun
Directed by Kevin S. Bright
Original Airdate: October 12, 2000

Episode 148: **"The One With Rachel's Book"**
Written by Andrew Reich & Ted Cohen
Directed by Michael Lembeck
Original Airdate: October 12, 2000

Episode 149: **"The One With Phoebe's Cookies"**
Written by Sherry Bilsing-Graham & Ellen Plummer
Directed by Gary Halvorson
Original Airdate: October 19, 2000

Episode 150: **"The One With Rachel's Assistant"**
Written by Brian Boyle
Directed by David Schwimmer
Original Airdate: October 26, 2000

Episode 151: **"The One With the Engagement Picture"**
Teleplay by Patty Lin
Story by Earl Davis
Directed by Gary Halvorson
Original Airdate: November 2, 2000

Episode 152: **"The One With the Nap Partners"**
Written by Brian Buckner & Sebastian Jones
Directed by Gary Halvorson
Original Airdate: November 9, 2000

Episode 153: **"The One With Ross's Library Book"**
Written by Scott Silveri
Directed by David Schwimmer
Original Airdate: November 16, 2000

Episode 154: **"The One Where Chandler Doesn't Like Dogs"**
Written by Patty Lin
Directed by Kevin S. Bright
Original Airdate: November 23, 2000

Episode 155: **"The One With All the Candy"**
Written by Will Calhoun
Directed by David Schwimmer
Original Airdate: December 7, 2000

Episode 156: **"The One With the Holiday Armadillo"**
Written by Gregory S. Malins
Directed by Gary Halvorson
Original Airdate: December 14, 2000

Episode 157: **"The One With All the Cheesecakes"**
Written by Shana Goldberg-Meehan
Directed by Gary Halvorson
Original Airdate: January 4, 2001

Episode 158: **"The One Where They're Up All Night"**
Written by Zachary Rosenblatt
Directed by Kevin S. Bright
Original Airdate: January 11, 2001

Episode 159: **"The One Where Rosita Dies"**
Teleplay by Brian Buckner & Sebastian Jones
Story by Sherry Bilsing-Graham & Ellen Plummer
Directed by Stephen Prime
Original Airdate: February 1, 2001

Episode 160: **"The One Where They All Turn Thirty"**
Teleplay by Sherry Bilsing-Graham & Ellen Plummer
Story by Vanessa McCarthy
Directed by Ben Weiss
Original Airdate: February 8, 2001

Episode 161: **"The One With Joey's New Brain"**
Teleplay by Andrew Reich & Ted Cohen
Story by Sherry Bilsing-Graham & Ellen Plummer
Directed by Kevin S. Bright
Original Airdate: February 15, 2001

Episode 162: **"The One With the Truth About London"**
Teleplay by Zachary Rosenblatt
Story by Brian Buckner & Sebastian Jones
Directed by David Schwimmer
Original Airdate: February 22, 2001

Episode 163: **"The One With the Cheap Wedding Dress"**
Teleplay by Andrew Reich & Ted Cohen
Story by Brian Buckner & Sebastian Jones
Directed by Kevin S. Bright
Original Airdate: March 15, 2001

Episode 164: **"The One With Joey's Award"**
Teleplay by Brian Boyle
Story by Sherry Bilsing-Graham & Ellen Plummer
Directed by Gary Halvorson
Original Airdate: March 29, 2001

Episode 165: **"The One With Ross and Monica's Cousin"**
Written by Andrew Reich & Ted Cohen
Directed by Gary Halvorson
Original Airdate: April 19, 2001

Episode 166: **"The One With Rachel's Big Kiss"**
Written by Shana Goldberg-Meehan & Scott Silveri
Directed by Gary Halvorson
Original Airdate: April 26, 2001

Episode 167: **"The One With the Vows"**
Written by Doty Abrams
Directed by Gary Halvorson
Original Airdate: May 3, 2001

Episode 168: **"The One With Chandler's Dad"**
Teleplay by Brian Buckner & Sebastian Jones
Story by Gregory S. Malins
Directed by Gary Halvorson & Kevin S. Bright
Original Airdate: May 10, 2001

Episode 169: **"The One With Monica and Chandler's Wedding—Part 1"**
Written by Gregory S. Malins
Directed by Kevin S. Bright
Original Airdate: May 17, 2001

Episode 170: **"The One With Monica and Chandler's Wedding—Part 2"**
Written by Marta Kauffman & David Crane
Directed by Kevin S. Bright
Original Airdate: May 17, 2001

The Triumphant Triumvirate: Executive Producers David Crane, Marta Kauffman, and Kevin Bright on that familiar orange couch in Central Perk. "There would be no six of us without the three of them," says Lisa Kudrow.

BRIGHT KAUFFMAN CRANE

The F·R·I·E·N·D·S Exit Interviews

It's hard to pinpoint what Bright Kauffman Crane have done right, because the thing is they've done **just about everything right.** They made this a great show and they kept it a great show. Marta and David have made sure that the writing staff is the best around year after year. And along with Kevin, they always fought to keep this show something that we could all be proud to have done together."

—Matthew Perry

Kevin Bright

To you, what was the beginning of *Friends*?

There's a song called "Closing Time" which includes the lyric, "Every new beginning comes from some other beginning's end." **The beginning of *Friends* was the end of *Family Album*.** We had this show on CBS...at least we had it for six episodes.

And when the *Album* got scratched?

When Marta, David, and I began our partnership, we agreed that the only type of show we did not want to do was your typical "family in a living room" sitcom. Then CBS pushed us to do *Family Album* and we learned that in television you could never say never. When *Family Album* was cancelled, our determination was that **whatever we do next, it's got to be something that comes from our experience, something we care about.** In November 1993, David and Marta came to me with an idea for a new show. Our previous series, *Dream On,* was about a man getting divorced in the middle of his life and being forced to start over and re-enter the world of dating. What they were interested in now was the other side of that coin: when people are in their 20s and they leave home for the first time and start their own lives. It's a time when your friends become your surrogate family. That was the beginning of *Friends*.

Why do you think the partnership has worked between you three?

The partnership evolved out of the amazing experience we had working together on *Dream On*. Before *Dream On*, David and Marta had primarily worked in musical theater while I had been working in variety television for

13 years. It seemed because of our backgrounds, from a professional standpoint we perfectly complemented each other. There was no ego but there was a lot of passion. When we disagreed, the passion always won. We also liked each other and knew how rare it is to find people whose work you respect and whose company you enjoy, so we just wanted to grab on and we did.

Did the division of labor happen pretty naturally?

Everything flowed seamlessly. My responsibilities were in the business, production, post-production, and directing end of it. David's love was always in the writer's room, and Marta's was split between the room, production, and being on stage with the cast, working out script problems. However, the key to our working relationship was our ability to challenge each other, which always resulted in making the show and us as individuals better.

You've been doing TV long enough to know the vast majority of shows fail. What went right with *Friends*?

Timing, talent, and luck. When *Friends* went on the air in September 1994, there was no other comedy on network television about people in their 20s, and I think the audience was ready for something different. Also, we were able to find these six incredible actors whose talent and charisma took the show to another level. After finding the actors, we were able to get them all signed, which was tricky because of the strict budget limitations on *Friends* in the first year.

I believe I read that they've gotten raises since then.

Yes, I believe those have been pretty well docu-

The Bright Stuff: Executive Producer Kevin Bright refers to the script before directing another episode during Season Nine of *Friends*. "The secret to directing this show is to remember that at its foundation, it's about the relationship between the characters."

always won

Director to Director: David Schwimmer and Kevin Bright on the set of "The One On the Last Night."

mented. Going back to the beginning, Jennifer and Matthew had already done pilots that season and actually, the other shows had first dibs on them. So when we taped the pilot with Jennifer and Matthew, we were taking a calculated risk that we might not have them for the series. If the other two shows got picked up, we would lose them. Fortunately for us, those two shows failed. Our good fortune continued when Jim Burrows wanted to direct. Jimmy is the king of network comedy pilots, and having the director of *Cheers* and *Taxi* on our team only increased NBC's confidence in the show.

And still the network had some questions?

In the beginning there were a few questions about the show from them. **Is the NBC audience really ready for a show that's about these twentysomethings who hang out in this coffee shop?** I remember there was great concern that nobody would really understand what the coffee shop was. Are they going to get it in the Midwest? This was before Starbucks populated the entire country, so they really wanted it to be more of a diner like *Seinfeld.* They were also nervous that there was no older continuing character for the over-49 audience to relate to. They were trying to push us in the direction of having a mailman or a cop on the beat who comes in and gives the friends sage advice when they have problems. Ultimately, **it was yes on the coffee shop and no on the older character.**

Did the network support your casting choices?

We brought 12 or 13 actors to the network and there was no question about who was getting the parts when we were done. The harper pace

only one that we were definitely locked into prior to going to the network was David Schwimmer. He lost out to his friend Jonathan Silverman on a pilot we did called *Couples*, but when Marta and David started writing Ross, they already had David Schwimmer in their heads. Then Lisa Kudrow auditioned for us. We already were fans of her Ursula character on *Mad About You* and we loved her as Phoebe.

Who came next?

Next, the part of Chandler was offered to Craig Bierko, and he turned it down. The funny part about it was that Matthew Perry was Craig Bierko's good friend and he was actually reading with Craig and helping him with his lines, and thinking the whole time, "This is *me*. This is *me*." So after Craig turned the part down, Matthew finally came in, and he *was* Chandler. I mean, he already knew it. And he *was* it. Then we saw Courteney. We knew Courteney from *Family Ties* and we thought, she's the perfect Rachel. Courteney said, "No, I don't want to read Rachel. I'm Monica." And Courteney was right. After that we had a long drought before finding our Rachel, and then Jennifer read for us and just knocked Rachel out of the ballpark. Although there was not a lot of Joey in the pilot script, Matt LeBlanc made him come to life at the network audition. Finally, we had our six cast members.

What was the experience of finding these actors like?

First, there was a lot of frustration. At the time, there were not a lot of parts available to 20-year-olds on TV, and yet we saw hundreds of actors and kept asking ourselves, "Where are the fresh faces to make this funny?" Barbara Miller, the head of Warner Bros. casting had an expression, **"God does not give with both hands,"** meaning we could get attractive or funny but it's going to be tough finding both in six actors. After we had David Schwimmer, I remember being with Marta in session after session and finding nobody for about a month. We really started to think that maybe the script was the problem, not the actors. Then we found Lisa and we were reinvigorated. **After the cast came together and we saw that first rehearsal, it felt like they had already been on the air for five years.** God does give with both hands sometimes.

Did everyone realize you were on to something after the pilot?

NBC had only guarded enthusiasm at first. Don Ohlmeyer, the president of NBC Entertainment at the time, had reservations about the pilot and specifically about Monica. He felt that by sleeping with a guy on the first date, the audience would never respect the character of Monica after the pilot and she would be perceived as a slut. Don would not let go of this and he really wanted us to change it. The compromise was to pass out a questionnaire to the studio audience, which might as well have asked, "By sleeping with a man on the first date, do you think Monica is: A-a slut, B-a whore, C-a tramp, or D-are you fine with it?" The audience was unanimously fine with it. After crossing that hurdle the show was tested with focus groups. It did not test great, but NBC showed their faith by putting *Friends* in the coveted Thursday night slot after *Mad About You*.

How would you describe the usually fast pace of *Friends* which Marta has called "over-caffeinated"?

I think Marta and David established that pace in the writing in order to service the six characters equally. Traditionally, most sitcoms had an A and a B story but with *Friends*, a C story was added, which made it immediately feel different. We realized that in order to get three stories in, there needed to be a faster feel to the show. **Since there was more cutting back and forth between the stories, it created a rhythm in the editing that made *Friends* unique.**

How would you say all of you handled massive fame and success when it arrived?

Well, having not that long ago experienced failure, success is *so* much better. It's so much better than getting canceled. Success didn't suck, but at the same time you could kind of start to feel its weight. The actors certainly felt it. I remember in the beginning, after the show got on the air, Matthew Perry was fascinated with the whole concept of fame. He would purposely go to public places to see if people recognized him. At first he did not get much response, then when the show got hot it changed—oh *boy* did it change—and it was impossible for Matthew and the others to go out in public anymore. Unfortunately, then came all those magazine covers, all the talk about Rachel's hair, and the last straw—the Diet Coke commercial. It all became very self-conscious and fame just kind of bit us in the ass. Once we got past all the hype and back to the show, everything was great again.

You and your partners have been unusually accommodating of your stars' film careers. How did that come about?

In television, shows are always losing their original cast members, for example, Shelley Long left *Cheers* after the first couple of years. This usually happens because the actors are forced to choose between a feature film and a television career. We did not want that to happen with *Friends*. **So in order to keep the cast on the show, we had to embrace and incorporate the ability for them to do other things.** At times, it was disruptive. If a cast member was doing a movie and they couldn't be there that week when we were shooting, we'd have to pick up their scenes later. When we did, it was out of the flow of the show and that took a little bit of getting used to. But ultimately, we adapted and everything was fine. I think the harder part for the actors was that they wanted to do these other things, but in the beginning it was difficult for audiences to separate them from the characters on the show. It was David Schwimmer in *The Pallbearer*, not Ross in *The Pallbearer*. That's really unfair and hard for an actor, but I think they all rose above it. I remember when *The Opposite of Sex* came out. Lisa's performance was 180 degrees from what Phoebe is. I think it helped change the audience's perception. That was the first, really great film that came out of the *Friends* cast.

Besides the obvious financial rewards, what's kept everyone coming back for more all these years?

I think when it really gets down to it, it's the food. **No other show eats the way we do. If you want to have happy people, you must have good food.** Over the years we've always kept our Craft Services table well stocked and the writers get nice meals brought in for them because when they're sitting there knocking it out on 16-20 hour days you've *got* to have something that makes you smile. **So I attribute the success of *Friends* entirely to good food.**

Any favorite main courses?

A staple for the last bunch of years has been Mulberry Street Pizza. That seems to be a particular favorite with the crew.

Now that the end is near, what would you like the legacy of *Friends* to be?

Probably the greatest dream fulfillment that

It's about

How You Doin'?: Kevin Bright checks in with Matt LeBlanc on the set during Season Five.

I could have for *Friends* is that someday it could really become the *I Love Lucy* of its generation. It's full of stories that you can relate to and care about that aren't dictated by a period of time or what was happening in the world. It's about people, how they behave, and what happens in their lives. **I think that these actors will *always* be appealing. I think that the jokes will *always* be funny.** As crazy as some of the *Lucy* stories were, there's something about that cast that you connect with and will forever enjoy inviting them into your living room. If we can still laugh today at Lucy wanting to go to Ricky's club, then hopefully, my grandchildren will feel that same way about Ross telling Rachel, "We were on a break," Phoebe "having her brother's triplets," Monica and Chandler "in London," or Joey "going commando" in all of Chandler's clothing.

You've got a shot, and a better looking cast.

Yes, but only time will tell if any of them has the lasting vocal sex appeal of William Frawley. The pizza's here, you want a slice?

Marta Kauffman

What do you think makes you and David Crane such a winning writing team?

If I were being flip, I'd say it's because we were brother and sister in another life. It's probably the same thing about how *Friends* worked. **There *was* no formula. It just works.** The timing was right. And we are both very careful with each other. I think part of the reason there's been longevity in our relationship is that we're really careful. I believe the worst thing we've ever said to each other is *"Fine."*

So that's a big argument for you two?

Yep. As soon as we acknowledge that we're having one of those days where we can agree on nothing, it goes away. **We're very different, but there's no one in the world with whom I'd rather work.**

Are your senses of humor very similar?

Yes, but I think we bring different things to the party. I have nothing but respect and admiration for his gifts and his talent. We complement each other. David is more reasoned, logical, and clear thinking. I tend to get more emotional and passionate about things. When you put it together, it works. We finish each other's sentences, and we can still do that. We can still communicate with just a look.

Growing up, what TV show meant the most to you?

The Dick Van Dyke Show. I came home from school and watched *Gilligan's Island, I Dream of Jeannie,* and *Bewitched*, but *Dick Van Dyke* was the show. I can remember thinking it was the funniest thing in the world. Those people were so vivid and so real and I wanted to live their life. I wanted to grow up and work with people and have

no formula

it look like it was that much fun. You sing and you dance and you're funny, you work in television and goodness, just the capri pants alone were irresistible.

Is the life of a *Friends* writer just like that?

Nothing like it. This job is not like being Rose Marie, except for the deli sandwiches they bring in. It's so different. Over the years the writers' rooms have changed a lot. When we did *Dream On*, we started with a room of six people. We now have 14. It's equally collaborative, but we don't have the insane person that you have to bend to. I don't know if you ever heard about the network on *Dick Van Dyke*, or broadcast standards. They didn't even talk about ratings.

And you do?

We do look at the ratings. So it's completely different, except for the feeling of loving to be in that room. Those three people had so much fun. And so do we. **There's nothing more fun than being in that room.**

Which is good, because you spend a lot of time there.

Yes, we've spent an *enormous* amount of time in that room. But I don't do the same hours I used to do in the first few years. **When we started I was the**

Game Faces: Marta Kauffman works her winning way with the cast during "The One In Barbados—Part 2". For Kauffman, "We're blessed with a dream cast."

Talking It Through: Kauffman offers some friendly guidance to Courteney Cox and Tom Selleck on the set of "The One Where Dr. Ramoray Dies."

only mother in the room. And I would go home at three and four in the morning and still get up with my kids. After a while it was just too hard for me. Other people, God bless them, can do it. I couldn't do it. It really took its toll on my marriage. Thank God we're fine, but it's hard. The hours depend on the week. Hiatus weeks are very healthy—like 10:00 a.m. to 7:30 p.m. If it's a rough rewrite week, it can start at 10:00 a.m. and go till three or four in the morning. There were a couple of years that were *really* bad when we would go all the way through to seven in the morning. I can remember driving home from work and hitting rush hour. That was rough: pulling into my driveway, waking my kids for school, getting them dressed, getting into bed for two hours, and having to go back to work.

Do you think people have any sense of what work goes into a sitcom?

No. Even some actors who see the rewrites don't really understand the process until you've been in that room. And this is a *very* special room. I can remember arguing about punctuation at two in the morning. Some people get very passionate about the punctuation. We have learned over the years to let go a *little* bit, and there's always another rewrite until show night.

How did the experience of *Dream On* shape *Friends*?

Friends was definitely, to a significant extent a reaction to that show. *Dream On* was the same guy in every scene. He'd made all his decisions and he was living with his choices. **On *Friends*, we created an ensemble and chose people who had all their big choices in front of them.** But *Dream*

On was guerrilla television. We learned to be independent there. We didn't have networks and studios breathing down our necks. We had no money. We did it on a shoestring budget, and it was the best classroom we could have had because we learned to look at structure and how to make a scene work. It showed us comedy doesn't have to have a laugh track to be funny. It's about what makes *us* laugh. So that show was our teacher.

In between *Dream On* and *Friends* you had a few shows and pilots that didn't pan out. What did you learn from a small taste of failure?

To follow your heart. Those were other people's ideas—the ones I look at as failures. The other thing it taught me is that sometimes it's just about how the stars are aligned. Sometimes, like on *Friends*, everything just gels.

Once *Friends* gelled and became a smash, the next season there was a veritable tidal wave of fake *Friends*. Was imitation a sincere form of flattery?

Everybody said that *Friends* was a *Seinfeld* rip-off, but I took the *Friends* rip-off criticism with a grain of salt because I knew that ripping off *Seinfeld* was never our intention. I also know that studios and networks look at something and they go, "Well *that* worked. What's the formula? It's a group of young people. They're friends. Let's do that." That to me is what kills anything. That's what's going to happen with the reality shows. The creative can't work that way. Each idea is it's own individual thing. It's a silly way to create something.

How did the idea for *Friends* click?

It clicked for each of us in different ways. I think we were sort of dancing around the idea of a bunch of young people in their 20s with all their choices in front of them. One day I remember driving down

Moment of Truth: Kauffman and colleagues make some of their not uncommon on-set adjustments.

Beverly Boulevard with my husband, and I saw a sign in front of a storefront that read "Insomnia Café." For some reason, those words made me say, "Oh, *that's* what the show is." Up until that point I think we felt like anthropologists because we weren't in our 20s anymore—although we had been in our 20s in New York in a group of six people at a time when friends are like your family. **That was the moment I understood what the show is. So I remember in our pitch we described it as "overcaffeinated." It still feels that way to me.**

What do you remember about writing the pilot episode?

It wrote itself in three days. It just wrote itself.

Is it pretty much the pilot that we saw?

Yes, there was a lot of network red tape to deal with though. My favorite was in the pilot Monica sleeps with this guy that she's had a crush on for a long time and that's the end of their relationship. Our network person felt that Monica got what she deserved. **Thank God for David, because when I got the note from the network, fire came out of my nose. The executive literally thought that Monica was a tramp.** So the next night when we played it in front of an audience, the network passed out a questionnaire asking about the audience's view of Monica. No one cared that she

us laugh?

slept with him. We didn't want to completely change the story, but we did change her investment in this guy.

Speaking of sex, *Friends* was presenting positive gay characters before *Will & Grace*. Is that a point of pride?

I feel very good about that. I have three kids—one boy and two girls. My daughters' godmothers are gay. They were part of our group of six friends when we all lived in New York. Their daughters are my godchildren. Carol and Susan are very loosely based on our friends Deb and Rona. They're David's friends also. We never did it to make a point—it was just that these were the people in our lives and we thought this would be good material. Then my friend Deb said she was watching the show once with Avery—their oldest daughter—and Carol and Susan were on it. This was the second season when Carol and Susan had a baby. Avery looked at the TV with big eyes and said, "A family like *ours*." She had *never* seen that before. That was the best feeling. Also, when we did their wedding episode, NBC expected thousands and thousands of phone calls and hate mail. Four people called. People don't care as much as *other* people think they do.

How do you react to criticism of the show's sexual content?

These people are in their 20s and they're sexual. Actually they're now in their 30s and they're *still* sexual. When the V-chip stuff was happening, I was involved in a discussion with Joseph Lieberman and John McCain, and Senator Lieberman said he was watching TV with kids and the episode came on where Monica and Rachel fought over the condom. He was appalled and turned it off. My feeling was, well that's *exactly* what the on/off switch is for. But more important than that, these two women were fighting over the last condom because whoever didn't get the condom *wasn't* going to have sex. To me that is so much more responsible than *not* dealing with sexuality.

How instant was the chemistry between the six cast members?

The first time I saw the six of them in the coffeehouse during the first run-through, a chill went up my spine. And I don't think it was until that moment that I realized how important chemistry was. Now I've actually learned that lesson more since doing other shows. These six just worked. It's *enormously* important. Each one of them individually could be fabulous, and you could still come up with crap as a group. Here it was magic. And thankfully, the magic just never really wore off.

What will you miss most about writing for these characters?

I think what I'll miss most is the fun of writing with this group of people. They're just the greatest group of people in the world, and we have such a good time working together. That's going to be hard to imagine being without. We have this annual Labor Day picnic at my house at the beach, and we've already talked about doing it anyway—even without the show. And I think the other thing I will miss is the company of these characters. They're fun to hang with, and they're fun to think about. They're fun to approach and ruminate over.

Can you, anywhere in your mind, accept the idea of a reunion somewhere down the road? A movie or something?

No. Not because I wouldn't want to spend time with the characters again, I would love to. It's just that reunions tend to suck.

Put very delicately.

Thank you. Subtleties are what I bring to the table.

You know this cast as well as anyone. What do you see for them in the future?

That's tough. Not having my crystal ball with me. I think

The Write Stuff: Kauffman and David Crane lead the tireless writers through another episode. On writing and working with David Crane and Marta Kauffman, Executive Producer, Scott Silveri says, "You hear about kids who grow up in Texas who, from their childhood are bred to be a quarterback. If you tried, you couldn't breed to come up with a person better suited for this job than David. It's awe-inspiring and pretty damn annoying sometimes. And Marta is amazing because she brings a lot of the heart to it. She brings a warmth to the writing—a lot of times dummies like me will say, 'Let's just make it funny.' She'll step back and say, 'No, I don't care about this, so why are we even telling this story?'"

they are so talented that they can probably do whatever they set their minds to. My hope is they each take some time to have their lives.

Which have been put on hold to a certain extent?

Absolutely. I'd like them to have fun for a while and not think about working. They should enjoy the fruits of their labor. And my hope is that they don't ever feel that this show has gotten in the way of the rest of their careers. So I guess my hope is that they get an opportunity and that they are trusted enough by the rest of the world to reinvent themselves.

Well, the fact that you've given them so much time to do projects outside the show has given them a great shot.

I hope that's true, and I hope that it actually works for them. I know that there is always that fear when you've been doing one thing that that's all people will see you as.

Yes, I have heard of the *Seinfeld* Curse.

Yes.

Are people's emotional states any different now that the end is pretty much in sight?

Oh yeah. Oh absolutely. We were talking about an episode where Monica and Chandler are looking for a house outside the city, and we came up with the idea that at the very end of one of the episodes—at the very end of the series perhaps—one of the images that we leave with is Monica and Chandler's empty apartment. And every time someone says "empty apartment" I get tears in my eyes. It's a tough image.

How would you say *Friends* has changed your life?

***Friends* has changed my life in every way.** There is everything it's taught me as a writer. There are rules that we thought you had to follow and this show taught me no, no, no, every show has its own rules. It taught me how to collaborate on a large scale and how to trust and empower people around me, and how to give up control—that was a big one. Of course, financially it's had a huge impact on me and my family and enabled me to give to my family, and my aunts, my synagogue, my children's schools, and do good things for the world. And I feel so fortunate that this has enabled me to give back. **I can't think of a way that *Friends hasn't* changed my life.**

David Crane

What makes you and Marta such strong writing partners?

I think we have separate strengths that complement each other. There is stuff that she cares about and is good at that I don't care about and I'm not good at. She's much more intuitive about casting, and I am much more driven by the minutia of writing. I'm *obsessed* with structure. So there's a nice balance there. **We don't do the same job. At the same time, we share a sensibility. The same things make us laugh. I *love* making her laugh. One of the best things about writing together is cracking her up.** And my favorite time—and it doesn't always happen because we have so much we've got to do—is when the two of us are in a room together just writing.

You still share this office?

Yeah, this is it. I'm that side, she's this side.

Boy, you'd think you could afford your own digs by now?

Well, we've been writing together for over 25 years now. Twenty-five years—that's a long marriage. Like any marriage, it's evolved and changed and grown. You discover the stress points, but **the fact that we can share an office is the tip of the iceberg.** When we first got together we were just two kids in college. We were vaguely aware of each other and we started out directing a production of *Godspell* at Brandeis.

***Godspell* at Brandeis, huh?**

Correct. In fact, our Jesus—who is still a friend of ours—is now a very successful rabbi. We started out directing and then writing in college with some other friends. We wrote some musicals, but I don't think either of us imagined at

a real

Word Up: On the set of "The One With Rachel's Assistant," David Crane offers some assistance to Eddie Cahill—the man who would be Tag—David Schwimmer, and Jennifer Aniston.

that point that we were going to be writers. She wanted to be an actress. I had decided I didn't want to be an actor. So it was very much, "Hey we've got a barn, so let's put on a show."

And now you two have a big barn.

Yes, we've got a *very* big barn.

Now let's fast forward to *Dream On*. How did doing that show with Marta and Kevin impact *Friends*?

In many ways *Friends* was a reaction to having done *Dream On*. That show was about one character, Martin, and he was in every scene. That device of using black-and-white clips meant that all those things were going on in his head, so he's got to be in every scene. You reach a point where you wonder, exactly how many stories are there that start with "What *if* Martin…"? *That's* why we decided to do this as a pure ensemble.

I'm not sure people realize how unusual a real ensemble actually is?

I don't think there had ever been a show on television that was a pure ensemble—where there wasn't the lead character's name as the title. Even in *Cheers*, it was Sam Malone's bar. Here we set out to do a real ensemble. You could follow any one of these six people at any time. We tried to create a network of relationships between them—college roommate, brother-sister, best friend, roommate, high school friends—so that you just had an unlimited number of places to go for stories.

I imagine that can be a lot to cover in a half hour.

It's true. We're certainly not the first people to tell three stories a week—*Seinfeld* was telling three or even four

emotiona

stories, but none of their stories ever had to be emotionally resonant. That was just about comedy. For us, the difficulty about including three stories in an episode is at least one of them should have some resonance. That's really hard and it ups your chances of something *not* working on any given week. The odds of one of your stories blowing up, or having some fatal flaw in it, or being ill-conceived is *so* much greater when you're telling three stories than if you're telling two stories or one story.

Is that why on shoot nights, you and the writers are often doing a fair amount of rewriting on the floor?

By that point we're basically fixing jokes. It's really at the table read where you finally see the issues with the story we've been discussing ad nauseum. You hear the actors read it and you suddenly learn a whole host of new things. That's when these large, wholesale changes happen or even after the first run through. Sometimes you see there's a problem and suddenly you have to reconceive things. I can only think of a handful of times when we had a story not grabbing on show night, when we have to quickly scramble and rethink a story with the studio audience sitting there waiting. That's awful. That's hell.

The emotionality of *Friends* seems more connected to a show like *All in the Family* than *Seinfeld*.

Our first job in Los Angeles was working for Norman Lear, who of course did *All in the Family*. I think Norman always liked our writing but found it a little glib. Norman's best work was so satisfying dramatically, yet he had none of that compulsive need to undercut the serious moments with a joke. We only rarely allow ourselves to go quite that far. But in the end, **I've always felt that the thing that makes the show work is how much you care about these people.** I think it wouldn't work if it weren't as funny as it is, but I also don't believe people would be watching it in Season Nine or Ten if they didn't invest as much in the characters as they do. We're always sort of flip-flopping back and forth, trying to strike the right balance between the emotional stuff versus the pure funny.

***Friends* has always been a highly tolerant show. Before *Will & Grace*, you were featuring homosexuality without the usual homophobic clichés. As someone who's been open about being gay yourself, did that mean a lot to you?**

That was very important to me. On the other hand, there are times when people ask about certain elements of the show, "Can you show *that* to kids?" Whether it was something with a gay character or if it's when Rachel got pregnant, my feeling is that when it came down to it, there were questions raised about whether these characters are good role models. And I would make the argument that's *not* what our job is. **Our job isn't to create role models. Our job is to create funny, interesting television. But honestly, I really like to have it both ways.**

Let's talk about some of the *Friends* characters. Joey is the one that seems to have undergone the greatest change.

You have to give a lot of credit for that to Matt LeBlanc. In the beginning I think both David Schwimmer and Matthew Perry were a little bit flashier with their comedy skills. You were *so* aware of them. And I always looked at Matt as this almost stealth comedian. You just saw him quietly chugging along, scoring more laughs and more laughs and more laughs and more laughs until a certain point where you go, wow, *there's* Joey. We cast Matt because he was really funny and also because he brought an *enormous* amount of heart and sweetness to the part. When we wrote the part for the pilot, I don't think we resonance

imagined that. When we first wrote it, we saw Joey as this kind of sexy New York actor guy. Suddenly we met Matt and he's obviously sexy, but there's a goofy sweetness and he's so funny and it all comes across in a really unthreatening way. You have this stud character and he's got to be friends with these three women. Over the years we have done lots of jokes where he flirts with them and comes onto them, but it always feels entirely gentle. There's never any real sexual threat in it. And Matt's able to do that. He was also flat out the funniest person we saw for the part.

Was that always the guiding principle?

That's true for all six of these people: **The reason they got the parts is they were flat out the funniest people for these roles. And sometimes they were the only people who could read this material.** I mean, until Matthew Perry came along, there were people who were *good*, but we were left feeling like maybe the role of Chandler isn't all that funny. It was shocking because when we wrote it, I thought this will be the easy part to cast. Then we started hearing actor after actor read it. And it's *dying*. We knew about Matthew because he had done an episode of *Dream On*, and he was wonderful on it, but he already had a pilot that season. So initially we said, "We're not going to take him in second position, he's off the list." And then a little later we were just so desperate, and someone apparently saw the pilot that he was in and went, "It's *not* going to happen." That's when we brought him in. We heard him read it once and we said, "Oh there you go." He *was* Chandler.

How was finding your Phoebe?

Lisa was the same way. You've got this character that could be so by-the-numbers—this flaky New Age sort of stock character type. I look at the pilot and some of Phoebe's stuff is very much what you'd expect. But

Fine Tuning: Crane makes a script fix during the making of "The One With Phoebe's Birthday Dinner."

when Lisa read it we said, "Oh okay, this is something I had never seen before." This was different from the character she was doing on *Mad About You*, which we also adored—Ursula the waitress. This was different. It was weird, and yet you believed it. It wasn't just a sitcom character. You believed this person existed in the world.

So *Friends* is reality TV, really?

Each of these actors in their own way has the same combination of two things—the ability to be hilariously funny and the ability to be hilariously funny in dramatic situations. You have to believe them. Look at Jennifer. She was *amazing* in so many of the scenes we did regarding Rachel's pregnancy, like when she's looking for the first time at the sonogram of the baby, and she can't find the baby. And she's crying. It's so moving because it's *so* real and it's hilarious at the same time. That's an amazing skill, and a rare one. With most actors, you get one or the other: crying is sad and comedy is funny. As Rachel, she was able to sort of embody all of it. And there's a warmth to Jennifer that comes through the screen. And that's crucial because if you look at the character of Rachel, a lot of what she does is *not* that appealing. She can be selfish, she can be spoiled, and yet…

She's Jennifer Aniston.

Yes, she is. And because of her this character—coming from this pampered lifestyle and reluctant to cut up her credit cards—suddenly becomes so winning that you're rooting for her. You're not judging her at all. If you imagine what we've had the character do and then you slot in some other actresses, suddenly it could be very off-putting. It's similar with Courteney. It took us a while to figure out what was funny about Monica because early on she was more caretaking to the other characters. It wasn't until Thanksgiving of the first season, where we discovered the neurotic side of her character, the obsessive cleaning and control freak tendencies. And a lot of that obsessive behavior could be incredibly off-putting in other hands as well, but with Courteney the fact that she's so beautiful and so warm means you don't feel that way about Monica.

Now that you mention it, she's not rough on the eye.

True, and as a rule, we tend not to necessarily laugh at really attractive people. We think of them as pretty, not funny. And sometimes there's a distance with gorgeous people, but with Courteney, there's so much warmth there and so much heart that you're drawn in. You put another actress who is that stunning in a fat suit, and that could be a really off-putting bit. You could think, "Fuck you, you're so gorgeous." But Courteney embraced the character of Monica so thoroughly and created this whole persona that felt so genuine that you *totally* went with it.

Because this cast was so attractive, the media put them on so many magazine covers, and then the backlash began.

But that's the journey you go on: we built you up so we can knock you down. By now we've been through so many of these cycles where it's "We love you and you're the darling of the moment." Then they turn the other way and forget about us entirely. *Then* they come back and rediscover us as if we haven't been there doing this work all along. We used to call it a *Friend*aissance. "Oh, here comes another *Friend*aissance." And then again they turn. Interestingly enough, usually these backlashes occur around well-publicized renegotiations of the cast salaries. Maybe it's a coincidence, maybe it's not.

Was there a moment when you realized your

the show has

Mutual Admiration: Crane confers with Jennifer Aniston on the set of "The One Where the Stripper Cries." For Crane, "it's a privilege to write for these people."

creation was becoming a cultural phenomenon?

Actually, there *was* a moment. It was Thanksgiving the first season. My folks were out here and we were at a restaurant with my life partner, Jeffrey Klarik. All of a sudden, we overhear a conversation three tables away and someone's saying, "Oh and did you see the one with the laundromat?" And Jeffrey said, **"Okay, remember this moment." And I always have.**

Friends has clearly touched a huge, almost global nerve?

It's weird. It's surreal because that's the aspect of the show that I'm the least in touch with, and frankly it always surprises me when there's a situation that brings it to my attention. That's because mostly I feel like we're just trying to beat the jokes. Most of the time we're busy trying to come up with a good story. So I'm not aware of the global impact. Sometimes I'll see *Friends* on a magazine cover or someone will show me a tape of the show in Japanese, and it's hard to process because it feels so far from sitting in a room with a group of people trying to come up with a better joke.

What makes you proudest of what _Friends_ has accomplished?

I'm really proud that we've been able to sustain the quality of the show. I'm also proud that the show doesn't feel stale—that the characters have been able to grow and mature and go to new places. You don't feel as though you're telling the same jokes you told seven years ago and telling the same stories. And as the characters have gotten older and their lives have gone to new places, we're telling fitting kinds of stories. They don't feel like they did when they were 25.

Your kids have grown up before our very eyes.

Yes. The show has really evolved. And I'm really proud of that, because I think so often with a sitcom, you get trapped in a box, and you end up having to do a new version of that same story because you have nowhere else to go. I'm also really proud in the larger sense that we've been able to make people laugh as long as we have, and it's those moments when I am able to step back and recognize that people are extraordinarily invested in these characters. Hopefully we've been able to keep their faith and we haven't violated our characters too much, and told stories that they can care about. That we've been able to do that and at the same time really make people laugh is what makes me proudest.

What's this last season been like for you—trying to give _Friends_ the proper coda and under a different, tighter sort of schedule?

Well, the different schedule is not that big of a deal. But it's really bittersweet. **I absolutely know in my heart that it is the time to stop. Creatively this is the time to put a ribbon on it.** On the other hand, it's very poignant because I'm really in touch with how much I love doing this, and how much I love the people I'm doing this with.

And that experience is not easily replaceable.

Oh, I don't think it's ever replaceable. I think you can go on and do other things, and hopefully do good work that you're proud of, but we all know we'll never have this again.

evolved

SEASON EIGHT

Pregnant Pause: Rachel finds out she really is pregnant after Phoebe reveals that she's lied to her about the test results in "The One After 'I Do.'"

AT THEIR BEST,

sitcoms give people a place to go once a week where they can laugh and forget about their troubles for 22 minutes or so.

Perhaps that helps explain why Season Eight of *Friends*—which began in the wake of the tragic events of September 11, 2001—turned out to be arguably the show's finest hour. In Season Eight, *Friends* seemed infused with a renewed sense of purpose and viewers took note as ratings increased.

"I think *Friends* was like comfort food for people at that time," says Marta Kauffman. "And I was really honored to be comfort food. We *weren't* dealing with the larger issues. We were just doing comedy, and I think people wanted to laugh more than they wanted to see all the images over and over and over again of the Towers coming down. After a time, people really were ready to laugh, *needed* to laugh again. That was just a special season, a strong season. It's hard to look at all your children and wonder which one is strongest, but I really did love Season Eight."

"If I had to pick a favorite *Friends* season, I suppose for me it would be Season Eight," Matthew Perry offers in a concurring opinion. "We were perceived as having a big comeback year. Everybody was watching the show again, and there was a little bit of that comfort vibe after the 9/11 trauma. That was also my first full, complete sober season which was obviously very rewarding for me personally."

All around, Season Eight was what David Crane has called "a *Friend*aissance"—an especially golden age of admiration for the show by those on the inside and the outside. Monica and Chandler were enjoying a first season of marital bliss. Rachel was going through her pregnancy—until "The One Where Rachel Has a Baby—Parts 1 & 2" which ended the season. "Rachel's pregnancy was *very* productive—it brought us some great stories," says Marta Kauffman. "We had a field day."

During Season Eight there were also great guest stars like Sean Penn in "The One With the Halloween Party" and "The One With the Stain," Alec Baldwin in "The One With the Tea Leaves" and "The One In Massapequa" and in "The One With the Rumor," a strong, surprising performance from Brad Pitt, a promising young actor who apparently scored the gig through a family connection.

"Brad was actually really nervous," recalls Matt LeBlanc. "I don't know if that was because Jen is so good and he didn't want to get shown up by the Mrs. But ultimately Brad was really great on the show." One hopes Pitt didn't take *too* Method an approach to the role, as he played Will, co-founder (with Ross, no less) of the "We Hate Rachel" club back in high school.

"It was perfect because the role wasn't what you'd expect from Brad Pitt," says Kevin Bright. "Brad is really sweet. He comes to pick up Jennifer every Friday night. He kind of sneaks in the back door and he hangs out in her dressing room because he doesn't want to steal the thunder from the show. He's a really sweet guy. He even calls my wife 'Ma'am.' I think she'd prefer he call her something more intimate."

Season Eight also saw the start of Joey and Rachel as a potential item. As Lisa Kudrow recalls, "Some of us were worried with Joey and Rachel because it was like, 'Oh no, now is it just like pairing *everybody* ɔff?' But that really worked out well. I think it was a risk that paid ɔff. Then again Matt and I always thought Joey and Phoebe should get together, but that's not happening—*damn*."

For all the good work in Season Eight, *Friends* would finally win its first Best Comedy Emmy—a long delayed honor considering the show's overall quality and massive popular success.

"That was a great moment for the show," says Jennifer Aniston. "They sure took their time, didn't they? I guess it's sort of like, good God, *they're* still here. I guess we *should* throw them a bone. But the thing is that *we knew*. It can't be the number one comedy on television and not be loved by people. So that spoke for itself. For years, that was our Emmy, you know. Thankfully it wasn't what was driving us, this need for an Emmy, but boy, when it happened, we were sure happy."

First Dance: Despite his slippery shoes, Chandler and Monica survive their first dance as husband and wife in "The One After 'I Do.'"

Dancing Shoes: Ross dances with young Melinda at the wedding, in hopes of impressing Mona in "The One After 'I Do.'"

Cover Story: Rachel has trouble telling her father—played by Ron Leibman—that she's pregnant in "The One With the Stripper" so she tells him she's got TiVo instead. As for the impact of *Friends*, Leibman notes, "I may have played Shylock at the New York Shakespeare Festival or won a Tony for *Angels in America* but people ask me, 'Aren't you Rachel's dad?'"

Tough Guy: Monica tries to convince Chandler not to arm wrestle with Ross because it's his inner strength that counts with her in "The One With the Halloween Party."

Calling Doctor Love: Rachel hits on another doctor—make that TV doctor—in "The One With Rachel's Date." Johnny Messner, who played the doctor, recalls, "After I did *Friends*, I started getting calls from people I hadn't talked to since grade school. It was crazy!"

Thin Line Between Love and Hate: Ross and his former high school buddy Will—played by Brad Pitt—catch up in "The One With the Rumor." Will can barely contain himself when Rachel—who sickens him—enters his view. "That was definitely Brad Pitt going against type," says David Schwimmer.

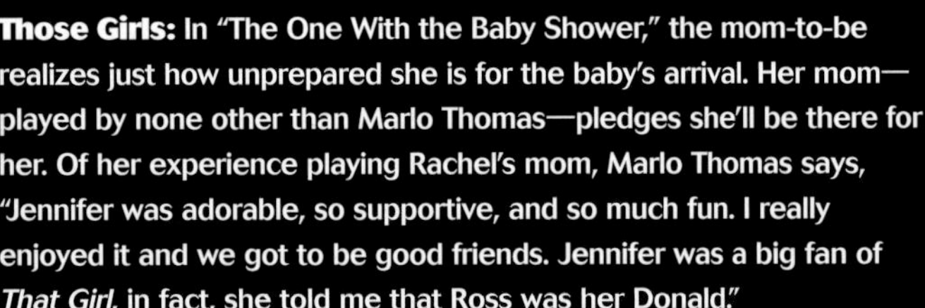

Those Girls: In "The One With the Baby Shower," the mom-to-be realizes just how unprepared she is for the baby's arrival. Her mom—played by none other than Marlo Thomas—pledges she'll be there for her. Of her experience playing Rachel's mom, Marlo Thomas says, "Jennifer was adorable, so supportive, and so much fun. I really enjoyed it and we got to be good friends. Jennifer was a big fan of *That Girl*, in fact, she told me that Ross was her Donald."

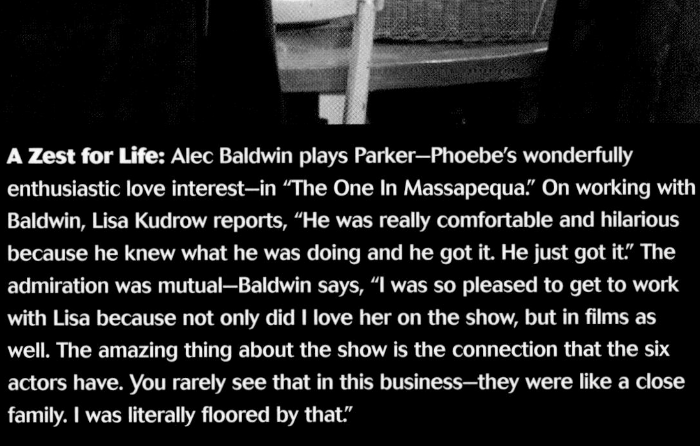

A Zest for Life: Alec Baldwin plays Parker—Phoebe's wonderfully enthusiastic love interest—in "The One In Massapequa." On working with Baldwin, Lisa Kudrow reports, "He was really comfortable and hilarious because he knew what he was doing and he got it. He just got it." The admiration was mutual—Baldwin says, "I was so pleased to get to work with Lisa because not only did I love her on the show, but in films as well. The amazing thing about the show is the connection that the six actors have. You rarely see that in this business—they were like a close family. I was literally floored by that."

Key Exchange: In "The One With Ross's Step Forward," Ross fails to keep things casual with Mona, played by Bonnie Somerville, by spontaneously offering her his apartment key. As David Schwimmer notes, "You could definitely say Ross has had more than his share of girl trouble." "Working on *Friends* was the most fun I've ever had on a TV show," recalls Bonnie Somerville. "I especially enjoyed working with David Schwimmer, who was so warm and giving—he also directed the episodes I was in and he's a great comedy director. It was surreal going to the *Friends* stage every day and parking right next to the cast. I couldn't get over the fact that everyone was so normal and down to earth. I had never worked with stars at that level of fame and they were all so nice."

A Double Act of Desperation: Monica and Chandler track down a couple they met on the plane while on their honeymoon in "The One With the Videotape." Monica wants to set up a double date—she doesn't realize the couple intended to ditch them by giving a bad phone number.

Whole Lot of Kickin' Goin' On: Rachel wakes up Joey in the middle of the night to feel her baby kicking in "The One With the Secret Closet."

The Big Sting: In "The One With Monica's Boots," Phoebe pretends to be Ben's lesbian mother in order to try and get Sting tickets from the singer's real-life wife Trudie Styler. Styler notes of her appearance on *Friends*, "It was great working alongside Lisa. She is an inspired comedian. I feel privileged for playing a role, albeit a small one, in such an important part of TV history. So many people all over the world have seen me on *Friends*, it's staggering!"

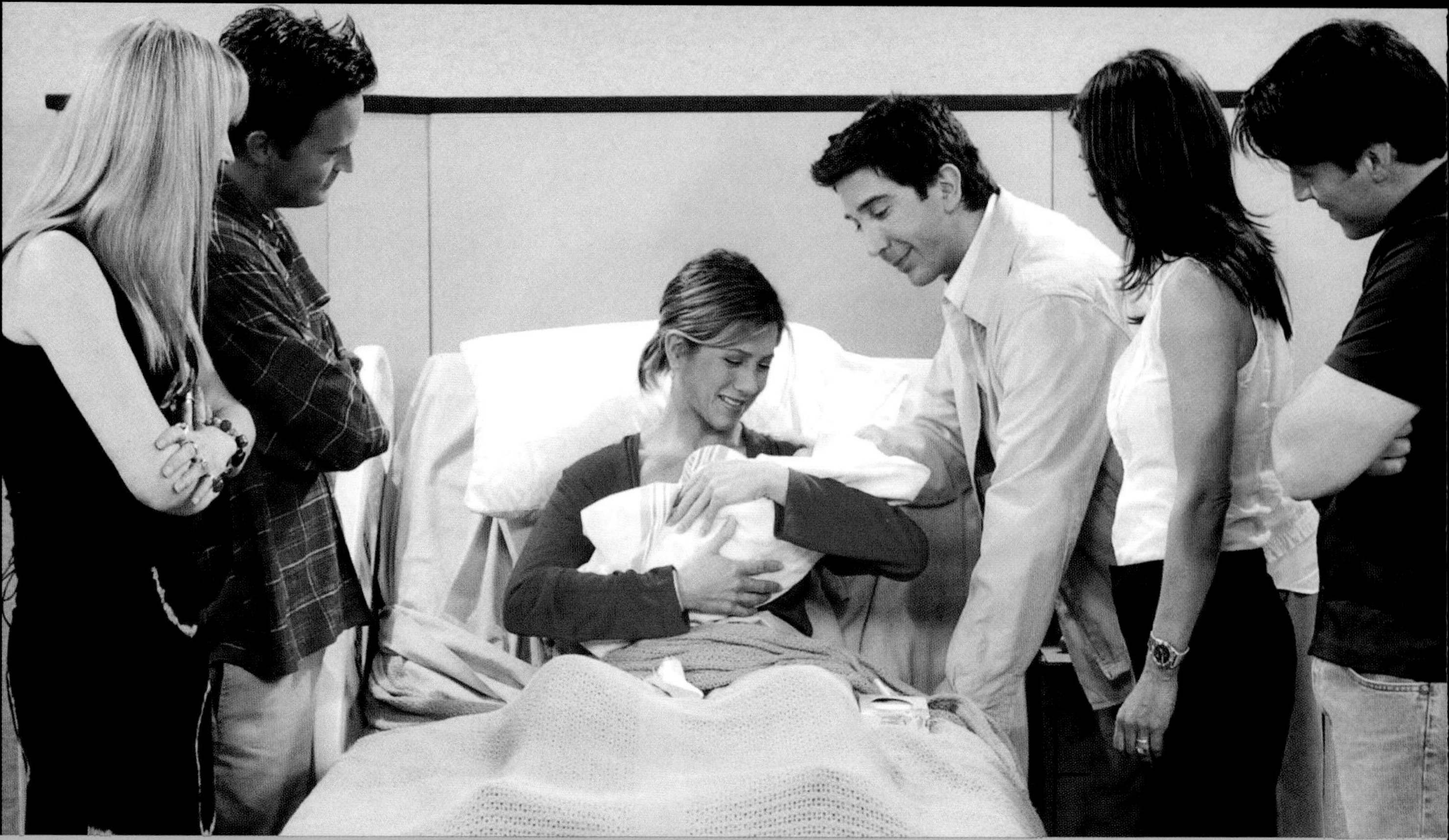

The Name Game: In "The One Where Rachel Has a Baby—Part 2," Rachel finally picks Emma's name with more help from Monica than Ross. Monica tells the gang, "I've had [my kids' names] picked out since I was 14." She's okay with giving Rachel her girl's name—Emma—because, she explains, "Nothing goes with Bing, so I'm screwed."

Cashing In: Rachel and Ross gradually get comfortable with the checks given to them by his parents' friends who have been led to believe they just got married in "The One in Massapequa."

Sister Act: Phoebe exposes her twin sister Ursula's bad behavior to her besotted beau, Eric, played by Sean Penn in "The One With the Halloween Party."

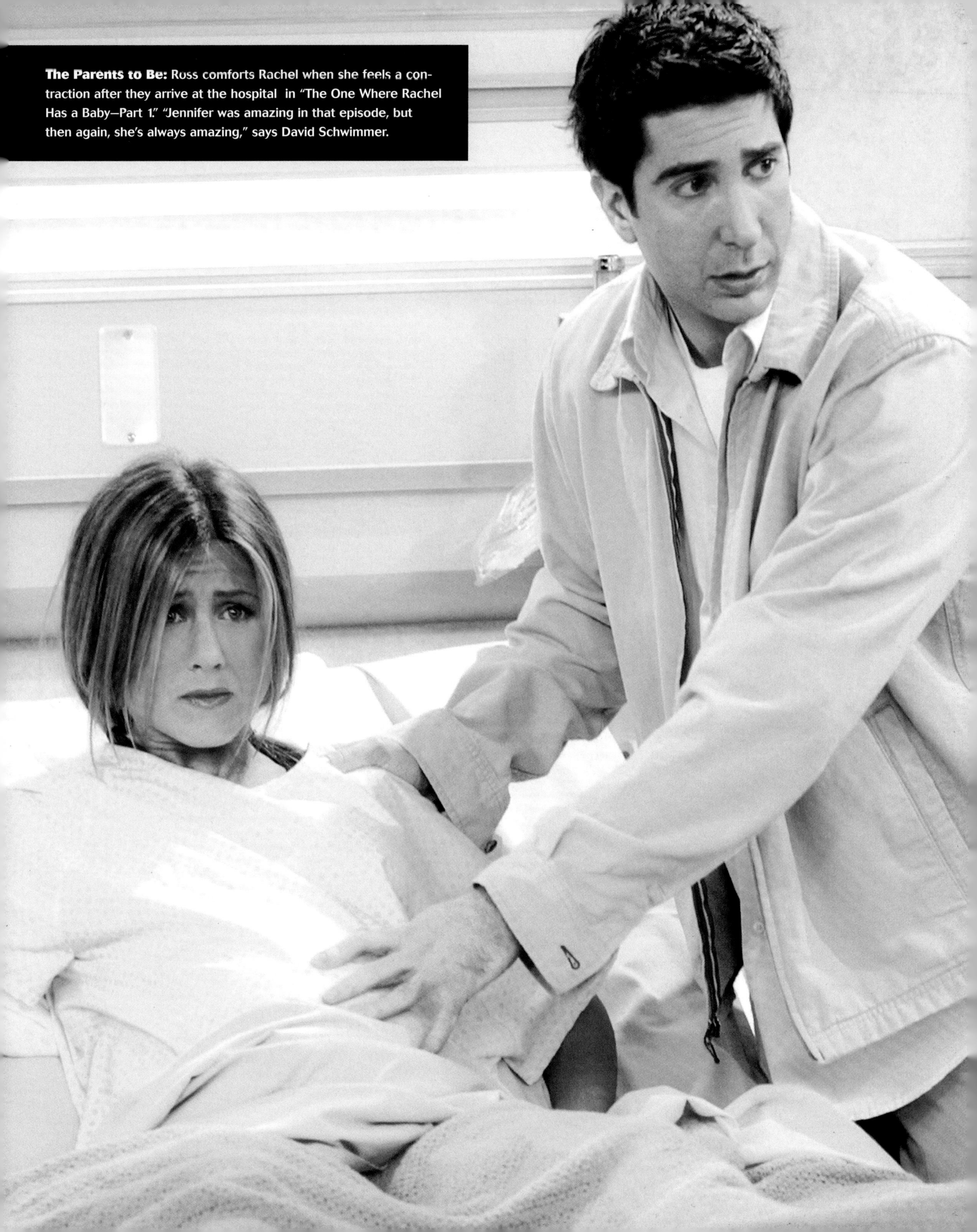

The Parents to Be: Ross comforts Rachel when she feels a contraction after they arrive at the hospital in "The One Where Rachel Has a Baby—Part 1." "Jennifer was amazing in that episode, but then again, she's always amazing," says David Schwimmer.

F·R·I·E·N·D·S

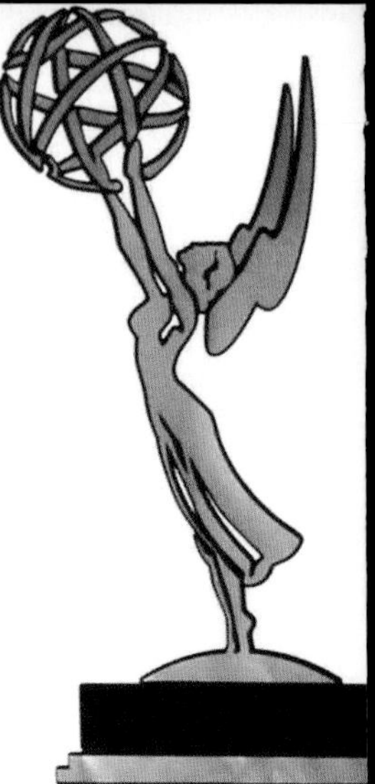

Congratulations to All!!

A Rewarding Night: The six stars of *Friends* not only present an Emmy, but the show also wins the Emmy for Outstanding Comedy Series in 2002.

EPISODE GUIDE

Episode 171: **"The One After 'I Do'"**
Written by Marta Kauffman & David Crane
Directed by Kevin S. Bright
Original Airdate: September 27, 2001

Episode 172: **"The One With the Red Sweater"**
Written by Dana Klein Borkow
Directed by David Schwimmer
Original Airdate: October 4, 2001

Episode 173: **"The One Where Rachel Tells Ross"**
Written by Sherry Bilsing-Graham & Ellen Plummer
Directed by Sheldon Epps
Original Airdate: October 11, 2001

Episode 174: **"The One With the Videotape"**
Written by Scott Silveri
Directed by Kevin S. Bright
Original Airdate: October 18, 2001

Episode 175: **"The One With Rachel's Date"**
Written by Brian Buckner & Sebastian Jones
Directed by Gary Halvorson
Original Airdate: October 25, 2001

Episode 176: **"The One With the Halloween Party"**
Written by Mark Kunerth
Directed by Gary Halvorson
Original Airdate: November 1, 2001

Episode 177: **"The One With the Stain"**
Written by R. Lee Fleming, Jr.
Directed by Kevin S. Bright
Original Airdate: November 8, 2001

Episode 178: **"The One With the Stripper"**
Written by Andrew Reich & Ted Cohen
Directed by David Schwimmer
Original Airdate: November 15, 2001

Episode 179: **"The One With the Rumor"**
Written by Shana Goldberg-Meehan
Directed by Gary Halvorson
Original Airdate: November 22, 2001

Episode 180: **"The One With Monica's Boots"**
Teleplay by Brian Buckner & Sebastian Jones
Story by Robert Carlock
Directed by Kevin S. Bright
Original Airdate: December 6, 2001

Episode 181: **"The One With Ross's Step Forward"**
Written by Robert Carlock
Directed by Gary Halvorson
Original Airdate: December 13, 2001

Episode 182: **"The One Where Joey Dates Rachel"**
Written by Sherry Bilsing-Graham & Ellen Plummer
Directed by David Schwimmer
Original Airdate: January 10, 2002

Episode 183: **"The One Where Chandler Takes a Bath"**
Written by Vanessa McCarthy
Directed by Ben Weiss
Original Airdate: January 17, 2002

Episode 184: **"The One With the Secret Closet"**
Written by Brian Buckner & Sebastian Jones
Directed by Kevin S. Bright
Original Airdate: January 31, 2002

Episode 185: **"The One With the Birthing Video"**
Written by Dana Klein Borkow
Directed by Kevin S. Bright
Original Airdate: February 7, 2002

Episode 186: **"The One Where Joey Tells Rachel"**
Written by Andrew Reich & Ted Cohen
Directed by Ben Weiss
Original Airdate: February 28, 2002

Episode 187: **"The One With the Tea Leaves"**
Teleplay by Steven Rosenhaus
Story by R. Lee Fleming, Jr.
Directed by Gary Halvorson
Original Airdate: March 7, 2002

Episode 188: **"The One In Massapequa"**
Teleplay by Mark Kunerth
Story by Peter Tibbals
Directed by Gary Halvorson
Original Airdate: March 28, 2002

Episode 189: **"The One With Joey's Interview"**
Written by Doty Abrams
Directed by Gary Halvorson
Original Airdate: April 4, 2002

Episode 190: **"The One With the Baby Shower"**
Written by Sherry Bilsing-Graham & Ellen Plummer
Directed by Kevin S. Bright
Original Airdate: April 25, 2002

Episode 191: **"The One With the Cooking Class"**
Teleplay by Brian Buckner & Sebastian Jones
Story by Dana Klein Borkow
Directed by Gary Halvorson
Original Airdate: May 2, 2002

Episode 192: **"The One Where Rachel is Late"**
Written by Shana Goldberg-Meehan
Directed by Gary Halvorson
Original Airdate: May 9, 2002

Episode 193: **"The One Where Rachel Has a Baby—Part 1"**
Written by Scott Silveri
Directed by Kevin S. Bright
Original Airdate: May 16, 2002

Episode 194: **"The One Where Rachel Has a Baby—Part 2"**
Written by Marta Kauffman & David Crane
Directed by Kevin S. Bright
Original Airdate: May 16, 2002

Welcome to the real world. It sucks. You're gonna love it.

—MONICA'S REALISTIC BUT WELCOMING WORDS TO RACHEL IN "THE PILOT"

Okay. Rock. Hard place. Me.

—CHANDLER EXPRESSES AN EXISTENTIAL CRISIS AFTER UNSATISFACTORILY COMPLIMENTING RACHEL'S ACCIDENTALLY VIEWED BOOBIES IN "THE ONE WITH THE BOOBIES"

Guys, rules are good. Rules help control the fun.

—CONTROL FREAK MONICA OFFERS HER VIEW OF LIFE "THE ONE WITH THE KIPS"

How you doin'?

—JOEY'S MINIMAL BUT OFTEN SUCCESSFUL PICKUP LINE IN NUMEROUS EPISODES STARTING WITH "THE ONE WITH RACHEL'S CRUSH"

JILL GOODACRE: Would you like to call somebody?

CHANDLER: Yeah, about three hundred guys I went to high school with.

—CHANDLER THINKS OF BUT DOESN'T SAY THE PERFECT ANSWER IN "THE ONE WITH THE BLACKOUT"

You ever wonder which is worse: going through labor or getting kicked in the nuts?…No one can ever experience both.

—CHANDLER MAKING SMALL TALK WHILE ERICA'S GIVING BIRTH IN "THE LAST ONE—PART 1"

PHOEBE: Stop being so testosteroney!

CHANDLER: Which by the way is the real San Francisco treat.

—A SUBTLE RICE-A-RONI REFERENCE IN "THE ONE WITH THE EVIL ORTHODONTIST"

One thing led to another and, before I knew it, we were… shopping.

—MONICA ADMITS TO THE ULTIMATE BETRAYAL OF BEFRIENDING ROSS'S NEW LOVE INTEREST JULIE TO RACHEL IN "THE ONE WITH THE BREAST MILK"

You have to stop the Q-tip when there's resistance!

—CHANDLER RESPONDS TO JOEY'S RAMBLING, DENSE SARTORIAL ADVICE IN "THE ONE WITH ROSS'S NEW GIRLFRIEND"

GREAT LINES

If I were a guy and…Did I just say 'If I were a guy?'

—Chandler bends gender again in "The One Where Rachel's Sister Babysits"

ON life

maggie

WHEELER

Friends of F·R·I·E·N·D·S

How do you explain the fact that Janice seems to be just about everywhere the *Friends* go?

You know, it's one of life's mysteries. She's become dear to everyone's hearts. This character just serves the story line in a unique way. I think from time to time the writers will be hashing out a script and looking at all the various directions that they can go, and somebody will just throw in the idea of bringing Janice back. And to that person, I am always grateful.

I do believe in Greek drama they called it *deux ex machina*?

That's right, exactly. I come in. And I am dropped down from above, with angel wings.

Tarnished angel wings?

Tarnished angel wings and leopard boots.

What do you love about Janice?

As an actress it's so wonderfully liberating to play somebody who is as annoying as Janice is and I've had such a blast doing this. The writers give me such great material. **What I love about Janice is that she is so unaware of the effect she has on the world around her–she just barrels through with her agenda–**and it's wonderful.

When did Janice come alive for you?

The audition material included the scene in which Chandler and Janice were breaking up in the coffee shop and she brings him a pair of Bullwinkle socks and she says "mix and match moose and squirrel, squirrel and moose, whatever you want." I read that particular line, and I just heard her in my head.

Vintage Whine: Oh sweet bird of paradox, Janice grows tired of Ross's whining and wants to break up in "The One With Chandler's Work Laugh."

I imagine it could be a scary thing to hear Janice in your head.

Yes. Well, it doesn't frighten me, but I can understand how it might frighten others. Her voice, her rhythm, all of that I really had when I went in to audition for the role, but the laugh came when we were rehearsing a scene, there was a moment when Chandler's bringing me coffee—he's had about 77 espressos by that time, and he's bringing me a cappuccino that was filled to the brim—and before I could even get it to my mouth—he asked me if I wanted another one. It was a funny moment. It was funny in the writing and in the way Matthew did it. And Janice needed to respond, and I responded with a laugh. That's where Janice's laugh was born.

Do fans on the street want to hear the laugh?

Yeah, they want to hear the laugh and they

want to hear "Oh my God." They also ask me to say, "You love me Chandler Bing." That's a popular request.

Are you in touch with your inner Janice?

Well, I was born and raised in New York City. I think I met Janice in many forms along the way. She's a combination of lots of people I have known.

Do these people know who they are?

It seems to me that the people who are most like Janice don't know that they're like Janice. Just like Janice doesn't know she's like Janice. And that's the beauty of it.

What's it been like to watch this cast?

Their historic rise to fame? I have to say, I feel very fortunate that I was introduced to this cast and had the great pleasure of working with them at the very beginning when the green room was a crappy little room with broken down couches and everybody was in there playing poker from dawn 'til dusk. It felt like a frat house. Not that I ever was in a frat house. The dressing rooms have gone from just a little cubicle to sort of fully decorated designer show rooms. But the people have essentially not changed.

When the end comes, do you believe Janice will be there too?

Yes. I don't know what the end is. Just as **I never know what Janice's next move is going to be until the script arrives on my doorstep,** sometimes the night before we go to work.

Finally, from your point of view does Janice believe she is the seventh *Friend*?

Yes, she believes she is. She thinks she's part of the family.

A sometimes scary part, but a part nonetheless.

That's the beauty of Janice—she's not afraid. 

The Heart Wants What It Wants: Chandler begs Janice to stay in "The One With the Giant Poking Device." On Maggie Wheeler's talent, Matt LeBlanc explains, "It's like she hits a switch and then shuts it off. It's so surreal and so over the top. It's been justified over the years because of her relationship with Chandler. She can go anywhere with it. She can do no wrong. She knows that and just lets it fly. It's great."

Straight Talk Express: Rachel, Ross, and Joey try to figure out what exactly is going on between them all in "The One Where No One Proposes." "Schwimmer and I were both worried about the Joey-Rachel thing," recalls Matt LeBlanc "I said, wait a minute, man, that's my buddy's girl—that's not right. And the writers' response was, 'We know it's dangerous, that's what's exciting.' Finally, David Crane, said, 'It's like playing with fire,' and then I got it."

SEASON NINE

IT WAS THE LAST

season that wasn't. When it began, Season Nine was going to be the final season of *Friends* but it soon became apparent that NBC didn't want to bid a fond farewell to *Friends* just yet

So after one more renegotiation for good measure, the show's hard-core fans were given a reprieve—they would get one more season before confronting their separation anxiety.

"What was a little difficult was not knowing in advance so that we could plan out the season," says Marta Kauffman. "It was also emotionally tricky to actually make the decision: are we or are we *not* going to do one more season? Making that decision so late puts a strain on things. It was a tough decision to make because we have a good time doing this show and we're well paid. Nobody really wants to say goodbye, but then sometimes in life you have to do it."

The actors also spent some time early in Season Nine thinking the end was near. "I thought wow, it's really going to be over," recalls Matt LeBlanc. "I definitely wasn't ready to accept that the show was going to end. Although, I guess you can never really be ready–I know when the end comes, it will be sad no matter what." LeBlanc wasn't the only one who wanted to keep things going. "The idea of the spin-off came up then too."

Other cast members were somewhat more reluctant to keep the show going one more season. "Truthfully, I deferred to the group this time," says David Schwimmer. "I was like, 'Whatever you guys want to do.' Because I really felt we were done last year. But I was not going to be the one person that stands in the way of the other five. I really was okay either way.'"

Eventually the decision was made to proceed, but to do a shortened season on a compressed schedule. But in the meantime, there was a ninth season to do.

Season Nine followed Rachel through her early days of motherhood, while sorting out her personal life right from the opening episode, "The One Where No One Proposes." The season also saw Chandler and Monica weathering some marital stresses together, through Chandler's exile to Tulsa, then his stay-at-home career crisis and their difficulty having a child. "Your heart goes out to them," says Marta Kauffman. "And they play it so beautifully."

"It's been great to see Chandler grow up," says David Crane. "It may have taken him a while, but he got there."

Some old and new friends of *Friends* stopped by along the way. Jon Lovitz—not seen since the first season as stoner restaurateur Steve—popped back in briefly. Christina Applegate—star of Bright Kauffman Crane's series *Jesse*—was charmingly self-obsessed in "The One With Rachel's Other Sister."

"That was like old home week," says Kevin Bright. "It started out that Reese Witherspoon, who'd played Rachel's sister in Season Six, was going to come back, but I think she was doing *Legally Blonde II* and couldn't work out the schedule. We liked the story the writers had and didn't want to lose it. And we never said that Rachel didn't have more than *one* sister. So enter Christina, who was thankfully available and who's the sort of total pro who brings everyone's game up."

One of Season Nine's most winning episodes was "The One With the Male Nanny" which featured a hilariously sensitive turn by Freddie Prinze, Jr.

A couple other guests would stick around considerably longer. Paul Rudd turned up as a last minute blind date for Phoebe and soon became a fixture. "It is rare that we find people who fit in with this cast," says Kauffman. "I just feel like he's a part of this group." Aisha Tyler first appeared as Charlie—the lovely young paleontologist—in "The One With the Soap Opera Party." Soon Ross and eventually Joey were smitten, setting up a triangle that would last to the end of the season. The casting of Tyler was also significant because it was the largest part a black actor or actress has had on the show—a point of some criticism over the years. "Hiring Aisha wasn't so much a response to that—Aisha was the best actress that we auditioned for the part," says Kevin Bright. "Aisha was funny and fresh and no one had really seen her before and that's what made it exciting to us. She's been great, and one very attractive paleontologist."

The Fab Four: The three women of *Friends* welcome a new addition—Emma—back home and admire how cute she is in "The One Where Emma Cries."

Emma's Fan Club: In "The One Where No One Proposes," the gang marvels at Emma. Jack Geller (played by Elliott Gould) is thrilled with his "first grandchild," until Ross reminds him about his son Ben. Says Gould of the cast, "They stuck together in the most proactive, positive, and loyal way on so many different levels—in the face of the materialism, the shallowness, and the coldness of the business. By their sticking together as a unit of people—that really brought them over the top and gave them the everlasting success that each of them has worked for, earned, and deserved."

A Stage with a View: The *Friends* sets from the perspective of the show's live audience during the filming of "The One With the Blind Date."

Look Back in Cuteness: Mike and Phoebe talk about her fake imaginary past relationship, then get real and swap spit in "The One With the Sharks." On Mike's relationship with Phoebe, Paul Rudd, who plays Mike explains, "The writers and producers may have thought it was a good match to put her with somebody who could appreciate her eccentricities, but who's also sweet milque-toast. Lisa and I get along really well and I would hope that comes through—that we are actually friends."

Heart to Heart: Rachel and Ross discuss "the Joey thing" in "The One Where Emma Cries."

There is Superstition: Phoebe and Joey make a wish that they win big in "The One With the Lottery." Phoebe wants in because "Vegetarians never get to do the wishbone."

The Good Dad: Chandler—hurt that Rachel and Ross don't want to leave Emma to him in their will if Ross, Rachel, and Monica were all to die—worries about not being a good father in "The One With Rachel's Other Sister."

A Hard Time: In "The One With Phoebe's Rats," Rachel gives Gavin, played by Dermot Mulroney, grief for checking out an assistant's rear—and he takes her to task for Tag. Dermot Mulroney says, "It's a fantastic cast. What I was struck with is how well they got along. And of course Jen is just a delight all around. It's not just her charm and her good looks—it's that other kind of unique appeal."

A Second Opinion: In "The One Where Rachel Goes Back to Work," Joey begs his director—played by Evan Handler—not to fire Phoebe from her role as an extra on *Days of Our Lives*. According to Handler, "It's hard enough to work with a lot of people for just a few days. Somehow, those guys have managed to be co-workers, confidantes, and deeply trusting collaborators for ten years. Though, true to my personality, I got them all on edge at least a few times over the course of the week—somehow they managed to survive, and thrive, in spite of me. *Friends* caught me in the waning moments of my career playing guest roles on television. I was extremely glad to have gotten the chance to appear at least once on such a well-loved show, with such a loving group. And, well, getting to play straight man to Lisa Kudrow is reason enough to get out of bed in the morning."

A Bad Night at the Theater: Chandler is about to get stuck being the only one to attend the one-woman play "Why Don't You Like Me: A Bitter Woman's Journey Through Life" in "The One With the Soap Opera Party."

Comedy of Errors: Chandler wrongly comes to think Monica wants money for some breast work in "The One With the Boob Job." "I'm glad that Monica's changed a lot over the years. She's still obsessive and neurotic but she's gotten herself a life," says Courteney Cox

True Confession: Charlie tells Ross that she and Joey broke up because, "I started to realize that I was having feelings for someone else" in "The One in Barbados—Part 2." "When I auditioned for the show," recalls Aisha Tyler, who played Charlie, "I didn't know my character was going to be in a love triangle with Joey and Ross. I thought I was just auditioning to play Ross's girlfriend. My first day on the set, Matt LeBlanc told me the Charlie-Ross-Joey-Rachel story line, and I just about died. Because I was just a guest star on the show, I didn't really expect much of a reaction—boy was I wrong! Things changed almost overnight. Big burly men, teenage girls, moms, little kids, grandparents—you name it—would constantly come up to ask me who Charlie was going to end up with, or breathlessly accuse me of breaking up Ross and Rachel—at which point I would have to gently remind them that it was a television show and that I was not a home wrecker."

The Options: Chandler and Monica discuss their options for childbirth with Dr. Connelly, played by Andy Umberger, in "The One With the Donor." His professional advice: "Above all, even though your chances of conceiving through natural means aren't great, you never know! So, keep having sex on a regular basis."

Top of the World: A bird's eye view of the cast during the filming of "The One With the Lottery."

it ain't over yet

EPISODE GUIDE

Episode 195: **"The One Where No One Proposes"**
Written by Sherry Bilsing-Graham & Ellen Plummer
Directed by Kevin S. Bright
Original Airdate: September 26, 2002

Episode 196: **"The One Where Emma Cries"**
Written by Dana Klein Borkow
Directed by Sheldon Epps
Original Airdate: October 3, 2002

Episode 197: **"The One With the Pediatrician"**
Written by Brian Buckner & Sebastian Jones
Directed by Roger Christiansen
Original Airdate: October 10, 2002

Episode 198: **"The One With the Sharks"**
Written by Andrew Reich & Ted Cohen
Directed by Ben Weiss
Original Airdate: October 17, 2002

Episode 199: **"The One With Phoebe's Birthday Dinner"**
Written by Scott Silveri
Directed by David Schwimmer
Original Airdate: October 31, 2002

Episode 200: **"The One With the Male Nanny"**
Written by Marta Kauffman & David Crane
Directed by Kevin S. Bright
Original Airdate: November 7, 2002

Episode 201: **"The One With Ross's Inappropriate Song"**
Written by Robert Carlock
Directed by Gary Halvorson
Original Airdate: November 14, 2002

Episode 202: **"The One With Rachel's Other Sister"**
Written by Shana Goldberg-Meehan
Directed by Kevin S. Bright
Original Airdate: November 21, 2002

Episode 203: **"The One With Rachel's Phone Number"**
Written by Mark Kunerth
Directed by Ben Weiss
Original Airdate: December 5, 2002

Episode 204: **"The One With Christmas in Tulsa"**
Written by Doty Abrams
Directed by Kevin S. Bright
Original Airdate: December 12, 2002

Episode 205: **"The One Where Rachel Goes Back to Work"**
Teleplay by Peter Tibbals
Story by Judd Rubin
Directed by Gary Halvorson
Original Airdate: January 9, 2003

Episode 206: **"The One With Phoebe's Rats"**
Teleplay by Brian Buckner & Sebastian Jones
Story by Dana Klein Borkow
Directed by Ben Weiss
Original Airdate: January 16, 2003

Episode 207: **"The One Where Monica Sings"**
Teleplay by Steven Rosenhaus
Story by Sherry Bilsing-Graham & Ellen Plummer
Directed by Gary Halvorson
Original Airdate: January 30, 2003

Episode 208: **"The One With the Blind Date"**
Written by Sherry Bilsing-Graham & Ellen Plummer
Directed by Gary Halvorson
Original Airdate: February 6, 2003

Episode 209: **"The One With the Mugging"**
Written by Peter Tibbals
Directed by Gary Halvorson
Original Airdate: February 13, 2003

Episode 210: **"The One With the Boob Job"**
Written by Mark Kunerth
Directed by Gary Halvorson
Original Airdate: February 20, 2003

Episode 211: **"The One With the Memorial Service"**
Teleplay by Brian Buckner & Sebastian Jones
Story by Robert Carlock
Directed by Gary Halvorson
Original Airdate: March 13, 2003

Episode 212: **"The One With the Lottery"**
Teleplay by Sherry Bilsing-Graham & Ellen Plummer
Story by Brian Buckner & Sebastian Jones
Directed by Gary Halvorson
Original Airdate: April 3, 2003

Episode 213: **"The One With Rachel's Dream"**
Teleplay by Mark Kunerth
Story by Dana Klein Borkow
Directed by Terry Hughes
Original Airdate: April 17, 2003

Episode 214: **"The One With the Soap Opera Party"**
Teleplay by Andrew Reich & Ted Cohen
Story by Shana Goldberg-Meehan
Directed by Sheldon Epps
Original Airdate: April 24, 2003

Episode 215: **"The One With the Fertility Test"**
Teleplay by Robert Carlock
Story by Scott Silveri
Directed by Gary Halvorson
Original Airdate: May 1, 2003

Episode 216: **"The One With the Donor"**
Written by Andrew Reich & Ted Cohen
Directed by Ben Weiss
Original Airdate: May 8, 2003

Episode 217: **"The One in Barbados–Part 1"**
Written by Shana Goldberg-Meehan & Scott Silveri
Directed by Kevin S. Bright
Original Airdate: May 15, 2003

Episode 218: **"The One in Barbados–Part 2"**
Written by Marta Kauffman & David Crane
Directed by Kevin S. Bright
Original Airdate: May 15, 2003

RACHEL: Lately, with this whole pregnancy thing, I'm just finding myself...how do I put this, erotically charged.
JOEY: Is that college talk for horny?

—SOME AROUSING WORDPLAY IN "THE ONE WITH ROSS'S STEP FORWARD"

GREAT LINES

Well, if you can't talk dirty to me, how you gonna talk dirty to her? Now tell me you want to caress my butt.

—JOEY TRIES TO LOOSEN UP HIS PAL ROSS IN "THE ONE WITH THE STONED GUY"

Well, it was the only thing to do there that didn't have a line.

—ROSS EXPLAINING WHY HE HAD SEX WITH CAROL IN DISNEYLAND AND WAS BANISHED FROM THE MAGIC KINGDOM IN "THE ONE WITH THE BLACKOUT"

A 'no sex' pact, huh? I actually have one of those going on with every woman in America.

—ROSS ON STRIKING OUT IN "THE ONE WITH ROSS & MONICA'S COUSIN"

Yeah, but Monica, do you really want to be in a relationship where you can actually use the phrase, 'That's not how your dad used to do it'?

—PHOEBE OFFERS A FATHER AND SON MOMENT IN "THE ONE WITH CHANDLER IN A BOX"

CHANDLER:
I just walked in the bathroom and saw Kathy naked. It was like torture.
ROSS:
You know, if we ever go to war and you're captured, you're in for a big surprise.

—SOME NAKED TRUTH IN "THE ONE WHERE CHANDLER CROSSES THE LINE"

MONICA TO JOEY: I can't believe this! I mean, someone asks you in for lemonade and to you that means they want to have sex?

—HOT BEVERAGE TALK IN "THE ONE WITH THE FLASHBACK"

ROSS:
Didn't you read *Lord Of The Rings* in high school?
JOEY:
No, I had sex in high school.

—SOME STRAIGHT BOOK TALK IN "THE ONE WHERE THEY'RE GOING TO PARTY"

Hey, I'm not one to kiss and tell…But I'm also not one to have sex and shut up. We totally did it!

—ROSS REVEALS THAT HE SLEPT WITH RACHEL THE NIGHT BEFORE IN "THE LAST ONE—PART 1"

RACHEL:
Uni-sex!
JOEY:
Maybe you need sex. I had sex a couple days ago.
RACHEL:
Oh, no, Joey. U-N-I- sex.
JOEY:
Well, I ain't gonna say no to that.

—AN ACCIDENTAL COME ON IN "THE ONE WITH JOEY'S BAG"

james michael

TYLER

Friends of F·R·I·E·N·D·S

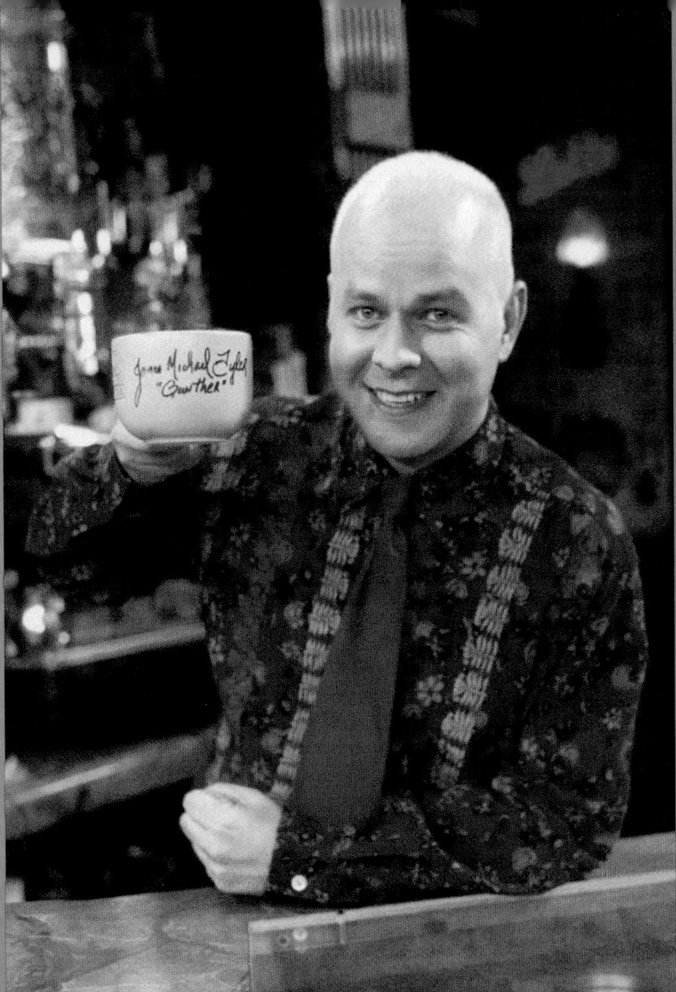

World Cup: Of James Michael Tyler, Matt LeBlanc says, "He's been a great guy. He has always helped us support the cause. I love when I have a joke with Gunther."

Is it possible that all of *Friends* is just something Gunther imagined?

That would be a good ending—Gunther wakes up and it's all been a big dream of his. But I'm not going to hold my breath.

How much thinking have you done about Gunther's back story?

Actually, I created this whole little world for him. Now whether or not it matches up with what the writers think about him or not, I don't know.

For you, who is this guy?

I think Gunther is repressed, a little sad but actually a really nice guy. He's inexperienced in the ways of the world, and of course, the ways of love. He's probably never been kissed. He's settled into his fate in many ways.

Is it true you won the role because you knew how to use a cappuccino machine?

In a way. Early in the first season, an assistant director I had worked with on another show knew about the coffeehouse set. At the time I was actually managing a coffeehouse here in Hollywood called The Bourgeois Pig. I don't know if at the time they planned to actually have an operational machine on the set, but I think they wanted somebody who could naturally look like they were working a cappuccino machine. He called me up and said, **"Do you want to come and do this? It's background work and it will probably go for about six episodes at least." I actually said to him, "Let me think about it, because I'd have to take a day off of work in order to do this."** But I have a Master of Fine Arts in acting anyway, and I thought, "Well, I can maybe jump on this thing and who *knows* what can happen?" And fortunately for me it did pan out, because they expanded my character.

Yet you've managed to keep your negotiations significantly more low-key than the other cast members.

Yeah, I stayed out of the papers as far as that goes. Seriously though, I think the cast deserves everything that they've gotten. I really do. I'm very happy for their success.

For you, what are Gunther's greatest hits? I love when he reveals that he was on a soap opera.

Oh yeah, that was actually one of my first lines. I think Gunther had a couple of lines prior to that, like "Here you go," or "Good night Rachel." But that was really the first time that the writers flirted with Gunther's back story.

Was there a time when you thought Gunther might remain a silent TV star?

Yeah, actually. The writers came up with a story arc when they first established Gunther's obsession with Rachel, which was supposed to be for about four episodes, but they've just sustained it. I still don't speak much. Gunther really is a man of few words. But when Gunther says something, he means it.

Gunther also helped break up America's favorite couple—Rachel and Ross.

Yeah, I was a little worried about that at the time, because I'm getting this character established and then, all of a sudden all of America is going to *hate* me. **I thought I would get hate mail and death threats for being the one who led to their breakup.** Fortunately that didn't happen.

In your mind, does Gunther still hate Ross?

I think that Gunther *tolerates* Ross at this point, but there's still animosity there.

Is there any chance that slow and steady will win the race and Gunther will end up with Rachel?

I think that would probably be quite a shock to a lot of people. I don't see it happening. As James Michael Tyler, I don't think that Gunther *deserves* Rachel. I don't think that Rachel deserves Gunther either. But there's still an obsession, a longing there.

In real life, have you found any place as welcoming as Central Perk?

Yeah, actually, the place where I worked is a very friendly neighborhood type of place.

What do *Friends* fans ask you on the street?

"Is that your real hair color?" I say it is as real as bottled hair can be. Yes, I bleach it. And they want to know, "Are they *really* friends?" Which, of course, they are.

Confessions of a Coffee Stud: Gunther tells Rachel he's kissed Phoebe and tries to make sure they are "cool" in "The One With Joey's New Girlfriend."

How do you view the ending of this show?

Honestly, it's sad. It's very sad, because I have made such good friends on *Friends*. The crew and the cast.

Any personal hopes to see how it will end?

I'd like to see Ross and Rachel get back together. That's me saying that of course, *not* Gunther.

And you'll be up for a Gunther spinoff if one would be requested?

If the phone rings, I definitely would listen to what they have to say.

Finally, do you consider Gunther the seventh Friend?

Well, I'm the seventh acquaintance. Gunther is more of an acquaintance—more a friend of a friend.

SEASON TEN

Talking Turkey: The gang finally sits down for their big meal at the end of "The One With the Late Thanksgiving." Rachel proposes a toast, "To Monica and Chandler—and that knocked-up girl in Ohio."

IN THE FALL OF

2003, the time had come for *Friends* to face its not so long goodbye.

And inevitably, the need for some sort of comedic closure shaped an abbreviated season that consisted of only 18 new episodes. As Season Ten unfolded, our gang of six wasn't exactly breaking up, but rather moving on with their lives in various ways. Monica and Chandler continued on their long and emotional path to parenthood and, yes, a home in the suburbs. Ross and Rachel were busy bringing up Emma and at times reconsidering their long and famously complicated relationship. Phoebe actually got married to her shockingly stable significant other, Mike, and settled down—insofar as Phoebe could ever settle down. And finally, of course, Joey was busy being, well, *Joey*.

The production schedule for *Friends'* last season was uniquely compressed—part of the previous season's last-minute deal for there to be a tenth season. Yet in the end, it wasn't the schedule that made the show's final season challenging; it was the elevated emotional mood of those for whom *Friends* has become a way of life.

"We all love *Friends*, and it's always hard to say goodbye to something or someone that you love," said Marta Kauffman.

"This has been such an extraordinary and meaningful experience for all of us," David Crane explained. "And we all want to do what it takes to bring it to the right conclusion."

"It's been such an amazing ride," says Kevin Bright. "We sure don't want to blow it now."

The media countdown to the end of *Friends* began in earnest with a *Newsweek* cover in October and grew louder during the season with assorted print and on air meditations regarding what it all meant—including an emotional group appearance by the stars of the show on a special *Oprah* shoot on the *Friends* set.

Oprah Winfrey asked what the cast thought the atmosphere on the set would be for their final show. "I think Jennifer probably won't be able to breathe," Courteney Cox told her. "I think she started crying the first day we got here this year."

Aniston was clearly the most openly sentimental of the castmembers—as Matthew Perry explained, "Jennifer is like, 'You know, this is the *last* bagel I'm going to eat on the second day of rehearsal'—there's a lot of that stuff." On- and off-screen, Season Ten was the show's most emotional.

The final season began with "The One After Joey and Rachel Kiss," yet over the course of the next few episodes it became clear that Joey and Rachel were destined to remain more friends than lovers. Rachel and Ross's daughter celebrated—sort of—her first birthday in "The One With the Cake." Phoebe and Mike got engaged in "The One Where Rachel's Sister Babysits." Charlie, played by Aisha Tyler, ended up going back to her old boyfriend Dr. Hobart, played by Tyler's *Talk Soup* predecessor Greg Kinnear.

About midway through, Season Ten seemed to take on added *gravitas* and resonance; the mood heightened as the characters headed towards their eventual imaginary destinies. Beginning with "The One With the Birth Mother," Anna Faris (*Lost In Translation*) appeared as Erica, the young pregnant woman who would finally help Monica and Chandler become parents. Phoebe got married movingly—if frigidly—in "The

One With Phoebe's Wedding." The show seemed to be hitting its stride effortlessly on the way to the finish line.

As 2003 came to an end, Marta Kauffman and David Crane sat down together and wrote the show's final hour-long episode. Kevin Bright would direct the episode—a reaffirmation of the partnership that had brought them to this rarified and special place.

Everyone at *Friends* was united in their shared desire to go out in style. "You can get caught up in the hoopla and packaging and all that, but at the end of the day, it has to be a good, satisfying finale," says Executive Producer Shana Goldberg-Meehan. "And that's what I would hope—that it's satisfying for fans and us."

Asked to describe the considerable challenge of giving *Friends* a proper ending, Executive Producer Andrew Reich responded, "Probably impossible, but what the fuck, we gotta shoot something."

Days before filming began on the two-part finale of *Friends*, accurately titled "The Last One," the cast and Bright Kauffman Crane met with the press on Stage 24.

"It feels kind of bittersweet," Matt LeBlanc said. "It's a chapter closing."

For Jennifer Aniston: "It's just hard, absolutely painful, in the weirdest way. Because it's the most fun and joyous place to be."

But the time had arrived for new joys and for one final chance to say goodbye to *Friends*.

Locked Out: Monica and Chandler punish their friends for being late to dinner in "The One With the Late Thanksgiving."

And They Call It Joey Love: Executive Producer Kevin Bright, Donny Osmond, and Matt LeBlanc hang out on the *Pyramid* set during the filming of "The One Where the Stripper Cries." "The first thing that happened when I came on the set was the cast sang, "A Little Bit Country, A Little Bit Rock & Roll" to me," recalls Donny Osmond. "Matthew Perry came up and said, 'We may be the hot show now, but we all grew up watching you and Marie.' It was nice of him to say that and it was an honor to be a part of television history in the 21st Century—a real slice of pop culture. Plus, now I'm the cool dad in the neighborhood because I've done *Friends*."

A Flock of Losers: In "The One Where the Stripper Cries," Chandler and Ross strike a deal as they hand out fliers for their almost certainly dismal college band.

Flesh for Fantasy: Danny DeVito plays veteran male erotic dancer, Roy, a.k.a Officer Goodbody—who makes quite an impression at Phoebe's bachelorette party in "The One Where the Stripper Cries." "Being on *Friends* was a wonderful experience and I feel honored to have been part of such outstanding television history," says Danny DeVito. "Three luscious babes, it made me feel like a sultan in a tent full of beautiful women."

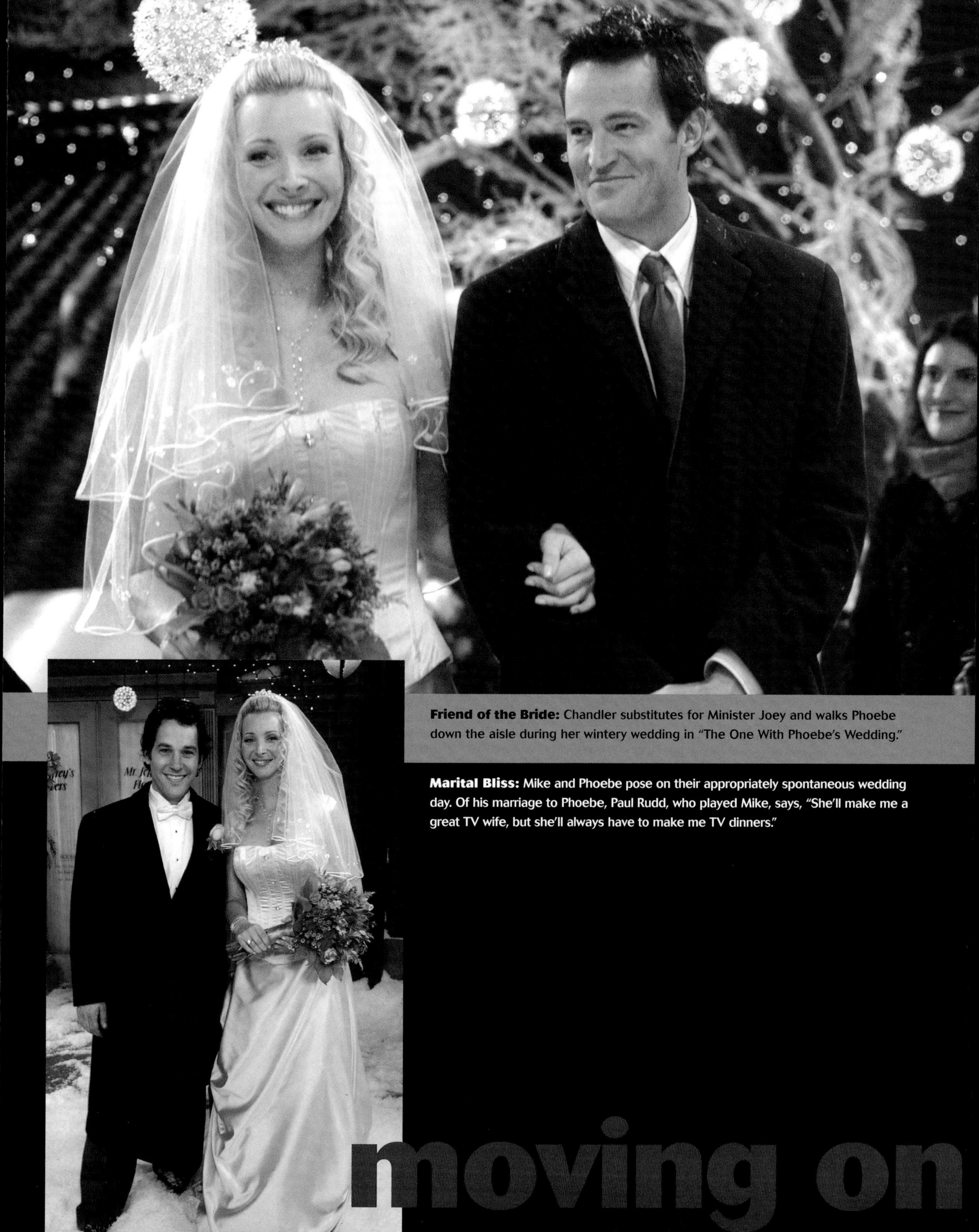

Friend of the Bride: Chandler substitutes for Minister Joey and walks Phoebe down the aisle during her wintery wedding in "The One With Phoebe's Wedding."

Marital Bliss: Mike and Phoebe pose on their appropriately spontaneous wedding day. Of his marriage to Phoebe, Paul Rudd, who played Mike, says, "She'll make me a great TV wife, but she'll always have to make me TV dinners."

moving on

A Conflict of Interest: Ross really wants a grant from Dr. Hobart, played by Greg Kinnear, while Dr. Hobart really wants Charlie in "The One With Ross's Grant." Kinnear, who was thrilled to be part of the shortened final season of *Friends* offers his kudos: "Putting on a great quality show for ten years isn't brain surgery. It's far more difficult. Congratulations. Dr. Greg Kinnear, MD."

Comfort and Joy: Kevin Bright and Jennifer Aniston grab a hug while shooting "The One Where Estelle Dies."

All's Well That Ends Well: In "The One With the Late Thanksgiving," a lousy evening is redeemed by a dream call to Monica and Chandler from the adoption agency. Monica rejoices, "This Thanksgiving kicks last Thanksgiving's ass!"

A New Friend: In "The One With Princess Consuela," Joey bonds with Mackenzie, played by Dakota Fanning, the daughter of the owner of the house Chandler and Monica want to purchase.

M&M: Matthew Perry and Marta Kauffman share a moment on the set of "The One With Princess Consuela."

Almost Neighbors: In "The One Where Estelle Dies," a desperate Chandler hits on Janice, hoping she'll be convinced not to buy the house next door and Janice, played by Maggie Wheeler, seizes the opportunity for one last kiss. "It was tremendously satisfying that they wrote me such a great parting scene," says Maggie Wheeler. "It was a poignant, funny, and weighty moment knowing that this was Janice's exit. I would like to say that working with Matthew Perry has been one of the great joys of my acting career. It's too bad Chandler had to be recoiling from Janice at that crucial moment."

Sisterhood: Jennifer Aniston and Christina Applegate give director Roger Christiansen a fair hearing on the set of "The One With Rachel's Sister." "It was great to work with Jennifer and be around *Friends* one last time," recalls Christina Applegate.

International Relations: In "The One Where Estelle Dies," Rachel and Ross go back and forth on a big question: will she stay or will she go to Paris.

A Priceless Present: Joey comes up with a meaningful gift for Emma on her first birthday—a dramatic reading of a storybook that uses his "talents as an actor." Amazingly, it worked in "The One With the Cake."

Preparing for the Inevitable: Our gang gets ready for the scene where Phoebe reads about the death of Joey's agent in "The One Where Estelle Dies."

Between the Lines: A script conference on the set of "The One Where Estelle Dies."

Good News, Bad News: Ross cracks open a bottle of Israeli champagne to celebrate getting tenure, but the gang tries not to get too excited since Rachel has big career problems in "The One With Princess Consuela."

One Love: Emma finally gets her just dessert in "The One With the Cake."

Got Milk?: In "The One Where Joey Speaks French," resumé padder Joey attempts to prove to Phoebe he does have valuable skills—such as chugging a gallon of milk in ten seconds.

moving on

EPISODE GUIDE

Episode 219: **"The One After Joey and Rachel Kiss"**
Written by Andrew Reich & Ted Cohen
Directed by Kevin S. Bright
Original Airdate: September 25, 2003

Episode 220: **"The One Where Ross is Fine"**
Written by Sherry Bilsing-Graham & Ellen Plummer
Directed by Ben Weiss
Original Airdate: October 2, 2003

Episode 221: **"The One With Ross's Tan"**
Written by Brian Buckner
Directed by Gary Halvorson
Original Airdate: October 9, 2003

Episode 222: **"The One With the Cake"**
Written by Robert Carlock
Directed by Gary Halvorson
Original Airdate: October 23, 2003

Episode 223: **"The One Where Rachel's Sister Babysits"**
Written by Dana Klein Borkow
Directed by Roger Christiansen
Original Airdate: October 30, 2003

Episode 224: **"The One With Ross's Grant"**
Written by Sebastian Jones
Directed by Ben Weiss
Original Airdate: November 6, 2003

Episode 225: **"The One With the Home Study"**
Written by Mark Kunerth
Directed by Kevin S. Bright
Original Airdate: November 13, 2003

Episode 226: **"The One With the Late Thanksgiving"**
Written by Shana Goldberg-Meehan
Directed by Gary Halvorson
Original Airdate: November 20, 2003

Episode 227: **"The One With the Birth Mother"**
Written by Scott Silveri
Directed by David Schwimmer
Original Airdate: January 8, 2004

Episode 228: **"The One Where Chandler Gets Caught"**
Written by Doty Abrams
Directed by Gary Halvorson
Original Airdate: January 15, 2004

Episode 229: **"The One Where the Stripper Cries"**
Written by Marta Kauffman & David Crane
Directed by Kevin S. Bright
Original Airdate: February 5, 2004

Episode 230: **"The One With Phoebe's Wedding"**
Written by Robert Carlock & Dana Klein Borkow
Directed by Kevin S. Bright
Original Airdate: February 12, 2004

Episode 231: **"The One Where Joey Speaks French"**
Written by Sherry Bilsing-Graham & Ellen Plummer
Directed by Gary Halvorson
Original Airdate: February 19, 2004

Episode 232: **"The One With Princess Consuela"**
Teleplay by Tracy Reilly
Story by Robert Carlock
Directed by Gary Halvorson
Original Airdate: February 26, 2004

Episode 233: **"The One Where Estelle Dies"**
Teleplay by Marta Kauffman & David Crane
Story by Mark Kunerth
Directed by Gary Halvorson
Original Airdate: April 22, 2004

Episode 234: **"The One With Rachel's Going Away Party"**
Written by Andrew Reich & Ted Cohen
Directed by Gary Halvorson
Original Airdate: April 29, 2004

Episode 235: **"The Last One–Part 1"**
Written by Marta Kauffman & David Crane
Directed by Kevin S. Bright
Original Airdate: May 6, 2004

Episode 236: **"The Last One–Part 2"**
Written by Marta Kauffman & David Crane
Directed by Kevin S. Bright
Original Airdate: May 6, 2004

INSIDE "THE LAST ONE"

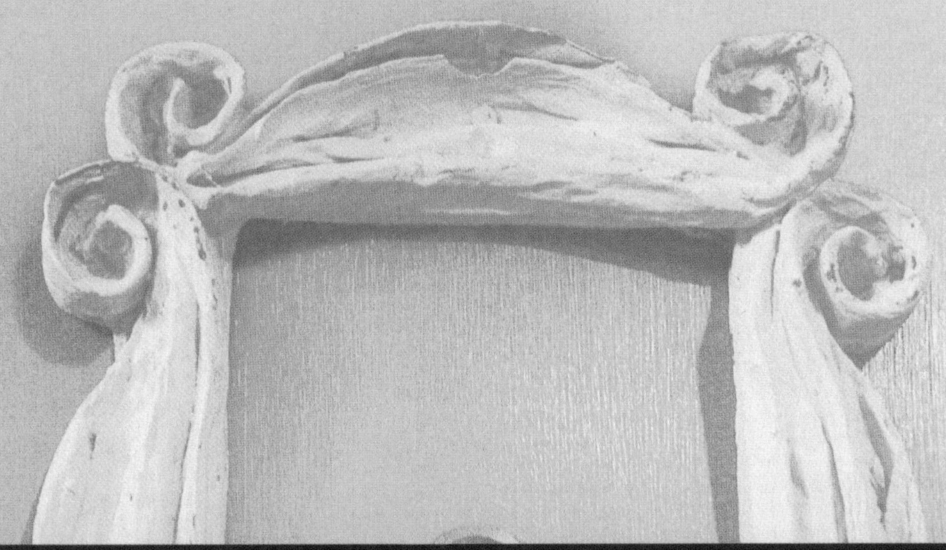

A Farewell to FRIENDS

PART ONE

In the end, as the Beatles once helpfully pointed out, the love you take is equal to the love you make. Over ten seasons *Friends* made a *lot* of love in every sense of the word, and in the end there was about as much love as anyone could take. Indeed, during the final days of *Friends*, life on Stage 24 can most accurately be described as one raging and tearful lovefest.

"It feels so sad and it feels so right." That's how David Crane describes the scene in front of Central Perk on January 16, 2004 as filming begins on the *Friends* finale. When the shooting stops tonight and Kevin Bright yells "Cut," the show's famed coffeehouse set will be torn down and consigned to TV history.

The End—or "The Last One" as the *Friends*' final one-hour episode is fittingly titled—comes in two parts. "Part One"—in which Monica and Chandler become parents *twice*, and Ross and Rachel do it yet again—will be filmed tonight amid lots of laughter and no shortage of open weeping.

On-screen and off, *Friends* has always been a highly emotional show. Lots of touching, lots of hugging, and some actual growth. **In a medium that can be cool or even chilly, this has been a warm show, as well as a hot one.**

As the cast and crew prepare for the show's live audience to be brought in, the reality of the situation seems to

That's our show

It's a Boy: For Monica and Chandler, it's love at first sight when they see baby Jack for the first time. Anna Faris, who played Erica, the twins' surrogate mother recalls, "It was a very short pregnancy, but a lot of fun. I loved being on *Friends* and it was an honor to be included in such an important episode."

hit home. Before the taping begins, cast, crew, and even your shameless author take a turn on the imaginary coffee shop's famed orange couch for a soon to be historic *Friends* photo op.

Stage 24 is especially frigid today. When someone mentions the temperature, Warner Bros. Television President Peter Roth is overheard to say, "Comedy is *cold*, babe."

But when the filming begins, things warm up quickly and the mood becomes more focused. David Crane, Marta Kauffman, and the writers are still playing their winning game of Beat The Joke. After the first take of the episode's teaser in which Joey and Phoebe are packing for Monica and Chandler, David Crane asks for the group's best judgment on whether it would be funnier for Joey to mark a moving box "Box of Crap" instead of "Box of Stuff." In the end, "Crap" gets a shot too.

Under Kevin Bright's direction, the episode flies by in

Handle with Care: Chandler and Monica hold Jack and Erica tightly after briefly considering a mid-air switch. "I think Monica and Chandler will be great parents," says Matthew Perry.

The Morning After: Rachel praises Ross on his new moves after they end up spending the night together.

so much as anything that takes more than five hours can fly by. Tonight's episode "gets off like a rocket," Bright notes between shots. "We'll hit a few snags, but this is going great. This is the way you want it."

The snags are few and the scenes click quickly—though there are a few unavoidable slowdowns, such as when either the baby chick or the duck pees on Matt LeBlanc.

During the delivery room scene, David Arquette takes the opportunity to take home movies of his actual pregnant wife becoming a TV mother. "I'm bootlegging," he explains with a friendly grin. "This stuff will be in Taiwan by the morning."

As one might expect, the audience is full of friends and family: Marta Kauffman's son Sam—a toddler when the show began—is looking ultracool as he hangs out on the floor in a Ramones T-shirt. David Schwimmer's parents sit up front in the audience, right next to Jennifer Aniston's dad. During a brief break, Schwimmer runs over to chat with his parents, then heads backstage towards his dressing room. As he passes Inger's craft services table, he is asked how he's doing. "I say I'm doing okay, but then I go back here and I'm a *wreck*. But I'm also happy because for these last episodes, they *really* nailed the comedy and the heart of the show."

Love Triangle: Once again, Ross is upstaged by Gunther, played by James Michael Tyler, who tells Rachel he loves her just as Ross was about to utter the same words. "It was a very fitting closure for Gunther's story line," recalls James Michael Tyler. "Jennifer Aniston made it both very easy and very difficult at the same time. Our scene went beyond acting—the emotion was real—it was a moment I will never forget."

The crying floodgates open wide during Scene K—the *Friends'* final appearance of Central Perk. The popular *Friends* hangout goes out in a high note, with a classic scene in which Gunther finally reveals his long-simmering love to Rachel at *exactly* the worst moment for Ross, who's only a few feet away to a similar moment of truth with her.

Before the scene begins, the cast is reduced to tears. "It's a *total* breakdown," Bright reports as he returns to his colleagues from talking to the actors. "Matt LeBlanc told them, 'Do you realize this is the last coffee shop

Packing It In: Courteney Cox takes a break on the set of "The Last One." "It's so hard saying goodbye to all of this,"says Courteney Cox.

A Friendly Reception: Babies Jack and Erica come back to the apartment that will only briefly be their home.

Kiss and Tell: Ross finds out he's about to be an uncle and then shares the news that he and Rachel "totally did it." "Part of the joy of *Friends* is we could always make each other laugh," says David Schwimmer.

scene?' and now they're *all* just gone." A few minutes later, while attempting to film Gunther's big confession, Aniston and James Michael Tyler dissolve once again.

After the scene, LeBlanc lingers with his arm around his stepdaughter on the couch, dabbing his eyes. And while Ross and Rachel's future is still up in the air, David Schwimmer and Jennifer Aniston hug each other for comfort.

Watching the waterworks, a cynic might note this is just the end of a TV show, not the end of the world. That's true enough, but for those who spent much of the past ten years right here, it's the end of *this* little world and the end of an era too.

"This is absolute chaos," First Assistant Cameraman René Menoni cries out at one point to a huge reaction on the floor.

At 10:30 p.m., Kevin Bright calls "Cut" and declares, "That's our show." The cast take their bows together and head upstairs.

Downstairs, the crew begins the poignant process of tearing down Central Perk. Then, just after the couch is taken away, Jennifer Aniston comes down to pay her Central respects. Before long she's joined by her cast-mates, Bright, Kauffman, and Crane, and much of the *Friends* crew. They come out of the woodwork and sit together on the hard floor where the coffeehouse rug used to be.

Many of the assembled toast with Patron tequila. Set decorator Greg Grande offers this toast. "The memories we made on Stage 24," he says, "are better than any dreams we ever had."

Later, the cast and crew take turns writing notes on the back of the *faux* Central Perk walls before they're taken away.

David Schwimmer writes, **"The best ten years of my life...Love to all involved. Schwim."**

"This has been great!" adds Jennifer Aniston, followed by kisses symbols and a promise of **"More To Come."**

Matt LeBlanc tried to keep things a little lighter: "I shat here," he writes.

Marta Kauffman's note is far more emotional, as if overwhelmed, she writes simply, **"Too much love."**

Clinging to Each Other: Aniston, Perry, and LeBlanc grab some last couch time.

The Huddle: The *Friends* cast in one of their last group hugs on Stage 24. "I couldn't love these five people any more," says Jennifer Aniston.

Last Call: The gang together for their final scene on the set of Central Perk. "This stage became a home for us," says Kevin Bright.

Airport Sendoff: Aniston, Kudrow, and Schwimmer huddle on the Newark airport set. "I'm going to miss everyone on *Friends*, but I'm especially going to miss Phoebe," says Lisa Kudrow. "I love that girl."

Chins Up: Jennifer Aniston gives Matt LeBlanc some moral support on the set of "The Last One—Part 1."

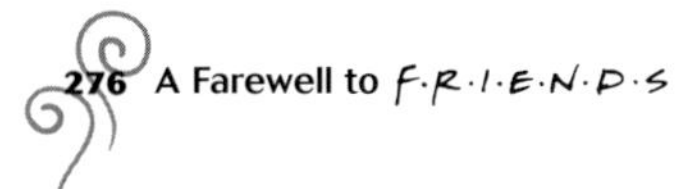

PART TWO

On January 23, 2004, their last day together, the writing staff of *Friends* reached a whole new high. As an oversized parting note, the scribes wrote—with the assistance of five skywriting jets—"Thank you David and Marta—Love, The Writers" high in the skies above the Warner Bros. lot.

Outside today in Burbank, California, it's sunny for the last day of *Friends*, though there's an unusual chill in the air. Inside Stage 24, David Crane declares that he's so thoroughly warmed by the writers' grand gesture that for once he has no notes to offer them. Marta Kauffman is similarly emotional, though she adds with a grin that she might have gone with an exclamation point in the skywriting instead of that dash. As Kevin Bright confers with his team of cameramen nearby, Marta grabs a few Kleenex from a nearby box and declares, "I'm going to need a *lot* of these."

At this point, everyone here appears to have shed a tear, with Jennifer Aniston setting the pace and Executive Producer Scott Silveri the last to fall. Still, the general mood on the set is more celebration than depression, but

Boarding Passes: Ross, at long last, declares his love for Rachel and pleads with her not to board the plane for Paris.

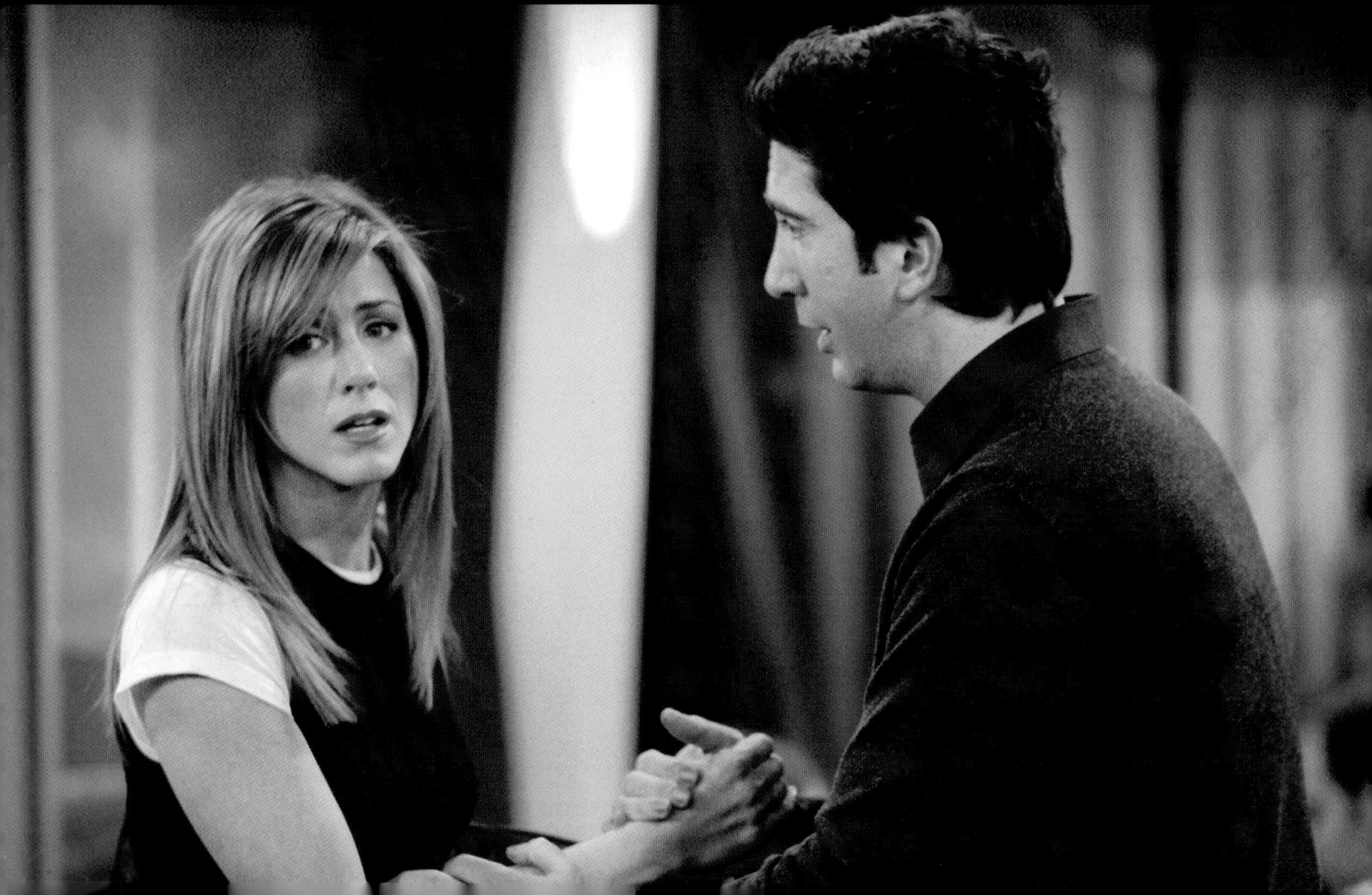

Rescue Mission: In order to save a chick and a duck, Joey and Chandler make the ultimate sacrifice—their foosball table.

it's a powerful, bittersweet mix. **Today, most people don't know whether to laugh or cry, so they generally do both.** "Congratulations or condolences, whatever works best," one visitor says to a group of writers. Many of the crew members are exchanging hugs and signing the special *Friends* staff yearbook assembled by producer Wendy Knoller.

This yearbook isn't the only very limited edition *Friends* finale memento around here. René Menoni's declaration "This is absolute chaos," has now become the slogan on the front of a T-shirt worn by much of the crew. On the back, the shirt says simply, "The Final Episode."

Pumping up the emotions further is the fact that these final, fleeting moments of *Friends* have become a sort of homecoming. James Burrows—who directed the *Friends* pilot and other classic early episodes and helped the cast bond in the beginning—is back here today, as are many other familiar faces from off and on screen. "I still consider the cast my kids. And I still am amazed that they're all friends and they've all united and banded together in spite of the fact that they all came in at the beginning of the show at a different level, but they're all going out at the same level", says James Burrows. Though they're not in the final episode, James Michael Tyler, Maggie Wheeler, Paul Rudd, and Aisha Tyler are all in attendance. At one point, Matthew Perry even discovers that Valerie Bertinelli—his onetime TV sister on the short-lived sitcom *Sydney*—is here too.

One of the original writers, Jeff Greenstein—who's now a big shot over at *Will & Grace*—takes in the scene with his wife. "It's like closing the circle," he explains looking on at the action. "Our little boys and girls have grown up." Maggie Wheeler approaches

Brothers in Arms: Schwimmer and LeBlanc during the filming of "The Last One—Part 2." "Whatever else was going on, we always had each other," says Matt LeBlanc.

The One We've All Been Waiting For: In the end, Ross and Rachel finally get things right. "From the beginning to the very end, there's always been a magic to Ross and Rachel," says Marta Kauffman.

Greenstein and says, "you gave me life," since he and his former writing partner Jeff Strauss created her character.

Later, Wheeler agrees to warm-up comic Jim Bentley's request for one last "Oh, my God" just for the live audience. Unsurprisingly, the crowd goes crazy for this whiny encore. "I already shot Janice's last episode," Wheeler says later. "But I felt like I was saying goodbye. I had to be here tonight. If I didn't see the tree fall myself, I might wake up and not believe it."

Other well-wishers who couldn't be here send their respects in various ways. A thoughtful fan sends a beautiful big floral arrangement that's put out on the craft services table. The gang at *Everybody Loves Raymond—Friends'* Warner Bros. lot-mates—has sent a lovely deli platter.

When the cast comes out to greet the audience, they receive a tremendous and enduring standing ovation that gradually reduces them, especially the women, to tears before a scene has been shot.

"Back to makeup," Co-Executive Producer Todd Stevens says with a laugh, and true enough all that crying required a quick trip backstage for some post-tears touch-up.

Central Perk is gone now, but some visitors can be seen scanning the remaining familiar set for any little keepsakes. Marta Kauffman's son Sam is far more practical and studious—he grabs a few dozen pencils. "I don't have any for school," he explains sweetly.

Others close to the show pop up on camera—Kevin Bright's lovely assistant Colleen is among the extras in the scene set in JFK Airport where Ross and Phoebe first go to catch Paris-bound Rachel. Meanwhile, over at Newark Airport—where Rachel's about to board her plane, David Crane's life partner, Jeffrey Klarik stands in line right in front of her.

Parting Thoughts: Matthew Perry and Matt LeBlanc enjoy one last script conference with Kauffman, Crane, and Bright. "Everything these actors did with our words was so much better than we could have ever imagined," says David Crane.

A Gathering of *Friends*: The producers and cast assemble together on the stage for their final bow after wrapping the "The Last One–Part 2."

Flashback: The *Friends* cast does a cold read from "The Pilot" during their wrap party. The party was held at the South Park Plaza in Los Angeles, where the entertainment included a set by Sheryl Crow and The Rembrandts singing "I'll Be There For You."

In the end, Ross and Rachel are of course reunited—or at least until the next "break."

Before the final scene of *Friends*, with the six stars together for the last time in Monica and Chandler's now packed up apartment, the strains of Donna Summer's "Last Dance" fill the stage. "Oh my God" says Paul Rudd "This isn't the end of *Friends*—this is the end of *Thank God It's Friday*." But of course, this *is* the end of *Friends*, which is why even a star like Rudd pulls out a video camera. "I'm not usually invited to witness television history," he explains.

During the final scene, emotion and nerves get the best of the typically unfailing Courteney Cox who keeps forgetting a line. Not for the first time—but possibly for the last—Matthew Perry lifts the mood on Stage 24 with the perfect joke. "*Somebody's* gonna get fired," he announces loudly with just the right taunting, little brotherly tone.

A little later, 'round midnight, after the last bows are taken, Matt LeBlanc takes a glass of champagne and hands a few around. He offers a toast to *Friends* itself: "There was magic here," he says quietly. "This was more than a TV show." He is speaking, likely for the first time ever, about *Friends* in the past tense.

Yes friends, *Friends was* more than a TV show, but what a TV show it was.

Curtain Call: The *Friends* cast takes their final bow.

As Good As It Gets: Says Todd Stevens, Co-Executive Producer, "For those of us lucky enough to have worked on the show, *Friends* has been a wild and amazing ride. In television, things rarely last long and even when they do, they're not always something you love the whole way through. This has been as good as it gets. It hasn't always been easy but it's always been interesting and worthwhile."

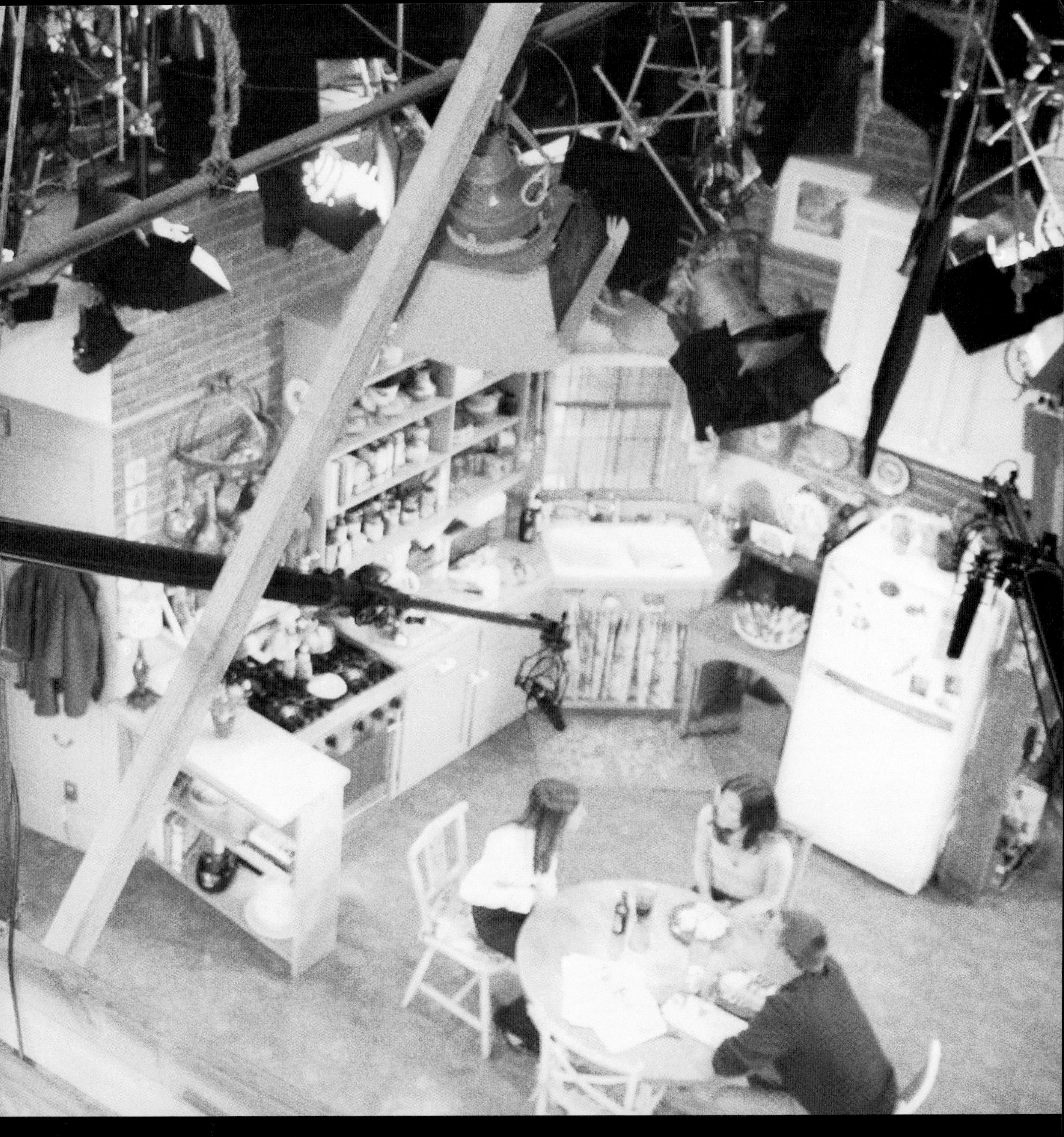

"THE WORLD'S BEST CREW"

—Jennifer Aniston

"The atmosphere around the set is really like a family. The crew, the producers, the writers, the security, wardrobe, make-up, hair, Inger (craft service), the assistant directors, the cast, and the set dressing guys all make the experience. The 'vibe' on the set is just a great time. It's a great group of people coming together to make some great entertainment and loving every moment of it."

—David Arquette

"I've run out of superlatives to adequately describe the catering—it was remarkable. In over 20 years on TV (and there were some great 'food' shows), none could compare with the variety, quality, and quantity that I enjoyed on *Friends*. It was an unending array of popular standards plus lovely gourmet surprises, served up with the same joy and enthusiasm that everyone else on the set exhibited in the performing of their functions."

—Steve Susskind, guest actor on "The One With Monica and Chandler's Wedding"

Stage 24—where *Friends* was shot—was also used for *A Star Is Born* (1954), *Now, Voyager*, and *The Big Sleep*. It is now officially known as "The *Friends* Stage."

"You know what they say—there's *Friends* and then there's all the other shows. Working here is the best experience and the most fun I could have—and it's been very rewarding looking out for such a high profile cast. The cast is very humble and they've tried to stay for the most part very open as people, which is hard when you're that famous. The show is very big in Israel where I come from—they call it "Haverim." My mother even sent me an article they did about me doing security for the show."

—Udi, Security

Tell me about one *Friends* behind-the-scenes hero.

"Oh, are you kidding? There are so many. Our props department—Marjorie—has been there forever—since the beginning. And Leslie and Kim are great. Ben Weiss, who is our first AD, and one of our favorite directors. They're all such important characters in our show. The second AD Carlos Pinero, he's been there forever with Ben. He takes a lot of shit, especially from me. But he's just as nice as he can be and he's great, and they just keep it running. And of course Inger who everyone calls Mama—she's unbelievable. Jennifer thanked her when she won her Emmy."

—Lisa Kudrow

"Well, Inger is the best. Inger is the catering table—she's the person who makes all the stuff. She's the cook."

—Matthew Perry

"The one thing I could never get over, and the one thing I've never had since, was the craft service on *Friends*. The food was great—they had whatever you wanted."

—Bonnie Somerville,
guest actor, Season Eight

Co-Executive Producer, Todd Stevens, explains that everything works on *Friends* because, "We've got Bright Kauffman Crane running things, we have a great crew, amazing writers, and this cast that you may have heard about somewhere."

"It's been really sad counting down to the end," says Ben Weiss. "I've spent more time with these people than any relationship I've ever been in—nine years. It's definitely a more emotional place this season. The reality is that this show is a once in a lifetime thing and we've got so close over the years. That last show—I don't know how the actors are going to get through it."

—Ben Weiss, Assistant Director and Director

Who behind-the-scenes deserves more credit?
"Well, our whole crew. The set department is pretty kick ass. They build, they turn around and they build more kick ass sets. And especially the set designer, Greg Grande, and his whole department also deserve more credit." —David Schwimmer

"This is a happy place. Our crew theme song is 'Dancing In The Moonlight'—'We have our fun/And we never fight.' That's our anthem."
—Kai Blomberg, Set Dressing

"I'm a *Friends* lifer and this has been quite a ride. It's been my life for ten years. I started the show single and now I have two children. And I've seen lots of others do the same. We've spent a quarter of our lives here, many of us. It's time for the show to end, but it will be very strange not to come here."
—Marjorie Coster-Praytor, "Prop Diva"

"This is not like the Beatles breaking up. They don't hate each other at the end—this cast could keep right on playing. Watching something so good end is bringing us even closer together. And it's sad because it's such an emotional place so close to the end."
—Gregg Bruza, Set Dressing

"It's mixed emotions for me. I've been doing this for four years and I love the job and the friends I've made. I'm getting close to retirement, but I'm still going to miss my kids. They're good kids who know how to behave. I would keep them all as my own. They like to eat."
—Inger, Catering

THIS BOOK WAS PRODUCED BY WARNER BROS. WORLDWIDE PUBLISHING

Vice President: Paula Allen
Production Director: Kevin Bricklin

Editor, Photo Editor, and Production Manager: Skye Van Raalte-Herzog
Director, Publishing Sales: Melanie O'Brien
Production Coordinator: Brittany Barr

Designed by: Design + Know-How
Design inspired by: James Gilbert, www.GoSandbox.com

Special thanks to: Vivek Mathur, Lisa Gregorian, Andrew Shipps, Brian Jamieson, Marcella Mparmperis, Mimi Slavin, Rosemary Markson, Diana Elizondo, Greg Dyro, John Eakin, Magy Perez, Tony Figueroa, Jack Teed

Episodic Photography Seasons Two–Ten by Danny Feld
Additional Episodic Photography by: Richard Cartwright, Byron J. Cohen, Bonnie Colodzin, Mitch Haddad, Robert Isenberg, Ron Jaffe, Justin Lubin, Craig T. Mathew, Oliver Upton, Joseph Viles
Additional Photography by Matthew Rolston
Back cover photograph by Mark Seliger © 2004

Special Thanks to Benay's Bird and Animal Rentals

President: Rob Gursha
Vice President, Branded Businesses: David Arfine
Vice President, New Product Development: Richard Fraiman
Executive Director, Marketing Services: Carol Pittard
Director, Retail & Special Sales: Tom Mifsud
Director of Finance: Tricia Griffin
Prepress Manager: Emily Rabin
Book Production Manager: Jonathan Polsky
Associate Product Manager: Victoria Alfonso

Special thanks to: Bozena Bannett, Alex Bliss, Robert Dente, Bernadette Corbie, Gina Di Meglio, Anne-Michelle Gallero, Peter Harper, Suzanne Janso, Robert Marasco, Natalie McCrea, Mary Jane Rigoroso, Steven Sandonato, Grace Sullivan

Published by Time Inc. Home Entertainment

Time Inc.
1271 Avenue of the Americas
New York, New York 10020

ISBN 1-932273-19-0
Library of Congress Control Number: 2004101646

Time Inc. Home Entertainment is a subsidiary of Time Inc.

If you would like to order any of our *Friends* Collector's Edition books, please call us at 1-800-327-6388 (Monday through Friday, 7:00 a.m.–8:00 p.m. or Saturday, 7:00 a.m.–6:00 p.m. Central Time).

Inside the Inner Sanctum: The Dressing Rooms

Jennifer Aniston

Courteney Cox

Lisa Kudrow

Matt LeBlanc

Matthew Perry

David Schwimmer